Primer to Developing a Successful Pre-Service Teacher Portfolio

James P. Takona and Roberta J. Wilburn

University Press of America,® Inc.
Dallas · Lanham · Boulder · New York · Oxford

KH

Library of Congress Control Number: xxxx
ISBN 0-7618-2798-6 (paperback : alk. ppr.)

8/21/05

Contents

Preface

Assessment is at the center of the current education reform movement, teacher preparation, good professional practice, legislative mandates. Our goal in this book is to provide foundational understanding of the principles and practice of the process of developing and using a portfolio in teacher education. For the pre-service teacher, portfolio development is a challenging and, sometimes, intimidating task. This text has the same focus as two previous editions titled: Pre-Service Teacher Portfolio Development—that is, it serves as an invitation extended to pre-service teachers to the portfolio world as a means of documenting growth and development for the teaching profession. *Primer to Developing a Successful Pre-Service Teacher Portfolio* seeks to provide the theory and experience necessary to develop an effective portfolio. It is more than a book of skills building. Rather, it is a text that reflects current theories and beliefs about learning and assessment amidst a dramatic change in the approach to the preparation of teachers and gauging professional development and growth.

While writing this book, we have aimed at assisting pre-service teachers who have had a limited number of professional education courses but who wish to learn more about the current reform movement that has led to an assessment practice that calls for tangible products evidencing what pre-service teachers know and can do. There are many ways to read this text. Cover to cover in a linear fashion is of course one way, but we encourage you to read it with your own questions in mind. We hope that you, as a prospective teacher, will gain new perspectives on assessment and especially when integrated with performance standards as benchmarks to professional growth and development.

Each chapter begins with a short orientation intended to orient students to information and ideas presented in the chapter. The following is a brief summary of the chapters:

Chapter 1—Describes the current education reform movement and its influence on teacher education. The current direction on that reform effort is defined by state and national mandates. These mandates are not tied to specific curricula, they do not provide a means for reaching them, and they do not suggest strategies for getting there. Rather schooling, if you like, must provide a standardized quality within an environment that is accountable.

Chapter 2—Provides a historical background of assessment practices, tracing it as far back as biblical times, through early civilizations and down to modern times. The content of the chapter reflect the idea that neither accountability nor assessment is new while describing that the current interest in accountability and assessment emanates for various socio-political, professional and legislative events amidst the belief by policymakers that schools will not be able to produce better-educated students without highly skilled, knowledgeable teachers who are treated as professionals.

Chapter 3—Examines the use of standards for PreK-12 students and pre-service teachers as they relate to teacher preparation and assessment. It also discusses the framework for determining knowledge and skills as a basis for preparation and professional development.

Chapter 4—Makes a sharp distinction between the various terms use to describe assessment while placing emphasis on performance assessment and the significant role it plays in learning and professional growth and development. In addition it provides a basis for gaining an understanding of the need for assessment and how it is done.

Chapter 5—Explores several fundamental purposes of a pre-service teacher portfolio including its ability to encourage the need for taking responsibility of ones own learning; promote partnership in assessment, encourage self-reflection, promote ownership of learning, encourage critical thinking, and is a key component of the licensing process and program assessment.

Chapter 6—This chapter examines the concept of competence and self-assessment as well as effective ways of gauging growth and development. It also discusses and expounds on the idea that the portfolio development process allows for the discovery the degree of mastery of a defined set of knowledge, skills, and dispositions. This chapter also describes how a portfolio affords an opportunity to examine thoughts and tenets regarding to issues in teaching and learning.

Chapter 7—Introduces a simple portfolio development model (PDC) which is founded on the belief that a portfolio is a purposeful engagement that calls for a collection of work samples to isolate tangible evidence of your progress in becoming a highly qualified teacher. The PDC model has four distinct stages, collection, reflection, reduction, and display. In addition, the chapter suggests ways of developing an exemplary portfolio and encouraging portfolio developers to seek help and input from various individuals.

Chapter 8—Provides a discussion on the content of a pre-service teacher portfolio while acknowledging that there is no single or right way to "do" a portfolio. This chapter includes suggestions to a layout for an effective portfolio, which may include the cover page, title page, and table of contents and the approach that you give to the development of your philosophy of education.

Chapter 9—Provides a model template of what could be included in a pre-service teacher portfolio with specific examples of various components typically found in a pre-service portfolio.

Chapter 10—Discusses methods used to evaluate pre-service teacher portfolios. It examines evaluation teams, tools including rubrics, and grading systems

Chapter 11—Gives guidelines for assisting pre-service teachers in doing a final analysis of their portfolio prior to submission. In addition, this chapter provides questions for self-evaluation to ensure that the portfolio is thorough and complete

Although this book's overall conception is the authors, any shortcomings should not be blamed on anyone else but us. It is a culmination of collaborative efforts from many. As we complete the preparation of this manuscript, we would like to make special acknowledgements to many contributors. Over the years, we have been able to depend on the support of our students and colleagues in the field of education. Our gratitude and acknowledgements go to undergraduate students at LeMoyne-Owen College, who challenged us to put course notes to a format that is accessible to them and have, indeed, helped us clarify the normative principles underlying authentic assessment. And to our colleagues—and we are hesitant to list them here without leaving others out—who read or heard us discuss a number of ideas we present in this text. Their generous comments and input helped make this text become a cohesive and consistent whole. Finally, thanks are due to all publishing professionals who made this work possible. To Vicky Burkholder for her editorial skills, constructive comments, and helpful suggestions. To Dorothy Albritton whose speed and diligence in manuscript preparation kept this project moving. And to the entire team at University Press of America, Inc., who have worked hard to make this text accessible to readers.

JPT & RJW.

Chapter 1

Introduction

Orientation

This introductory chapter is intended to provide a background on the American educational system and the incremental responsibility for accountability demanded by the current wave of educational reform. This discussion might probably leave you wondering why it is included in a text on portfolio development. Certainly, you might have expected that we might begin this textbook with a batter of practical tips on developing a portfolio. If so, you were mistaken as that comes later and will be covered very quickly in that regard. We have proposed, however, to confront you with a strong background on the state of education in America amidst a two-decade period of reform efforts aimed at improving the way we teach and the impact of our teaching on learning.

Focus Questions

- ▭ Why has the way to assessing pre-service teachers changed from the early 1980s?
- ▭ What must teachers, either in-service or pre-service, be taught about assessment?
- ▭ What ought to be considered a major function of a teacher education program?
- ▭ What are standards anyway and why are they important within the current reform movement?

Reform Movement

The education profession is vested by the American public with the responsibility and trust demanding the highest level of quality and professional service. Concern with the lack of quality and with alleged weaknesses and shortcomings in public schools continue to beleaguer the American educational system. The media continues to be dominated with discussions about how to fix schools and school systems. Vouchers, longer school days and other school reform ideas are the subjects of numerous talk shows and political columns. A dynamic and far-reaching reform movement seeking greater accountability and effectiveness in the learning and teaching environment has been underway in the United States since the early 1980's. This movement was first triggered into motion by the report of the National Commission on Excellence in Education, *A nation at risk: The imperative for education reform* (1983) when it decried the state of American public schools. The report claimed that U.S. students generally achieve at lower skill levels than those of other industrialized nations.

A decade after *A-Nation-At-Risk* report, Congress enacted the *Goals 2000: Educate America* Act to provide a framework for education reform for the 21st Century. This legislation called for the establishment of high quality, internationally competitive content and performance standards for all students, and promoted the use of technology to enable all students to achieve national goals. To accomplish this, the legislation emphasized the need for teacher education and professional development. A major function of a teacher education program is to change the prospective teacher by altering one or more of characteristics that make up his or her identity: knowledge, skills, dispositions and so on. It is the responsibility of teacher preparation programs to give pre-service teachers the opportunity to acquire the knowledge and skills needed to instruct and prepare students for the next century. The same applies to teachers themselves as they work with their school districts: they must have access to programs to improve professional skills and be encouraged "to use emerging new methods, forms of assessment and technologies" (The National Education Goals Panel, 1998).

An examination of the preamble of the *Goals 2000 Educate America* Act of 1994 reveals the following two proclamations:

❖ To improve learning and teaching by providing a national framework for education reform.
❖ To promote the development and adoption of a voluntary national system of skills standards and certifications.

Performance measures proposed in Goals 2000 are probably more appropriate for assessing learning than the traditional norm-referenced, standardized achievement test. The difference between performance measures when compared to the traditional pencil and paper tests is that performance measures are direct measures of student learning. Moreover, what are performance measures? How are they different from other tests? That is a straightforward question, which usually receives a not so straightforward answer. Of course, we do not intend to provide an all-satisfying answer either. However, we will restate here what Herman and his associates (1992) had earlier observed: that performance measures share common characteristics which may include: (a) asking students to perform, create and produce; (b) tapping into higher-level thinking and problem-solving skills; (c) using tasks that represent meaningful instructional activities; (d) involving real-world applications; (e) relying on people and human judgment rather than machines to score; and (f) requiring new instructional and assessment roles for teachers. This is certainly a better approach and has received become widely accepted across the nation. Since the passing of the "*Goals 2000 Educate America* Act, forty-nine states have now established state-level academic standards. Most of them have standards for all core subjects" (Falk, 2000).

At the dawn of the 21st century, American education has seen yet another re-authorization of the 1965 Elementary and Secondary Education Act (EASE) commonly known as Title I, when in January 2002, the Bush administration signed into law a landmark legislation—No Child left Behind Act (NCLB, 2002). The NCLB Act is intended to change the culture of America's schools and improve student learning. This new legislation (H.R. 1) focuses on improving performance of low achieving children in the nation's highest poverty schools and assuring that all students make progress and achieve rigorous standards (NCLB, 2002). The legislation demands accountability on the part of the teacher. The Act's overall purpose is to ensure that children in every classroom enjoy the benefits of well-prepared teachers, research-based curriculum and safe learning environments. The bill is both "a carrot and a stick" from the federal government for those districts participating in ESEA. This reform act is part of the most far-reaching federal education initiative in thirty years. For children already doing well in school, this law provides tools to help them do even better. In addition, the act targets those children who need extra help; it provides more training for teachers; and demands that a highly qualified teacher lead every classroom in America within four years. Furthermore, the No Child Left Behind Act requires schools to hire more teachers so that classes will be smaller and children will learn better; it empowers parents with more information about how their schools measure up, and provides public school alternatives for children in chronically troubled schools.

The NCLB legislation expects all fifty states to set their own standards—and set them high without yielding to the temptation of creating worthless standards just to ensure that they can be attained. These standards must be meaningful and challenging. Standards specify goals and objectives that students should meet. They do not mandate, however, a particular sequence of topics, curriculum, instructional approaches or textbooks. Effective standards must, however, be specific to the point that they identify what students need to learn and to determine when the standards have been met (Linn and Gronlund, 2000). The question then is: will states set their standards high enough? They have to and they must. That is not so they can make sure the NCLB Act works, but so students in the state are not short-changed. For math and reading, these standards had to be in place by fall 2002. By the end of the 2005-2006 school year, states are expected to have established science standards as well. Once states have standards in place, they must determine how those standards will be tested. That is a big question: what kind of test is appropriate? Generally, this comes down to two choices—criterion-referenced or norm-referenced exams. Criterion-referenced tests are tied directly to the state's standards. Norm-referenced tests are not tied to specific standards, but still provide results down to the individual student level. While criterion-referenced tests are likely to provide the most accurate assessment of student knowledge, they may need to be specifically tailored to standards delineated by each state. Of course, this is bound to be a very expensive process. However, it is a very promising route to obtain more a reliable and effective picture of student mastery of set standards. Norm-referenced tests, in contrast, are relatively easy to obtain "off-the-shelf," making them less expensive and more readily accessible. However, they are more general about what students know and can do.

Teacher Quality and Assessment

It will benefit you to know that the current reform movement has not been without a discussion of the most important issue—teacher quality. Public education today focuses on teacher quality and test scores, indicating that adults understand that children other than their own are in trouble. Underlying these reform agendas and policies is the idea about assessing teachers including what the appropriate outcomes of teacher preparation programs and curricula ought to be. In essence, these agendas, policies, and practices are placing intense and unprecedented demands on teacher preparation programs and their institutions to produce convincing evidence of their effectiveness in enhancing teacher learning. Central to this idea is the use of performance-based assessment approach.

In recent years, attention has widened to include a call for rigorous evaluation and improvement of teacher education and in the preparation of teachers and educational personnel in colleges and universities. The next time you have a casual discussion with faculty from your teacher education department try mentioning NCATE (http://www.ncate.org). NCATE is an acronym for the National Council for Teacher Education, a professional body that plays a major role in upgrading teacher preparation standards and accredits teacher preparation programs. NCATE, which has been in existence since the early 1950s, serves as the preeminent national accreditation body in teacher education. NCATE claims that it benefits education by: (1) ensuring that colleges of education meet external quality standards; (2) encouraging institutions to modify their programs to reflect changes in knowledge and practice; (3) providing a common set of national standards; (4) strengthening institutional self-evaluation and catalyzing program improvement; and (5) deterring decreases in resource allocations (Roth, 1996). Proponents have asserted that NCATE has led the way in changing teacher preparation to match more rigorous licensing and master teacher certification requirements and in encouraging links between student and teacher standards (Wise & Leibbrand, 1996). At all levels, there has been intense focus on two vehicles for improvement. The first of these has been the development and implementation of benchmarks for achievement, often referred to as standards-based reform.

The current reform movement in education is profoundly a blessing as well as a curse. Why do we so boldly say that? On the one hand, it serves to focus attention on a national level on schooling, learning, quality of teachers, funding, and the curriculum. On the other hand, it brings to bear what Machiavelli in his classic book, *The Prince,* said: "There is nothing more difficult to carry out, or more doubtful of success, or more dangerous to handle, than to initiate a new order of things." The need for 21st century skills creates an urgent demand to acquire the higher order thinking (Bloom, et al., 1956). This certainly may include bringing back a culture that is not popular to either the students or their instructors—assessment.

Beliefs about the purpose of educational institutions, student ability and potential influence the way teacher education programs are structured and the way instructors interact with pre-service teachers. These perceptions and beliefs guide the way teachers are prepared and defines what teaching is. Teaching is facilitating the development of knowledge, skills, and the intellect of students—bringing out the latent qualities that students already possess. All students have, existing within them, the capability and competence to fulfill their chosen career goals. Noble (1986) has expanded this when he asserts, "to be human is to possess 'will' and 'intent'—divine intelligence—and to have the capacity to develop and change" (p.92).

The last two decades have witnessed the process of assessing student learning and performance undergoing a paradigm shift—shifting the focus from what is taught (input) to what is learned (output). Assessment plays an integral role insofar as it shapes values and behavior. As psychologist Lauren Resnick puts it, ". . . what we assess is what we value. We get what we assess, and if we don't assess it, we don't get it" (cited in Wiggins, 1990). Resnick's comments refer to assessment of learning. You ought to recognize this just as much as your instructors do. This means that you need to see a connection between what you learn and what your instructors assess and expect as learning outcomes. Certainly, the same principles apply to the assessment of teaching. What we assess in teaching and the development of teachers reflects and influences what we value about teaching and, ultimately, affects the way we teach.

Unfortunately, traditional methods of evaluating learning are based upon antiquated and often fragmented conceptions of learning and teaching. More often than not, learning is construed as a batch of isolatable skills and personal qualities, enthusiasm for subject matter, and so on. These are typical dimensions in your report card as you came through PreK-12. Of course, these qualities have something to do with learning. The problem is that students, parents and even some teachers treat them as if they constitute the whole of learning.

Pre-service preparation represents the period of recruitment to a teacher education program, completion of professional program which includes the acquisition of content knowledge appropriate to the subject to be taught, clinical practice, graduation and entry into the classroom as a "highly qualified" teacher. One of the most significant innovations in thinking about the professional growth of a prospective teacher is the formal conceptualization of growth and development as continuous process extending from where you are right now as a pre-service teacher through your entire teaching career. An increasing demand by parents, communities, and policy makers for accountability on the part of educators—be they college professors or PreK-12 teachers, has become part and parcel of the standards movement in education. It is widely assumed that the adoption of standards and systematic assessment of learners' progress towards meeting the standards is a means by which a meaningful educational accountability system can be implemented. These standards are of various categories including performance, curriculum, delivery, and learning. Figure 1.1 provides a summarized description of the various categories. The first three descriptions are given by Sweeny (1999).

Figure 1.1: Categories of Standards and Their Description

Standards Category	Description
Performance	Describes how well how well students must know and do specific assessment tasks
Curriculum	Defines how teachers will reach desired results
Delivery	Describes what teachers must know and do if students are to performance at he desired levels
Learning	Describes student behavior and are associated to instructional objectives

Along with the standards movement is a growing national interest in alternative assessment as a means of determining the knowledge, skills, and dispositions of students. This interest stems in part from a subtle dissatisfaction with standardized achievement tests and originates in theoretical arguments about how children learn and what they learn. These alternative assessments are performance based. Rather than assessing what students know, performance assessment gives precedence to what students know and can do. Performances can be live or taped and represent evidence that students have integrated knowledge and skills and can apply them in useful ways (Wright, 1997). Portfolios are a good example of authentic assessment devices because they include concrete examples of students' work, which reflect what they know and are able to do. They are also authentic because they provide the student an opportunity to include "work that she sees fit to display and talk about to others" (Johnston, 1992, p. 129). Ideally, effective authentic assessment occurs at short intervals over time. These intervals are planned and systematic, not left to chance or whim, and include assessment sampling during instruction as well as sampling of the products of that instruction.

Summary of Key Points

School vouchers, longer school days, establishment of standards, change in assessment strategies, and other school reform ideas are subjects of the current educational reform movement. This movement was first triggered into action by the report of the National Commission on Excellence in Education, *A nation at risk: The imperative for education reform* (1983), which decried the state of American public schools. This legislation called for the establishment of high quality, internationally competitive content and performance standards for all students and called for increased use of technology to enable all students to achieve national goals. To achieve this, the legislation emphasized the need for teacher education and professional development

Recently, the American education has seen, yet another re-authorization of the 1965 Elementary and Secondary Education Act (EASE) commonly known as Title I, when the Bush administration signed to law a landmark legislation. The No Child Left Behind Act is intended to change the culture of America's schools and improve student learning. This new legislation focuses on improving achievement of low performing children in the nation's highest poverty schools and assuring that *all* students make progress and achieve rigorous standards (NCLB, 2002).

A review of the current reform movement is certain to lead to the conclusion that it is both a blessing and a curse. A blessing because of (a) its potential influence on the way teacher education programs are structured and the way instructors interact with pre-service teachers (b) the adoption of standards and systematic assessment of learners' progress towards meeting the standards is a means by which meaningful educational accountability system can be implemented. A curse because it is expensive to everyone—tax payers, parents, students and their teachers. Legislative mandates related to education and schooling are always expensive to implement. Often, as it is true for the current reform movement, these mandates are not tied to specific curricula; they do not provide adequate means for reaching them; and they do not suggest clearly defined strategies of getting there. These standards are of various categories including learning, performance, curriculum, and delivery. Along with the standards movement is a growing national interest in alternative assessment as a means of determining the knowledge and skills of students. Rather than assessing what students know, performance assessment looks at what students can do. A portfolio is a potentially capable intermediary for assessing performance.

References

Bloom, B.S., Englehart, M.D., Furst, E., Hill, W.H., & Krathwohl, D. R., (Eds). (1956). *Taxonomy of educational objectives: The classification of educational goals. Handbook I: Cognitive domain.* New York: David McKay.

Falk, Beverly (2000). *The heart of the matter: Using standards and assessment to learn.* Portsmouth, NH: Heinemann.

Herman, J. L., Aschbacher, P. R., & Winters, L. (1992). *A practical guide to alternative assessment.* Alexandria, VA: Association for Supervision and Curriculum Development.

Johnston, P. (1984). Assessment in reading. In P.D. Pearson (Ed.), *Handbook of reading research* (147-182). New York: Longman.

National Commission on Excellence in Education (1983). *A nation at risk: The imperative for educational reform.* Washington, DC: Government Printing Office.

Noble, Wade W. (1985). *Africanity and the Black family: The development of a theoretical model.* Oakland, CA: Black Family Institute.

Roth, R. A. (1996). Standards for certification, licensure, and accreditation. In J. Sikula, T. J. Buttery, & E. Guyton (Eds.), *Handbook of research on teacher education* (2nd ed., pp. 242-278). New York: Macmillan.

Sweeny, B. (1999). Content standards: Gate or bride? *Kappan Delta Phi.* 35(2), 64-67.

US Department of Education. (2002). *No Child Left Behind.* On-line document: http://www.nochildleftbehind.gov/next/overview/index.html.

Wise, A. E., & Leibbrand, J. (1996). Profession-based accreditation: A foundation for high-quality teaching. *Phi Delta Kappan, 78,* 202-206.

Wright, B. D. (1997). Evaluating learning in individual courses. *Handbook of the undergraduate curriculum.* J. Gaff & J. Ratcliff, Eds., San Francisco: Jossey-Bass.

Chapter 2

Evolution of Assessment: Retrospective and Prospective

Orientation

In Chapter 1, we noted that the American educational system continues to be in the midst of a reform process. The current direction on that reform effort is defined by state and national mandates. These mandates are not tied to specific curricula, they do not provide a means for reaching them, and they do not suggest strategies for getting there. Rather schooling, if you like, must provide a standardized quality within an environment that is accountable. In this chapter, you will learn that neither accountability nor assessment is new. What is new is its resurgence. This resurgence has been stirred by socio-political, professional and legislative events. Assessment reforms involve more than merely changing the nature of test taking tasks. It also involves curriculum content, process (delivery method), and the product (which is what students know and can do). Policymakers have become convinced that schools will not be able to produce better-educated students without highly skilled, knowledgeable teachers who are treated as professionals. The key aim of education is to construct a continuous path of development for each individual and to increase each person's experience base for meaningful learning that is guided by standards. What are standards anyway? This chapter will provide a simple definition of what standards are and their origin. Additional definitions and their origins will be identified in next chapter.

Focus Questions

- 📂 What is the relationship between the need for an increased and better-trained labor force, and what goes on in the classroom?
- 📂 How has improving the quality of education for all students been a priority for the past 20 years?
- 📂 How have political and education leaders have focused their attention on how well children are learning and what skills they are attaining?
- 📂 What other strategies should policy-makers pursue to improve student achievement?
- 📂 What are the predictors of superior academic performance?

Tracing Assessment Practices

What goes on in school today, be it at PreK-12 level or in higher education, is very much a result of the decisions made by professional educators, politicians, social commentators, and sometimes by average citizens who are committed to the vision of education. The vision, though described in many ways, is essentially the achievement of a preferred future. The path toward that future takes into consideration both input and output. Prior to the early 1980s, emphasis was skewed toward input—that which goes into supporting the vision, facilitating the learning environment, curriculum content and instructional methods length of the school day, and so on. Along with that emphasis were considerations of a mechanism for knowing if the impact of all such input. This mechanism is known as assessment. Assessment has a history and this history did not begin in American. Rather, it goes back to ancient societies. You would be short changed in a discussion on portfolio development and assessment if you are not familiar with the historical background of assessment and need for assessment.

Biblical Times

Some of the earliest records of testing are found in the Bible. God's creative act included a review that concluded with an attestation: "and all that God created was good." The occupants of the Garden of Eden found their demise following a content-based assessment. One of the clearest references of an assessment activity again is illustrated in the Old Testament:

> And the Gileadites took the passages of Jordan before the Ephraimites: and it was so, that when those Ephraimites which were escaped said, Let me go over; that the men of Gilead said unto him, Art thou an Ephraimite? If he said Nay; then said they unto him, Say now Shibboleth: and he said Sibboleth: for he could not frame to pronounce it right. Then they took him and slew him at the passage of Jordan: and there fell at that time the Ephraimites forty and two thousand.
>
> Judges 12:5-6

Undoubtedly this was an assessment with high-stakes. Look at that passage again and you will, certainly, notice that the sole test of a man being a Gileadite was his using the "h" sound in the word shibboleth. In this incident, the poor Ephraimite failed a performance-based test and the consequences were extended to a whole community.

Another example of how assessment practices were used in biblical times is described the book of Daniel. Daniel and his three friends had been captured by King Nebuchadnezzar While in captivity they refused to live according to the practices of their captors in regard to what they ate. Daniel challenged the king's officials to test them to determine whether their way of eating was healthier than the way the King proposed. Following the testing period, the King analyzed the derived data to form a basis upon which to make decision.

> But Daniel resolved not to defile himself with the royal food and wine, and asked the chief official for permission not to defile himself this way. . . . Please test your servants for ten days: Give us nothing but vegetables to eat and water to drink. Then compare our appearance with that of the young men who eat the royal food. So he agreed to this and tested them for ten days. At the end of the ten days they looked healthier and better nourished than any of the young men who ate the royal food.

> At the end of the time set by the king to bring them in, the chief official presented them to Nebuchadnezzar. The king talked with them and found none equal to Daniel, Hanniah, Mishael and Azariah, so they entered into the king's service. In every matter of wisdom and understanding about which the king questioned them, he found them ten times better. . . .
>
> Daniel 1:8, 12-15

From this passage it is evident that Daniel and his friends undertook a performance-base assessment. It involved not only a physical evaluation as a part of their assessment, but also included an oral interview to accurately determine their level of knowledge. Like current day assessment activities these early prophets were engaged in an assessment that allowed passage of time to determine if the treatment (or instruction) had any effect. After the treatment period, Daniel and his friends successfully passed the test and were rewarded with promotion to the king's service. Similarly, we teach our students, subject them varied assessment. If the gains made stand to expectations the students are promoted to the next grade level.

Ancient Times

An elaborate system of examination existed in ancient societies. About 2100 BC, the emperor of China is said to have examined his officials on a frequent basis and used the results to either promote or dismiss them from service (DuBois, 1966). We are not exactly sure what the content or the method of examinations was. What is certain is that the job security of one dependent largely on the performance on the examination. A millennium later, 1115 BC, at the beginning of the Chan dynasty, formal examining procedures for entry and remaining in office were established. Here the records are clear, the civil service required proficiency in five basic arts: Music, archery, horsemanship, writing, and arithmetic.

Testing was a normal part of the education of the ancient Greeks (Chauncey and Dobbin, 1963). The Socratic method involved the skillful interspersing of instruction with oral testing. Throughout educational history, great dependence has been place upon memorizing, and the role of the Roman and medieval teacher was practically that of a taskmaster whose chief responsibility was to punish those who failed to remember (Atkinson and Maleska, 1965).

Modern Times

The use of an examination system in the civil service reached Europe in the mid-nineteenth century and was quickly adapted in the United States by President Grant in 1871. However, assessment of academic achievement has come along way since ancient times. In the nineteenth century, annual public oral examinations of teachers were common. Teachers would assemble in the town hall for the examination and were questioned by the superintendent. This was a high stakes assessment where those who fell below the minimum standard of 75% were dismissed (Cureton, 1971).

The late 1800's and early 1900s saw the emergent of a wave of testing aimed at various problems in the school. One of these problems was that of classifying school pupils so that the dullest of them could be identified and separated from the others for special instruction. Horace Mann began using written standardized tests in Massachusetts and Connecticut in the 1830s, leading to the development of Mann's Boston Survey in 1846, the first printed test for large-scale assessment of student achievement in various disciplines. The tests were discontinued because the results were not used.

Standardized tests were again recommended after 1895 when Joseph Rice administered a form of standardized tests to a large school system. A decade later, Alfred Binet, a French psychologist began to develop complex tests for picking out children who were mentally unable to profit from regular instruction. At about the same time, a professor at Stanford University by the name of Dr. Lewis Terman was also developing similar test drawing heavily on Binet but extending the procedures for administering and interpreting the scores. By 1916, Terman's test, known as the Stanford-Binet, gained wide acceptance in the United States and quickly became the standard American "Intelligence test." Terman recognized the usefulness of a test in discovering children who were mentally deficient as well as the potential of such tests for the identification of superior students.

The Stanford-Binet in its current version continues to be the most widely used test of the mental ability of American children apart from its only rival, the Wechsler-Bellevue Intelligence Scale for Children (WISC), developed in 1949. Additionally, in the 1900s, Thorndike, often called the father of the educational testing movement, persuaded educators to measure human change. There was a call for immediate, demonstrable results and by 1915, testing had become a primary means of evaluating schools. A lack of trust in teachers developed because of the assumption that they were biased in evaluating students and standardized, norm-referenced tests emerged so that individual student groups could be compared with each other on a normal, bell-shaped curve. Dewey's progressive education movement in the 1930s favored education based on natural learning and practical problems, but the impetus in standardized assessment led to a boom in the technical development of tests to compare schools on a larger scale.

Since the 1920s, the field of testing has grown rapidly with the development of thousands of standardized tests to the extent that they are marketed in catalog books. For example, *Test in Print* (Buros, 1961), although a rather out of date volume, provides a descriptive list of commercially available tests up through 1961. Others include the volumes of *The Mental Measurements Yearbooks* (Buros, 1965) which provide assistance in the evaluation of specific test instruments as well overviews on test score interpretations. Moreover, more important are a number of professional journals that publish reviews of selected tests. These journals include the American Educational Research Journal, Journal of Educational Measurements and Personnel and Guidance Journal. Published catalogues and manuals have also become popular as they provide information and overview of available instruments.

Achievement tests are as varied as they are numerous. However, most early tests and many of those currently in use measure little more than recall of information (Takona, 1999). This has been so for two basic reasons: First, the retention and retrieval of information has been an important purpose of the school. Second, it is more difficult to measure other kinds of learning such as insights and reflection, point of view, or dispositions. A truly competent student is one who not only is able to retain and retrieve information, but one who is able to discuss it, classify it, apply it, manipulate it, and evaluate it appropriately.

A case in point, however, is that as educators realized that standardized test outcomes do not reflect the complexity of learning, opposition against standardized testing has steadily grown. The 1980s saw a rise in the use of criterion-referenced tests—that are in reality norm-referenced with a set of criteria instead of other students. Criterion-referenced assessments provide a description of what students can and cannot do. A criterion-referenced test is one that is

> . . . deliberately constructed so as to yield measurements that are directly interpretable in terms of specified performance standards. . . . The performance standards are usually specified by defining some domain of tasks that the student should perform. Representative samples of tasks from this domain are organized into a test. Measurements are taken and are used to make a statement about the performance of each individual relative to the domain (Glaser & Nitko, 1971, p. 653).

Norm-referenced test are standardized instruments that compare an individual's performance with that of others. Norm-referenced and criterion-referenced tests have certain characteristics in common. Gronlund (1981) describes those common characteristics as follows:

- Both require a relevant and representative sample of test items
- Both require specifications of the achievement domain to be measured
- Both use the same type of test items
- Both use the same rules for item writing (except for item difficulty)
- Both are judged by the same qualities of goodness (validity and reliability)
- Both are useful in educational measurement (p. 14).

By the 1990s, educators were raising and documenting problems with standardized testing in addition to claiming that they elicit only a limited category of behavior. In answer, educators explored alternatives to standardized testing which fall under the term "alternative assessment." Some examples of these are performance-based tests and portfolios. Different forms of alternative assessments are still being developed and used, but they too face opposition.

Assessment falls into two forms: content-based or competency-based. Throughout your educational career, you have certainly come across both forms of assessment. Most recently, competency-based assessment, also loosely called performance or outcome-based assessment has become vogue. Like local and state educational agencies, many teacher education programs have identified sets of content standards to support the organization of the body of knowledge, skills, and dispositions needed by pre-service teacher. Again, content-based assessment goes back to Biblical times. Remember the encounter of the serpent and the Eve at the Garden of Eden? Notice how the test was content-based.

Now the serpent was subtler than any beast of the field, which the Lord God had made. And he said unto the woman, Yea, hath God said, ye shall not eat of every tree of the garden? And the woman said unto the serpent, we may eat of the fruit of the tree which is in the midst of the garden: but of the fruit of the tree which is in the midst of the garden, God hath said, Ye shall not eat of it, neither shall ye touch it, least ye die. And the serpent said unto the woman, Ye shall not surely die: for God doth know that in the day ye eat thereof, then your eyes shall be opened, and ye shall be as gods, knowing good and evil. And when the woman saw that the tree was good for food and that it was pleasant to the eyes, and a tree to be pleasant to the eyes, and a tree to be desired to make one wise, she took of the fruit thereof, and did eat, and gave also unto her husband with her; and he did eat (Genesis 3:1-6).

Curriculum development in the United States before the mid-1960's can safely be characterized as content-based and relying heavily on the objective test format. Objective tests are often associated with content-based curriculum because they have the advantage and capability to test the greatest amount of content knowledge within the shortest period. Undoubtedly, objective testing is a product of a content- based assessment approach. The late 1970s brought about competency-based teacher preparation programs, which emphasized knowledge, skills, and dispositions. Knowledge is the quintessence of the cognitive domain which is one of the three human behavior domains (Bloom, Englehart, Furst, Hill & Krathwohl, 1956). Knowledge is at the core of most standardized test. Skills complement knowledge because they involve an act of doing, which is an active application of knowledge. Disposition is a member of the second human domain often referred to as the affective domain. The affective domain involves emotions as well as emotional tendencies and emotional intelligence such as attitude, perseverance, and motivation. Skills and dispositions are difficult to accurately measure in a content-based test such as a multiple-choice test. As such, the use of a given assessment tool for a particular purpose can be a contentious issue, particularly when assessments are used to make high-stakes decisions. When used for purposes of accurately determining student performance, testing instrument must be of high quality and validated for the intended purpose. Traditionally, the determination of the quality of an assessment instrument revolves around three questions (see for example, Linn and Grodlund, 2000):

1. **Is the instrument valid?** This is the overarching concern and it involves asking whether the instrument provides accurate information for the purposes for which it is being used. If a selected instrument is used to determine how well a learner has mastered standards, does it do a good job of covering

those standards? If we use a an assessment instrument such as the SAT for the purpose of college admissions, does it in fact predict something about a student's college performance? In other words, are the consequences of the assessment instrument—or inferences made from the results—reasonable given the particular test that was conducted?

2. **Is the assessment instrument reliable?** Reliability is related to the consistency with what a test measures and the confidence that one's obtained score is close to one's true score. If a learner took the test on more that one occasion, would the obtained scores remain consistent for every occasion? Moreover, do other learners with similar experiences and exposure score the same results time after time?

3. **Is the assessment instrument fair?** Is it free of biases that are inherent within the instrument that can create advantages or disadvantages based on individual learner characteristics such as racial background? Has the learner had an opportunity to learn what is being tested?

Events Impacting Assessment

Policy makers, at various times in the American history, have tended to believe that legislation is an effective way to provide effective schools. In that regard, therefore, a number of events and legislative mandates have had a profound impact on how we now approach learning and assessment. Here we will discuss several.

The Sputnik 1957

The American educational system has been characterized by a traditional emphasis on reading, writing, and arithmetic delivered in a classroom setting with a teacher at the front of a classroom containing neat rows of desks with students in them. Further, the act of listening to the teacher by students then repeated back to the teacher the information received has often characterized the informal assessment process that occurs in the classroom. America's assumption that school was and should be an unchanging institution that is "adequate today because it was adequate yesterday" changed when its position of world superiority was challenged with the Soviet launch of Sputnik I in 1957.

On October 4, 1957, the Soviet Union successfully launched Sputnik I, the first satellite to orbit Earth. This monumental accomplishment of a foreign, and not so friendly a nation, struck terror in the very fabric of American society leaving every responsive individual amused yet devastated. Bracey (2002) writes:

> Sputnik hit American schools like a tsunami. In early 1958, Life magazine launched a five part series entitled *Crisis in Education*. The March 24 cover showed photos of two teenagers, a stern-faced Muscovite, Alexei Kutzkov, and an easy-smiling Stephen Lapekas in Chicago. Inside, photos showed Kutzkov doing complicated experiments in physics and chemistry and reading aloud from Sister Carrie in his English class. . . . Stephen, by contrast, was shown walking his girlfriend home hand-in-hand and dancing in rehearsal for the school musical. One large picture caught him retreating, laughing, from a geometry problem on the blackboard (p. 38-39).

While the Russians were leading in the so-called space race, the American educational system was receiving a barrage of criticism for failing to establish standards which will enable students to remain competitive. In response to this criticism, and to remain competitive, the U.S. Congress earmarked over one million dollars during the 1960s toward the development and implementation of curricula in mathematics and science (Eisner, 1995). American education, even at the beginning of the 21st century, is still hounded by the Sputnik episode.

Elementary and Secondary Education Act of 1965

An enduring theme in the history of American education has been the effort by many educators and public officials to get the federal government to provide direct aid to public elementary and secondary schools. In the late nineteenth century, and then again in the early decades of the twentieth century, supporters of a substantial federal role in education attempted and failed to pass legislation. In the early 1960s, Presidents Kennedy and Johnson called on the public schools to take responsibility in doing their work and doing it right. This call was partly because of the international challenge that the US was confronting following the success of the Sputnik project by the Soviet Union and partly as a responsibility to improving the economic conditions of the American citizenry and, particularly, the minority groups. The major piece of federal legislation was the passing of the Elementary and Secondary Education Act of 1965 (ESEA) in response to public concern about the schooling of disadvantaged children. This law, representing a major federal commitment to the nation's elementary and secondary schools, has been reauthorized regularly since then, and most recently in January 2002 when President Bush signed it to into law under the No Child Left Behind Act. It would be, therefore, accurate to say that no other single piece of federal legislation reveals so clearly the peculiar commitment of the federal government to education. You might already be asking: what does this have to do with assessment? Remarkably, much! As it has always been, along with federal funding, comes the issue of accountability. To provide a means to document accountability standards must be established. Congress needs to know how well federal funding is being utilized. In essence, therefore, the standards movement, driven by the need for accountability, became a part of the educational landscape which requires that teachers be held accountable for their students' success.

Given the task to imagine what a successful student is, one is likely to paint a portrait which assumes that a successful student is one with a good grade record. Is that an accurate description of a successful student? Probably not. What is wrong with a good GPA as a measure of success? Most teacher education programs require a given GPA value to enter, remain, and successfully exit from the program; you need an attractive GPA to gain admittance to graduate school; and a good employer would like to see a strong GPA to offer the position. However, it is doubtful that a good grade point average describes ones abilities. Dressel (1983) has defined grades in a rather humorous way by saying:

> A grade is an inadequate report of an inaccurate judgment by a biased and variable judge of the extent to which a student has attained an undefined level of mastery of an unknown proportion of an undefined material (p. 10).

While this definition is humorous, it carries a strong element of truth. A GPA does not cover all types of successes relevant to the educational objectives and may reveal a limited dimension of what one knows and can do. This being so, teachers must demand tangible evidence of what the learner knows and can do.

The 1966 Equality of Educational Opportunity Survey

The year following the enactment of the Elementary and Secondary Education Act of 1965 (Title I), the U.S. Office of Education in accordance with the Civil Rights Act of 1964, commissioned an extensive national study lead by James Coleman, then a Hopkins University sociologist. With his colleagues, Professor Coleman issued the report titled: *Equality of Educational Opportunity,* which has come to be widely known as the Coleman Report. It is certainly interesting that the report was released at a time of national unrest. The issues of racial relations and equality were foremost in the public's consciousness and the Coleman's study added fuel, so to say, to the fire.

After analyzing data from some 600,000 students and 60,000 teachers in more than 4,000 schools, Coleman and his colleagues concluded that the quality of schooling a student receives accounts for only about ten percent of the variance in student achievement. To understand what this means, consider the following example: Assume that you are analyzing the mathematics achievement scores for a group of 100 eighth-graders from three different schools. These students will no doubt vary greatly in their mathematics achievement. Some will have very low scores, some very high scores, and some in the middle. The findings from the Coleman report indicate that only ten percent of these differences are caused by the quality of the schools these 100 students attend. In other words, going to the best of the three schools as opposed to the worst of the three schools, will change only about ten percent of the differences in student achievement.

Concluding that public schools did not make a significant difference, Coleman's report credited the student's family background as the main influence to student success in school. His findings suggest that children from poorer families and homes, lacking the prime conditions or values to support education, could not learn, regardless of what the school did.

With the publication of the Coleman Report—Equality of Educational Opportunity—in 1966, educators, especially in North America, were overwhelmed by the evidence that schools in the United States appeared to have far less impact on students' academic achievement than home and neighborhood factors. The notion that the public schools offered all children, regardless of background, the opportunity to become fully-participating citizens, literate, employable, tax-paying, and civic-minded, seemed to be so eroded as to leave many educators feeling in some considerable measure impotent and irrelevant to their students' futures.

The conclusions by Coleman paint a not so hopeful picture for educators and education. If most of what influences student achievement is out of the control of schools, why even try? In retrospect, fortunately, we now see some serious flaws in these conclusions. In fact, we now can look at the possible influence of schools and teachers with great hope. But how is this so? First, the technique used by Coleman of focusing on the percentage of explained differences in scores paints an unnecessarily gloomy picture. This point has been made quite eloquently and convincingly by researchers such as Brophy and Good (1986) who commented: "The myth that teachers do not make a difference in student learning has been refuted" (p. 370). Other researchers include Rosenthal (1991) and Hunter and Schmidt (1990). From such a perspective, schools definitely can make a difference in student achievement. The conclusion that individual teachers can have a profound influence on student learning, even in schools that are relatively ineffective, was first noticed in the 1970s when research focused more on effective teaching practices. Again, a need for standards is evident.

A Nation at Risk

The launching of Sputnik and the recognition of Soviet technology brought much concern on America's success in educating its youth into the spotlight of national concern. Educational critics point out in horror that accountability measures introduced in the mid-1960s were not working. There were widespread reports by employers that high school graduates had not learned the competencies necessary for everyday life and work. Soon after President Reagan went to the White House, he appointed Terrel H. Bell as Secretary of State and asked him to see what was going on with schools. Bell and his team formed the National Commission on Excellence in Education and embarked on their four major charges:

- ❖ Assess the quality of teaching and learning in the nation's schools
- ❖ Compare American schools to those of other industrialized nations
- ❖ Assess the degree to which major social and educational changes since Sputnik had impacted on pupil achievement

❖ Define problems that must be faced in order to attain excellence in education

As a result of those investigative efforts, Bell published in 1983—*A nation at risk: The imperative for educational reform* which confirmed that "Some 23 million Americans adults are functionally illiterate by the simplest test of everyday reading, writing and composition" and that "about 13 percent of all 17 year-olds in the United States can be considered functionally illiterate." Many could hardly fill out a job application or read a simple map. Bell's report presented strong and dramatic statements resembling a nation at war and with a warning:

> The educational foundations of our society are presently being eroded by a rising tide of mediocrity that threatens our very future as a nation and a people. If an unfriendly foreign power had attempted to impose on America the mediocre educational performance that exists today, we might well have viewed it as an act of war. As it stands, we have allowed this to happen to ourselves. We have even squandered the gains in student achievement made in the wake of the Sputnik challenge. Moreover, we have dismantled essential support systems, which helped make those gains possible. We have, in effect, been committing an act of unthinkable, unilateral disarmament (p.5).

The National Commission for Excellence in Education (NCEE, 1983) recommended that the American educational systems distances itself from accepting the minimum to demanding rigorous and measurable standards when it issued the following statement:

> Standardized tests of achievement . . . should be administered at major transition points from one level of schooling to another. . . . The purpose of these tests would be to: (a) certify the pupil's credentials; (b) identify the need for remedial intervention; and (c) identify the opportunity for advanced or accelerated work. The tests should be administrated as part of a nationwide . . . system of state and local standardized tests (p. 28).

Although accountability for test scores may serve as a catalyst for change by focusing the spotlight on academic success and failure, it is unlikely that it will provide any substantial inputs into the system. Testing is primarily an outcome-measuring device. Test scores alone are not a sufficient motivator of change. They merely highlight the need for a process that can take the raw data that is collected, analyze it, use that data to inform decision making, and redirect resources to address areas of need. In effect, standardized tests are simply one tool that ought to be supplemented with a variety of inputs that are necessary for continuous school improvement.

National Board for Professional Teachers Standards

In 1986, three years after *A Nation at Risk* the Carnegie Task Force on Teaching as a Profession issued a pivotal report, *A Nation prepared: Teachers for the 21st Century*. Its leading recommendation called for the establishment of a National Board for Professional Teaching Standards (NBPTS), which are high and rigorous in nature as expectations for what teachers need to know and be able to do.

The mission of the National Board for Professional Teaching Standards is:

* ❖ To establish high and rigorous standards for what accomplished teachers should know and be able to do.
* ❖ To develop and operate a national, voluntary system to access and certify teachers who meet these standards.
* ❖ To advance related education reforms for the purpose of improving student learning in American schools.

It is evident from this mission statement that educational reforms involve more than merely changing the nature of test taking tasks. It involves a defined framework which includes curriculum content, process (delivery method), and the product (which is what students know and can do). Removing any component of this framework, however, will severely weaken assessment (Takona, 1999) and require careful thought into the kind of changes in the scoring of performance tasks. How can one document achievement and consider both process and product? Because it is always not possible to analyze performance and categorize them into a series of separate attributes, rubrics are come to be considered as a useful method in evaluating student work. However, how can grades be standardized with this type of system? Essentially, there is no easy answer. Rubrics can serve in a holistic evaluation or guide a process that evaluates various parts that address specific skills. However, some of these begin to look standardized after they are broken down into many categories that address various skills and sub-skills.

In response, mainly, to the 1983 *A-Nation-at-Risk* report on the mediocre performance of American students on national and international tests, former President Bush and the nation's governors jointly convened the first National Education Summit in 1989 in Charlottesville, Virginia. The summit led to the establishment of several long-term goals for public education and spawned a host of national commissions, task forces and study groups, including the National Council on Education Standards and Testing. The main objectives of the plan were to improve student achievement in core subjects and to lead the world in math and science test scores by the year 2000, making America's children internationally competitive.

The goals are based on three basic premises: (1) that all children can learn, (2) that lasting improvement can be made only through the leadership and collaboration of local and state education departments with the support of their communities, (3) and that reform must take place at all levels (USDOE, 1998).

Goals 2000: Educate America Act

President Clinton, often considered an educational reformer, continued to make education an important part of his administration's agenda. Clinton favored national standards that were developed during the previous administrations. In his 1997 State of the Union message to Congress, he made strong recommendations for the establishment of standards for teachers based on the National Board for Professional Teaching Standards.

In the late 1980s, an educational partnership called Educate America 2000 was created between the nation's governors and the Bush administration. When President Bill Clinton entered office, he used the framework of the Educate America 2000 partnership to sign legislation into law.

The 1990s brought the *Goals 2000: Educate America Act* that sets standards as the centerpiece of educational reform efforts. The *Goals 2000: Educate America* Act, signed into law March 31, 1994, marked a major turning point in the focus of federal education legislation. The act endorses national education goals and procedures to establish education standards, provides grants to states and local districts to advance reform, promotes deregulation for improved flexibility with federal programs that serve the same children, and develops work-force skill standards. Through these provisions, *Goals 2000* is helping states and localities build a new capacity for an education system that promotes higher levels of performance by all students.

Goals 2000 is based on The National Education Goals initiative which outlines essentially an eight-point program to create and enforce "national standards" for all school children, in an effort to "reform" America's failing education system. The eight goals are as listed in Figure 2.1.

Figure 2.1: National Education Goals

GOAL #1: School Readiness-all children must be socialized by school age in order to be ready for what they will encounter in the schoolroom.

GOAL #2: School Completion-90 percent of American children will graduate from high school by the year 2000.

GOAL #3: Student Achievement and Citizenship-mandatory testing in grades 4, 8, and 12 to determine competency in humanities and sciences.

GOAL #4: Teacher Education and Professional Development-all teachers must participate in ongoing skills training.

GOAL #5: Mathematics and Science-U.S. students are to be "first in the world" in math and science by 2000.

GOAL #6: Adult Literacy and Lifelong Learning-claims that every American adult will be literate and socially equipped by the same year.

GOAL #7: Safe, Disciplined, and Alcohol- and Drug-free Schools-commits the federal government and allied agencies to enforce discipline in the classroom.

GOAL #8: Parental Participation-schools will promote "partnerships" with parents to increase parental involvement in "promoting the social, emotional, and academic growth of children."

Source: National Education Goals Panel. (1997). *National education goals: Building a nation of learners* [Online]. Available: http://www.negp.gov/negp/reports/97report.pdf [Retrieved November 30, 2002].

The primary aim of education is to construct a continuous path of development for each individual and to increase each person's experience base for meaningful learning. This legislation expects that educators at all levels be involved. Universities are one of the important partners in the implementation of Goals 2000 and the improvement of teaching and learning in schools.

These goals are expected to speak to teachers, instructors, and others involved in designing curriculum or implementing instruction. They contribute to understanding effective strategies that can address problems of low levels of academic achievement. Policy makers have become convinced that schools will not be able to turn out better-educated students without highly skilled, knowledgeable teachers. As a first step, all states are participating in Goals 2000 at the state or local levels. In addition many states are now setting stiffer requirements such as standardized tests, including the Praxis Series, for entry into and graduating from teacher preparation programs. In all estimates, these goals are difficult to reach. However, it is noteworthy to observe that in November of 1996, the annual report tracking the progress of Goals 2000 issued by the National Education Goals Panel stated that the overall national performance in the implementation of Goals 2000 objectives has been virtually static.

National Commission on Teaching and America's Future

In their work, *What Matters Most: Teaching for America's Future*, the National Commission on Teaching and America's Future (1996), articulates an imperative establishing high and rigorous standards for what teachers should know and be able to do and to advance related education reforms for the purpose of improving student learning. The report contains an analysis of a representative number of schools of education and finds them to have "unenforced standards for teachers" (p. 27), and "major flaws in teacher preparation" (p. 31). Beginning with the premise that the quality of teachers is the most important factor in children's education, the commission makes two recommendations to improve student learning. First, it calls for "renewing the national promise to bring every American child up to world-class standards in core academic areas" (p. 64). Second, it recommends "developing and enforcing rigorous standards for teacher preparation, initial licensing, and continuing development" (p. 64). A performance-based standards approach to teacher licensing and certification is a significant departure from traditional methods that have prescribed testing, credits, and courses as the primary requirements for becoming a teacher.

In his 1997 State of the Union message to Congress, President Bill Clinton, made strong recommendations for the establishment of standards for teachers based on the National Board for Professional Teaching Standards. Consistent with this call to action, the National Council for Teacher Education (NCATE, 2000) redefined its set of accreditation standards and required documentation of the impact of pre-service teachers on the learning of their students. Current NCATE standards (widely known as NCATE 2000) require that teacher preparation programs adhere to specified standards that include a requisite to assess the performance of pre-service teachers over time in a variety of ways using multiple measures and linking the expected performance on institutional, state, and professional standards. To effectively respond to these mandates, teacher education programs have responded by setting higher standards for pre-service teachers. Concomitantly, they have also developed and instituted assessment systems that yield defensible and credible evidence regarding pre-service teacher's abilities to meet those standards and impact PreK-12 student learning.

No Child Left Behind Act of 2002

To close the achievement gap with accountability, flexibility, and choice, so that no child is left behind, President George W. Bush has laid out four principles of education reform that provided the basis of the recently reauthorized Elementary & Secondary Education Act (ESEA) entitled the No Child Left Behind Act and signed into law on January 8, 2002. The principles are listed in Box 2.1.

Box 2.1

📁   Accountability for results
📁   Local control and flexibility
📁   Empowering parents to participate more meaningfully in their children's education
📁   Employing research-based practices that work to improve student performance

This law is founded on the premise that every struggling child can learn—and every struggling *school* can rebound. The No Child Left Behind Act presupposes to provide a roadmap and the resources for even the most troubled public schools in America to pull them up.

Further, the No Child Left Behind Act expects teachers in public schools to be experts in the subject areas they teach and are prepared to effectively engage in the challenges of a growing diverse population of students who may have a variety of multicultural, multi-linguistic, as well as multi-ability needs. This Act expects teachers to have an impact on student learning. Such and impact is only possible when teacher have a mastery of content knowledge and have pedagogical skills. Mastery involves performing at high levels. Citing the work of Engelman who likens mastery to a stairway, Martella and his associates (2003) have stated "mastery is the guarantee that students are able to reach each stair without falling" (p. 178). To that end teacher preparation programs play a significant role in the preparation of highly qualified teachers who can provide the necessary support called for by the complex 21st century society. A quality program ensures high-quality learning experiences and assessment based on sound and proven theoretical principles.

On July 1, 2002, the federal government began providing a portion of the $5 billion allocation making it the largest increase in funding in history of the United States, along with unprecedented local control and flexibility. In exchange, the No Child Left Behind legislation expects educational institutions to deliver better results for the nation's children.

Era of Standards

What are standards anyway and where do they come from? Standards are statements that identify the essential knowledge and skills that should be taught and learned in school. Essential knowledge is what students should know. Essential knowledge includes the most important and enduring ideas, issues, dilemmas, principles, and concepts from the disciplines. Essential skills are what students should have and be able to use. By definition what are skills? Skills are abilities that go beyond those commonly associated with work. Skills include ways of thinking, problem solving, investigation and analysis, and communication abilities. Skills can come from all aspects of your life, from courses, work experience, as well as from extra-curricula activities and interests. Standards lay the foundation and identify related behaviors and attitudes that assure success when skills are applied whether in or out of school. These include but are not limited to providing evidence to back up assertions and developing productive fulfilling relationships with others (Carr and Harris, 2001).

The standards-based reform effort has three essential components:

- ❖ What teachers should teach and what students should learn—that is the part that is content-standards;
- ❖ What the acceptable level of performance should be—that is performance standards
- ❖ How the content and performance is going to be evaluated—that is assessment.

The standards-based reform effort is, essentially, hinged upon a concrete model of educational practice that delineates a high standards curricula and meaningful instructional techniques into the classroom (Swanson and Stevenson, 2002). A meaningful interpretation of a learner's performance requires relating that performance to a reference point. In this case the standards are the reference point. The emphasis on alignment is based on the premise that what is taught influences by what is assessed. Therefore, an alignment of assessments with content standards is essential. According to the National Education Goals Panel (1993), "without high standards, we will not be able to rebuild America's education system—they are absolutely pivotal if we are to thrive and prosper."

How are We Doing?

From the background that described, it is reasonable to postulate that the cure to education in American lays in the teachers themselves and not the students or the curriculum. Goodlad (1984) gave an immediate response to the reform movement of the 60s and 70s "that the movement never became linked to the structures and institutions preparing and certifying teachers" (p. 293). Teachers entering the classroom were not prepared to implement an innovative curriculum. Earlier, Cohen (1978) had observed the preparation process of teacher as not doing its best and concluded:

Unfortunately, teacher education . . . remained unprepared for inter-disciplinary proposals. As a result, the successes of many interdiscipli-nary programs depend on the ad hoc inventions of imaginative and dedicated teachers, who must learn for themselves how to be inter-disciplinarians (p. 124).

Goodlad (1984) found that "teacher education programs are disturb-ingly alike and almost uniformly inadequate" (p. 315). He suggested that the improvement of schools depends upon innovative preparation of teach-ers. He called for major restructuring in the way teachers are prepared as while indicating skepticism when he state ". . . the relatively minor adjustments of the past have proven to be almost completely futile (p. 317).

How are institutions of higher education involving themselves in meeting such a colossal challenge? It might not appear apparent to you as a student that your college or university grumbles about and struggles to make this happen. Indeed, many colleges and universities are engaged with educators, policy makers, concerned citizens, and others in the de-velopment of content and performance standards in core academic areas. These standards are challenging and of high quality, asking all students to reach the level of academic achievement now reached by only a few who have access to better opportunities. Many teacher education pro-grams have developed a philosophical document commonly known as a conceptual framework. Examine a sample Conceptual Framework (LeMoyne-Owen College) contained in Appendix A. This document sets forth a training approach, performance standards and a path towards their attainment. These standards become a means of accountability.

Summary of Key Points

This chapter has presented important background on the history of as-sessment as it traced it as far back as the biblical times, through early civilizations and down to modern times. While the manner in which as-sessment has been administered has varied, a wide use of standardized testing may have first appeared in the United States when Horace Mann began using them in Massachusetts and Connecticut in the 1830s. This practice led to the development of the Mann's Boston Survey in 1846, thus becoming the first printed test for large-scale assessment of student achievement in various disciplines. Standardized tests were again recommended soon after Joseph Rice conducted tests in a number of large school systems in 1895. Shortly thereafter, the Stanford-Binet gained wide acceptance in the United States and quickly became the standard American "Intelligence test". Dewey's progressive education movement in the 1930s favored instruction that was based on natural learning and practical problems, but the boom in standardized assessment led to a boom in the technical development of tests to compare schools on a larger scale.

We have observed that the current assessment reforms involve more than merely changing the nature of test taking tasks. Opposition against standardized testing grew soon after educators realized shortcomings of standardized testing in reflecting the true picture. This realization lead to exploration of alternatives to standardized testing that fall under the term "alternative assessment." Most recently, standard-based assessment, also called performance-based assessment, is in vogue.

An enduring topic in the history of education in this country has been the effort to get the federal government to provide direct aid to public elementary and secondary schools. The last four decades have seen the emergence of a number of significant efforts and landmark reports initiated to address the effectiveness of the American educational system. Among the most significant reports is the 1983 report issued by the National Commission on Excellence in Education popularly known as *A-Nation-at-Risk*. The report issued a critical characterization of the American public citing mediocre performance of American students on national and international tests.

The report has continued to receive significant responses from both educators and policy makers. Some of its significant responses include the action of former President George Bush and the nation's governors who jointly convened the first National Education Summit in 1989 in Charlottesville, Virginia. The summit led to the establishment of several long-term goals for public education and spawned a host of national commissions, task forces and study groups, including the National Council on Education Standards and Testing. President Bill Clinton made education an important part of their administration's agenda. Clinton favored national standards that were developed during the previous administrations.

The *Goals 2000: Educate America Act*, signed into law March 31, 1994, marked a major turning point in the focus of federal education legislation. The act endorsed national education goals and procedures to establish education standards, provide grants to states and local districts to advance reform, promote deregulation for improved flexibility with federal programs that serve the same children, and develop work-force skill standards. Through these provisions, *Goals 2000* is helping states and localities build a new capacity for an education system that promotes higher levels of performance by all students.

It is certainly appropriate to refer to the current reform movement as an emerging era of standards. In this chapter we have defined standards as statements identify the essential knowledge and skills that should be taught and learned in school. Essential knowledge is what students should know. Essential skills are what students should be able to do. In this chapter, we have observed that the standards-based reform effort ranging from teacher's and student's skills to levels of acceptable performance to approach toward evaluating content and performance. The standards-based reform is founded upon a concrete model of educational practice that delineates high standards curricula and instructional techniques into the classroom. Alignment of assessments with content standards is essential.

This chapter has also reviewed the literature suggesting that the improvement of schools depends upon innovative preparation of teachers. Many teacher education programs have developed a philosophical document commonly known as a Conceptual Framework.

References

Atkinson, C., and Melaske, E.T. (1965). *The Story of Education.* New York: Bantam Books.

Bloom, B.S., Englehart, M.D., Furst, E., Hill, W.H., & Krathwohl, D. R., (Eds). (1956). *Taxonomy of educational objectives: The classification of educational goals. Handbook I: Cognitive domain.* New York: David McKay.

Bracey, Gerald. (2002). *The war against American public schools: Privatizing schools, commercializing education.* Boston, MA: Allyn and Bacon.

Buros, O. K. (Ed). (1965). *The mental measurements yearbook.* Highland Park, New Jersey: Gryphon Press.

Brophy, J., & Good, T. (1986). Teacher behavior and student achievement. In M. Wittrock (Ed.), *Handbook of research on teaching* (pp. 340-370). NY: Macmillan.

Carr, Judy F., & Harris, Douglas E. (2001). *Succeeding with standards.* Alexandria, VA: ASCD.

Chauncey, H. and J.E. Dobbin. (1963). Testing: *Its place in education today.* New York: Harper & Row.

Cohen, M. (1978). Whatever happened to interdisciplinary education? *Educational Leadership*, 36(2), 122-126.

Cureton, L.E. (1971). The history of grading practice. *NCME Measurement in Education*, 2 (4) 1-8.

DuBois, P. H. (1966). A test-dominated society: China, 115 B.C.— 1905 A.D. In A. Anastasi (editor). *Testing problems in perspective.* Washington, D.C.: American Council of Education.

Dressel, P. (1983). Grades: one more Tilt at the windmill. In A.W. Chickering. *AAHE Bulletin.* 35 (8), 10-13.

Goodlad, J. I. (1984). *A place called school: Prospects for the future.* New York: McGraw-Hill.

Eisner, E. W. (1995). Educational reform and the ecology of schooling. In A. C. Ornstein & L. S. *Behar* (Eds.), *Contemporary issues in curriculum* (pp. 390-402). Boston, Mass: Allyn & Bacon.

Martella, R. C., Nelson, J.R., & Marchand-Martella, N.E. (2003). *Managing Disruptive Behaviors in the Schools.* Boston, MA: Allyn & Bacon.

North Central Regional Educational Laboratory. (2002). *From High-Stakes Testing to Assessment for School Improvement.* http://www.ncrel.org/policy/pubs/html/beyond/stakes.htm [Retrieved July 7, 2003].

National Commission on Excellence in Education, (NCEE). (1983). *A Nation at risk: The imperative for educational reform.* Washington, DC: Government Printing Office.

National Commission on Teaching and America's Future. (1996). *What matters most: Teaching for America's future.* New York: NCTAF.

National Board for Professional Teaching Standards (1994). *What teachers should know and be able to do.* Detroit, MI.: NBPTS.

Rosenthal, D.M. (1991). *The nature of the mind.* New York: Oxford University Press.

Swanson, C.B., & Stevenson, D. L. (2002). Standards-based reform in practice: Evidence on state policy and classroom instruction from the NAEP state assessments. *Educational Evaluation and Policy Analysis*. 24(1), 1-27.

Takona, J. (1999). *Distribution of undergraduate Examination questions among the specified levels: A case of an African university.* Clearinghouse Research Report No HE033165. (ERIC Document Reproduction Service No. 444429).

National Education Goals Panel. (1997). *National education goals: Building a nation of learners* [Online]. Available: http://www.negp.gov/negp/reports/97report.pdf [Retrieved November 30, 2002].

U.S. Department of Education. (1998). Goals 2000: Reforming education to improve student achievement *http://www.ed.gov/pubs/g2kreforming/g2ch1.html*

Chapter 3

Setting Learning Expectations

Orientation

In the previous Chapter, we became aware of the dynamics of the current reform movement within the American educational system. Emphasis has been focused on quality education and accountability. Both quality education and accountability require standards. Increased calls for accountability in education are challenging teacher preparation programs to examine traditional methods of preparing teachers. Emphasis has shifted from the process of preparation of pre-service teachers to performance. In respond to these calls, teacher preparation institutions must assure that pre-service teachers have the knowledge, skills, and dispositions to impact learning for PreK-12 students. An almost universal action from a vast number of institutions has been the adoption of standards. These standards have either been delineated by professional education entities or the institution itself develops its own. In this chapter, we will examine where current standards come from and why they are important within an educational system. As a preface to the understanding of effective principles and practices in the development of a pre-service teacher portfolio, knowledge of this information is important in giving you a background on why and what standards you need to become aware of as you prepare for the teaching profession.

Focus Questions

- Who sets standards and why?
- Why are standards important within an educational system?
- How would you make a sharp distinction between a mission statement, standard, and performance outcomes?
- Who and how are accomplished teachers assessed?
- How are standards assessed and what do assessment results tell?

Keeping your Fours

Once upon a time in the land of Fuzz, King Aling called in his cousin Ding and commanded, "Go ye out into all of Fuzzland and find me the goodest of men, who I shall reward for his goodness."

"But how will I know one when I see one?" Asked the Fuzzy.

"Why, he will be sincere," Scoffed the king, and whacked off a leg for his impertinence.

So, the Fuzzy limped out to find a good man. But soon he returned, confused and empty-handed.

"But how will I know one when I see one?" he asked again.

"Why, he will be dedicated," grumbled the king, and whacked off another leg for his impertinence.

So the Fuzzy hobbled away once more to look for the goodest of men. But again he returned, confused and empty-handed.

"But how will I know one when I see one?" he pleaded.

"Why, he will have an *emphatic understanding of self-actualizing potential,*" fumed the king, and whacked off another leg for his impertinence.

So the Fuzzy, now on his last leg, hopped out to continue his search. In time, he returned with the wisest, most sincere, and more dedicated Fuzzy in all of Fuzzland, and stood him before the king.

"Why, this man won't do at all," roared the king. "He is much too thin to suit me." Whereupon, he whacked off the last leg of the Fuzzy, who fell to the floor with a squishy thump." (Mager, 1984, vii)

The moral of the fable is: if you can't tell one when you see one, you may wind up without a leg to stand on. Moreover, it is possible that you have heard someone say, "You can't define a good teacher." "Nobody can say what a good teacher is." Maybe you can answer those questions by saying: "It all depends on what your definition for competent is." The ultimate aim of any teacher education program, be it in a large university or a small liberal arts college, is to prepare competent, caring, and qualified teachers. Teacher quality is essential to student learning, to the future of our families, nation, and the ultimate destiny of our humanity and economy. The more teachers know and can do, and the better they are prepared, the more their students will learn. Conversely, the less teachers know and can do and the poorer they are prepared, the more their students will struggle with learning. Improving the quality of education for all students has been a priority for the past two decades as political and education leaders have focused attention on how well children are learning and what skills they are attaining. Among the strategies that have been used to respond to the demand of quality education is the introduction of rigorous standards for pre-service teachers by state legislatures, professional standards boards, state boards of education, licensing agencies, and colleges and universities. The general American public has come to believe that the key to educational improvement lies in upgrading the quality of teachers rather than changing the school structure or the curriculum. Public focus as evident in Gallup polls in recent years has consistently focused on high quality teachers. In the 2002 Phi Kappan Gallup poll, an overwhelming (96%) majority of the American public believes that qualified and competent teachers are key to improving public school achievement (Rose & Gallup, 2002).

Emergence of Standards

Soon after the Coleman report of 1966, new approaches to educational assessment emerged with a growing emphasis on assessing the outcomes of schooling at the local and the state levels. Such emphasis has continued to find further currency as research reveals a number of anomalies including SAT declines (NCEE, 1983; USDE, 1993; Doyle, 1994). With the dramatic national decline students are ill-prepared for higher education and the workplace. As we had observed Chapter 2, a great many legislations and public agendas catapulted the rise of standards. The landmark report, *A Nation at risk: The imperative for educational reform* (1983) called for rigorous and measurable standards. Although the term standard has been around the field of education for a long time, it has become more prominent in recent years as the authentic assessment movement has taken off. The term standards gained its prominence than missions, goals, or objectives for two reasons. First, like objectives, standards are amenable to assessment, which is a requirement to instruction (Tyler, 1950). Second, the broader nature of standards versus objectives is consistent with performance-based assessment's emphasis on complex, integrative authentic tasks that typically span the total breadth of the teacher education program. Performance-based assessments are, particularly useful when learners are working on long-term projects. Long-term projects provide the learner opportunities to bring into play a variety of resources thus giving them a fair means of demonstrating mastery of various concepts and principles. Authentic assessments are similar to performance assessments except that learners demonstrate their knowledge, skills and dispositions in a real-life context.

Arthur Wise, President of NCATE asserts that:

> The standards, which focus on candidate performance, represent a revolution in teacher preparation. . . . It is not enough for a faculty member to say, 'I taught the material.' Performance-based accreditation is based on results-results that demonstrate that the teacher candidate knows the subject matter and can teach it effectively in a real classroom. The institutions will need to provide credible evidence that their schools of education achieve this goal.

An initiative undertaken to strengthen the teaching profession embodied the establishment in 1987 of the National Board for Professional Teaching Standards (NTBTS). The primary focus of NBPTS (National Board for Professional Teaching Standards, 2001) is to develop standards for the advanced certification of accomplished teachers. This, then, provides the teaching profession the rigorous approach that professional certifying agencies do in assessing physicians, architects, accountants, and others. The National Board for Professional Standards has since developed standards and assessments for evaluating accomplished teaching. These standards articulate in performance-based terms what an accomplished teacher knows and is able to do. This focus on performance has the great advantage of illuminating what an expert teacher can do and how such a teacher uses knowledge to support learning for all students. A major question that arises regards standards.

In 1990, the Interstate New Teacher Assessment and Support Consortium (INTASC) began developing a set of standards (see Figure 3.1) for beginning teachers to serve as a framework for the systemic reform of teacher preparation and professional development. The core standards are now broadly recognized as providing a sound framework for reforming teacher education. The momentum generated by the articulation of the core standards establishes the imperative that performance-based licensing becomes a reality.

Moving toward performance-based licensing in teaching is quickly becoming a driving force in the general vision for rethinking the design of teacher preparation programs and for restructuring the systems by which departments of education train teachers and the kinds of practices licensing agencies must engage in. It lays out the components of a performance-based licensing system, including the use of performance-based assessments for licensing and the replacement of course-counting strategies. Moreover, it describes the policies necessary to enact and maintain such a system: the redesign of licensing, the redesign of program accountability requirements, and the creation of incentives for ongoing professional development.

Finally, it considers some of the factors that determine the success of standards-based reforms. The ten standards articulated by INTASC are performance-based and are built upon and compatible with those of the major national organizations. Their intent is to articulate what entering teachers should know, be like, and be able to do in order to practice responsibly, and to begin the journey toward deepening expertise that will enable highly accomplished practice as the teacher's career evolves. Most teacher education programs in the United States are incorporating INTASC standards into their assessment systems to achieve a broader effect on the preparation and professional development of teachers. In many cases, teacher education programs and many school districts that have adopted INTASC standards require that pre-service teachers develop their portfolio around these standards.

Setting standards is like building a pyramid. Each layer depends on the strengths of the others. Students will not be able to achieve higher standards of learning unless teachers are prepared to teach in new ways

Figure 3.1: INTASC Standards

Standard #1—Knowledge of Subject Matter -The teacher understands the central concepts, tools of inquiry, and structure of the discipline(s) he or she teaches and can create learning experiences that make these aspects of subject matter meaningful for students.

Standard #2—Knowledge of Human Development and Learning—The teacher understands how children learn and develop, and can provide learning opportunities that support their intellectual, social, and personal development.

Standard #3—Adapting Instruction for Individual Needs—The teacher understands how students differ in their approaches to learning and creates instructional opportunities that are adapted to diverse learners.

Standard #4—Multiple Instructional Strategies—The teacher understands and uses a variety of instructional strategies to encourage students' development of critical thinking, problem solving, and performance skills.

Standard #5—Classroom Motivation and Management Skills—The teacher uses an understanding of individual and group motivation and behavior to create a learning environment that encourages positive social interaction, active engagement of learning, and self-motivation.

Standard #6—Communication Skills—The teacher uses knowledge of effective verbal, nonverbal and media communication techniques to foster active inquiry, collaboration, and supportive interaction in the classroom.

Standard #7—Instructional Planning Skills—The teacher plans instruction based on knowledge of subject matter, students, the community, and curriculum goals.

Standard #8—Assessment of Student Learning—The teacher understands and uses formal and informal assessment strategies to ensure the continuous intellectual, social, and physical development of the learner.

Standard #9—Professional Commitment and Responsibility—The teacher is a reflective practitioner who continually evaluates the effects of his or her choices and actions on others (students, parents, and other professionals in the learning community), and who actively seeks out opportunities to grow professionally.

Standard #10—Partnerships—The teacher fosters relationships with school colleagues, parents, and agencies in the larger community to support students' learning and well-being.

Source: Interstate New Teacher Assessment and Support Consortium. (1998). *Model standards for beginning teacher licensing and development: A resource for state dialogue.* Washington, DC: Council of Chief State School Officers

and schools are prepared to support high-quality teaching. The National Commission on Teaching and America's Future affirmed this when it stated "higher standards for students must ultimately mean higher standards for teachers and schools" (NCTAF 1996, p. 27).

In addition, the need for standards emanates from the belief that there are competencies that those who enter the workforce must possess to be successful. In 1990, Elizabeth Dole, then secretary of the Department of Labor, established the Secretary's Commission on Achieving Necessary Skills (SCANS) which developed a set of generic competencies and foundation skills that all workers will need in the future (U.S. Department of Labor, 1991). These skills include flexible problem solving, respecting the desires of the customer, working well on teams, taking responsibility for one's own performance, and continuous learning and have been developed to guide the efforts of educational reform in the direction helping more students to make the transition to work successfully. Collectively, the need for standards and effort to achieve them represents a substantial challenge for the American schools. The use of standards implies that all students must achieve at much higher levels.

Mission Statement

Few, if any, universities and colleges in the United States are without a mission statement. Individual units, for example a teacher education program, have their own mission statements that draw from the broader statements of the institution. What are mission statements for and why are they so popular? The idea of a mission statement has been around for long time. Businesses, religious institutions, and schools have historically formulated their own mission statements for various purposes. Mission statements are developed to serve a purpose – to direct and guide the operations of an institution. When careful thought is not exercised, these statements often degenerate to mere marketing slogan purposed, at best, to make stakeholders feel good. Some mission statements are short and cute. For example, you might recognize this popular business mission statement: "We like to see you smile." Or this other: "Satisfaction or your money back guarantee."

Figure 3.2
Graduating Senior competencies for LeMoyne-Owen College

- Think creatively, critically, logically, and analytically using both quantitative and qualitative methods for solving problems.

- Communicate effectively (listen, speak, read and write) on formal and informal levels.

- Distinguish, clarify, and refine personal values for the attainment of richer self-perception and relate those values to the value systems of others.

- Appreciate, understand, and know the foundations of the Afrocentric perspective.

- Appreciate, understand, and know the foundations of diverse cultures in the context of a global community.

- Appreciate, understand, know, and pursue the principles, methods and subject matter that underlie the major discipline(s).

- Accept social responsibility and provide service to humankind.

- Maintain levels of literacy that allow them to understand the impact of science and technology on individuals, society and the environment.

- Attain motivational, personal management, interpersonal skills, professional development and research experience, as well as resourcefulness that will form the basis for a career and/or further educational experiences.

- Attain critical skills, frame of reference, and understanding needed to appreciate and discriminate between artistic achievements.

Typically, mission statements are broad, lofty, and difficult to understand, yet very inspirational. Have you ever wondered who writes them? Ideally, mission statements are a product of consensus. Mission statements are often written by a cross-sectional team of faculty, administrators, staff, other educators, and concerned citizens to ensure that everyone is represented. Having participated in the development process these various constituencies are assured a command of ownership. A vast majority of institutions publish their mission statements in catalogues and other widely published documents. A mission statement is typically the broadest statement of what students are intended to know and be able to do when they graduate. The purpose of mission statements is changing constantly though. Commonly, they are used for internal as well as external purposes. Mission statements let faculty, administration, staff, students and other stakeholders know what the purpose, goals, and values of their institution are. They unify and define the institution, its course, and vision. Mission statements attempt to communicate to all constituencies the purposes of education. Listed below are examples of a mission statement:

. . . to prepare students in a nurturing and student-centered community for lives of success, service and leadership.

—LeMoyne-Owen College

. . . is a learner centered community dedicated to continuing improvement in meeting student needs. Preparing individuals to serve in a changing world, the institution provides a quality educational experience in an innovative culture and a technologically enhanced environment

—Valley City State University

. . . seeks to be a premier institution for helping students gain the knowledge, skills, and the moral and ethical attitudes necessary to achieve their personal goals and contribute to the welfare of their communities in the global society. The College endeavors to impart a desire for life-long learning and an enhanced capacity for critical and creative thinking so that students can reap the reward of intellectual growth and professional effectiveness.

—Wesley College

. . . our mission, therefore, is the search for truth, the discovery and sharing of knowledge, the fostering of personal and professional excellence, the promotion of a life of faith, and the development of leadership expressed in service to others.

—Marquette University

A well articulated mission statement provides a useful guide against which progress can be compared to determine if the institution is and its programs follow a consistent and productive path. Along with the mission statement, most universities develop competencies statements that accurately define dimensions of gains expected of their students upon graduation. A university whose students, upon graduation, can demonstrate an acceptable level of proficiency, as reflected by performance competency statements, can justify its claim to have prepared students well. Performance outcomes often identify a set of goals that specifically, yet still broadly, define expectations for students. Figure 3.2 provides an example of performance competencies expected of graduating seniors at LeMoyne-Owen College. A clearly written, purposeful statement can serve as an excellent starting point for curriculum development, instruction and assessment.

If your institution has a set of competencies, sometimes referred to as performance outcomes, they may have been written broadly enough to accommodate various program content areas. Some institutions or programs within institutions explicate these competencies in various ways. Some choose to define them in rubric form while others selectively redefine within curricula. Redefining them within curricular includes breaking the broader competency statements into simple objective statements. The statements of what students must know and be able to do are explicated in standards and consequently, more numerous within a curriculum. The most specific and numerous are the *objectives*. Objectives are typically written at the level of a course and may be outlined in a course syllabus.

Figure 3.3 provides a comparative summary of the characteristics of mission and objective statements. Mission and purpose statements are typically written to serve as benchmarks to be measured. Furthermore, they are written as a declaration of a broader vision of an institution. Moreover, their language does not usually make them amenable to assessment. On the other hand, standards and objectives are written with measurements in mind. Effective standards are written in a manner that describes observable behaviors.

Figure 3.3 Comparative Characteristics of Mission and Objective

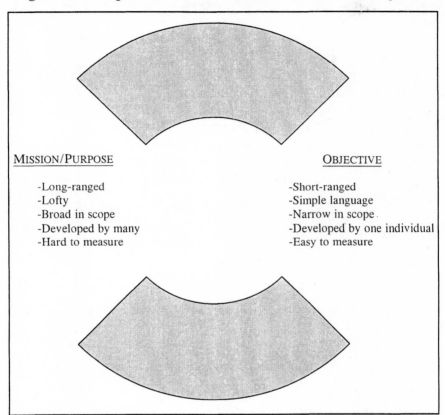

MISSION/PURPOSE

  -Long-ranged
  -Lofty
  -Broad in scope
  -Developed by many
  -Hard to measure

OBJECTIVE

  -Short-ranged
  -Simple language
  -Narrow in scope
  -Developed by one individual
  -Easy to measure

Role of Standards

Why are standards important? Two important principles have often been advanced for the development of standards: standards serve both to clarify and to raise expectations, and standards provide a common set of expectations. Ravitch (1996) in her book *National standards in American education: A citizen's guide* provides this explanation:

> Americans . . . expect strict standards to govern construction of buildings, bridges, highways, and tunnels; shoddy work would put lives at risk. They expect stringent standards to protect their drinking water, the food they eat, and the air they breathe. . . . Standards are created because they improve the activity of life (pp. 8-9).

Just as standards improve the daily lives of Americans so too will they improve the effectiveness of American education. As Ravitch asserts: "standards can improve achievement by clearly defining what is to be taught and what kind of performance is expected" (p. 25). Standards provide a way of connecting the entire education system. If decisions have to be made on what students should know and be able to do, what must be included in the curriculum and textbooks and tests and teacher education programs must also be defined. Students benefit most from a structure that has high and clearly articulated academic standards. In many professions, standard setting are a hallmark and continue to pay constant dividends in terms of promoting safe, effective, and competent practices and serves a vital function in terms of protecting public interests. Standards are currently the staple of educational conversation. Textbook and test publishers often develop their products with intent of aligning them with national and state standards. States are trying to align curriculum frameworks and assessments to their standards.

Fox (1999) describes performance-based assessment in the following manner:

> In performance assessment, students construct, rather than select, responses. Students may write, give a speech, solve a problem, or do a project to show what they know. Teachers observe student behavior on those tasks and systematically record information about the student's learning gained from the observation. Teachers are able to see patterns in students' learning and thinking. This method of assessment is ongoing, built as a part of the instructional process. It also drives the instructional process. Students are well prepared for what is expected of them and understand criteria that will be used in assessment. Rubrics explain how tasks will be assessed by defining exemplary, competent, minimal or inadequate performance or other delineations such as advanced, proficient and partially proficient, as required by the U. S. Department of Education (p. 2).

Most teacher education programs and licensing agencies emphasize what teachers need to know and are able to do to help their students learn. Teacher education preparation standards describe the goals of the program, the destinations at which pre-service teachers should arrive at the end of their preparation for the teaching profession and performance expectations in their teaching engagements. A performance standard measures how well pre-service teachers meet the content standard. Performance standards are often depicted by levels—4, 3, 2, and 1; or advanced, proficient, novice, and basic—and are explicated in performance descriptors. These descriptors may be explicated in rubric form. Rubrics describe what pre-service teachers work or performance must consist of to achieve a given score. Performance standards rubrics list expected characteristics, for example, problem-solving skills, communication skills, etc. All examples of problem-solving or communication skills, no matter what the topic, should contain these characteristics.

Wiggins (1993) makes a strong case for implementing performance standards that build accountability when he writes:

> Too many teachers and administrators are in the habit of accepting praise for student success while explaining why student failure is not their fault . . . . In the absence of an accountability system that would make teachers worry more about the effects of teaching than the intent, many educators still do not understand their jobs: many wrongly come to think that their purpose is to teach what they know and like, on a relatively fixed schedule—irrespective of the learning that does or does not ensue. Far too many persist in resolutely moving through the syllabi even when things are clearly not working, when important ideas are not yet understood. They will tell you that they cannot slow down because they must cover the content, yet it is not quite clear why . . . (p. 276).

Moreover, the cumulative effect of performance standards setting have been catalogued into four major uses by Linn (1990). These include:

- ❖ Exhortation, in order to motivate teachers, students, and so on, to greater levels of accomplishment;
- ❖ Exemplification, in order to provide clarity to achievement expectations;
- ❖ Accountability, in which the standards permit schools to be rewarded or sanctioned based on performance;
- ❖ Certification, when standards are associated with decisions for individual students, such as whether to award a diploma, promote to the next grade level, and so on.

So far, we have learned that standards are statements written in terms of what students should know and are able to do. A key role of standards is to provide guidelines and direction for curriculum and assessment development. Beyond this they serve as looking glass into learners' acquisition and mastery of knowledge and skills. The current standards culture also defines standard for teacher knowledge and skills while setting requirements that are linked to standards for PreK-12 student learning. The implicit assumption is that teachers who are knowledgeable and skillful will be successful in helping their students.

Summary of Key Points

Among the strategies commonly used to respond to the demands of quality education is the introduction of rigorous standards for pre-service teachers by state legislatures, professional standards boards, state board of education, licensing agencies, and colleges and universities. The term *standards* gained its prominence more than *mission*, *goals*, or *objectives* for two reasons. Standards are currently the staple of educational conversation. Teacher knowledge and skills requirements are continuously being linked to standards for PreK-12 student learning. Interstate New Teacher Assessment and Support Consortium (INTASC) developed a set of standards for beginning teachers to serve as a framework for the systemic reform of teacher preparation and professional development. The core standards are now broadly recognized as providing such a framework for reforming many aspects of teacher education. Most teacher education programs across the country incorporate INTASC standards into their assessment systems to achieve a broader effect on the preparation and professional development of teachers. In some cases, teacher education programs and many school districts that have adopted INTASC standards require that pre-service and beginning teachers develop their portfolio around them. The standards, which focus on pre-service teacher performance, represent a revolution in teacher preparation. Other standards have been put in place for experienced teachers. NBPTS, for example, has developed standards for the advanced certification of accomplished teachers.

In addition, this chapter has examined the concept of mission statements from whence institutional standards are derived. We described the fact that mission statements are not mere marketing slogans intended to please stakeholders. Rather, mission statements serve as guides and give direction to an institution in its effort to meet its purpose. Further, we examined the role of performance outcome statements as a set of criteria that are intended to motivate teachers, students, and others to greater levels of accomplishment. These statements provide clarity to achievement expectations and permit institutions to either be rewarded or sanctioned based on performance. Finally, performance outcome statements are associated instruments used to base decisions for individual student's promotion and awarding of credentials.

References

Fox, Sandra J. (1999, March 10). Math problems often linked to language. *What works in teaching and learning*, pp. 1-2.

Interstate New Teacher Assessment and Support Consortium. (1998). *Model standards for beginning teacher licensing and development: A resource for state dialogue*. Washington, DC: Council of Chief State School Officers.

Mager, Robert F. (1984). *Goal analysis*. Belmont, CA: David S. Lake Publishers.

Rose, L. C. & Gallup, A. M. (2002). The 34th Annual Phi Delta Kappa/ Gallup Poll of the Public's Attitudes Toward the Public Schools. *Phi Delta Kappan*, 84 (1), 41-56.

National Commission on Teaching and America's Future. (1996). *What matters most: Teaching for America's future*. New York: NCTAF.

Chism, N. (1999). *Peer review of teaching: A sourcebook*. Bolton, MA: Anker.

Martin, Bill. (1983). *Brown Bear, Brown Bear, what do you see?* New York: Henry Holt & Company, Incorporated.

Ravitch, D. (1996). *National standards in American education: A citizen's guide*. Washington, D.C.: The Brookings Institute Press.

Wiggins, G. (1993). Assessing *student performance: Exploring the purpose and limits of testing*. San Francisco, CA: Jossey-Bass Publishers.

U.S. Department of Labor. (1991). *Secretary's commission on achieving necessary skills*. Washington, D.C.: Government Printing Office.

Chapter 4

Assessment in Teacher Education Programs

Orientation

Following nearly four decades of education reform aimed at raising the performance levels of American public school students in area subjects, there has emerged a broad consensus for improving the quality of teachers. In many traditional school settings, students are virtually powerless over what they will learn, how they will learn, how they will demonstrate their learning, and how they will be assessed. In all cases, relationships between teachers and students are usually quite formal. Teachers take the dominant position of transmitters of knowledge while students take the subordinate role of passive recipients of that knowledge and are assumed to consistently strive for excellence with little emphasis on the expression of that knowledge. Further, the teacher takes the active role of examining and grading. Notice the two terms just introduced—examining and grading. Neither one of the two terms truly means assessment (Takona, 2001). True, they are components of assessment. In this chapter, we will look at assessment in relation to learning. After reading this chapter, you will have an understanding of the need for assessment and how it is done. We encourage you to supplement your reading with hands-on performance. As you read, find the answers to the following questions:

Focus Questions

- ☞ What is the difference between the following terms: Assessment, measurement, evaluation, testing, and measuring?
- ☞ Why is authentic assessment becoming a preferred way of assessing students?
- ☞ What kind of assessment are Praxis series examinations?
- ☞ What impact have educational reforms had on assessment?
- ☞ How do students benefit from performance assessment?
- ☞ Where does assessment fit into the overall system of teacher preparation in America? What roles does it play?
- ☞ How has your own experience of assessment affected your teacher preparation opportunities?
- ☞ Have your experiences of assessment affected any other opportunities?

Is this Going to be in the Test?

"Is this going to be on the test?" Doesn't this sounds familiar. It is the kind of phrase repeatedly stated by your peers in the classroom. How about this one: "Pay special attention to this . . . You might want to write it down; it is very important." This statement might have come from your instructor. It could, as well, be the answer to the first question. This is what goes on in the classroom. Statements like these describe that learning is followed by testings and what is learned is done selectively depending on if it going to be required—on the test! If it is not on the test, then you do not need to know or retain it. What should you really know and be able to do? A common mistake made by a vast cross-section of educators—be they PreK-12 or college—as they search for ways to create productive learning opportunities for students, is to consider the partnership of learners in what they learn and the assessment process. When you think about 'assessment' what goes through your mind? Certainly, few might claim a sense of pure joy. How many would rather put off thinking about it if they possibly could? Is that not interesting? Many approach assessment with fear and trepidation viewing it as an unavoidable if not a necessary evil in formal education.

Assessment is a human encounter where the teacher seeks to find out more about the student's abilities (Takona, 2001). Certainly, this is a thorny encounter. Among the thorns in this concept is the endeavor to determine which abilities to assess and how to do it. For instance, should the ability to actively participate in the learning experience be evaluated and graded? If so, how can it be done effectively? What about the ability to speak and write fluently? Is mastery of the discipline-specific knowledge and skills sufficient for awarding a degree or should generic abilities (e.g. problem-solving skills, critical thinking, computer skills, etc) be considered?

Many college courses have both continuous assessments and end-of-semester examinations purposed to determine the final grades. Continuous assessment may include quizzes, short reports on lab experiments, individual or group presentations, book reports, and others. A key responsibility of course instructors is to determine the number and type of assessments appropriate for the aims and objectives of the course. Many instructors struggle with the question of how many and how varied the assignments and assessments for formative and summative purposes are needed. The key is determining appropriate ways of imparting sound educational practices while striking a balance between providing sufficient opportunities for students to develop and demonstrate their abilities without overloading them with work. Of course, you might not think that this is the case, but it is!

Terminologies and Concepts

When we talk about assessment, we place ourselves in a position that lend itself to discussions of what most people consider to be arcane technical topics that include testing, evaluation, and measurement. These terms are frequently used interchangeably. However, these terms have different meanings. Assessment is an integral process that goes on in the educational milieu and is the umbrella term used to describe the process of collecting and synthesizing information to help understand and describe the information being analyzed. Any specific component in an educational environment can be assessed. These components may include curricula, specific courses, equipment, buildings, teachers, staff, and administrators and must all be assessed at various times. A Test is a type of assessment that often uses the paper-and-pencil format and is vulnerable to time limits and may require restricted access to resources. Evaluation relates to a systematic and objective process of making judgment on quality, value or worth of something based on defined criteria. Evaluation is not expressing a personal attitude or feeling. Rather, it involves recognizing and using criteria in different instances (Jonassen, 2000) to make a judgment. Although many regard evaluation as analogous to an activity leading to the assignment of grades, assessment is used to perform a wide variety of functions. Eisner (1994) has articulated some of these functions that are listed in Box 4.1.

Box 4.1

📁   To diagnose
📁   To revise curricula
📁   To compare
📁   To anticipate educational needs
📁   To determine if objectives have been achieved

There is no better way to distinguish the worthwhile from the worthless (Scriven, 1991) without such a process. Typically, assessment can occur in the absence of a test or other objective information. For example, your instructors may assess your progress based on activities that may include systematic assessment. The resulting product of their assessment would be a judgment of quality rather than a measurement. This judgment may be given in qualitative terms such as outstanding, proficient, satisfactory, good, okay, needs improvement, terrible, etc. Of course, we could assign these qualitative terms a number for the purpose of quantification. In quantitative terms, such a number has a property of an arbitrary zero as opposed to an absolute zero (meaningful zero).

Linn and Grodlund (2000) define measurement simply as the "assigning of numbers to the results of a test or other type of assessment according to a specific rule (e.g. counting correct answers or awarding points for particular aspects of an essay)" (p. 31). These assigned numbers are usually called scores and they have the function to describe the degree to which that test demonstrates the attributes of the individual taking it. An important concept about these assigned numbers is that they maintain the same order that exists in the real world among those being measured. For example, if your average score is better than that of the class, it then follows that their average scores are lower in value than yours.

Importance of Assessment

In the years following *A-Nation-at-Risk*, virtually every agenda implemented in the current reform movement in the American education has relied on the need for sound assessment as a force for accountability. Assessment in education has become increasingly important due to several fundamental assumptions including three that have been defined by Alverno College (1996):

- ❖ Knowledge and its application are inseparable; students should be able to do something with what they know
- ❖ Ability is the complex integration of knowledge, dispositions, skills, and self-perceptions
- ❖ Assessment is integral to learning, both as a means of helping students learn and as a way of validating their achievement
- ❖ Two frequent themes found in reform reports are to increase education standards and to improve means to measure these standards.

Improve Educational Standards

Assessment of pre-service teacher's progress under the old paradigm was, typically, nothing more than a measurement of classroom performance. While this kind of assessment is necessary, it is certainly not adequate. It is more than possible to be a good student while not having the qualities that are needed to become an effective teacher. It is also very likely that a good student may not even have attained the goals that the instructor has placed in the front of the syllabus. Diez (1994) has observed that the points awarded for various activities that add to a grade in a course have little or nothing to do with the goals at the front of the syllabus" (p. 21f.). The new assessment paradigm addresses this problem. Rather than looking solely at course completion, it focuses on qualities of effective teaching and measures the extent that pre-service teachers have achieved them. Portfolio development and assessment have, in most recent years, become a major component of the reform process.

As you develop and advance in your preparation for the teaching profession, you will, certainly, come across all kinds of calls to improve educational outcomes by measuring learners' and school performance. Certainly all of these are based on good intentions. And, of course, as you become familiar with higher education literature, you will quickly learn that in the last two decades, two major themes have gained prominence: assessment and accountability. For various historical reasons, and the source of considerable confusion, both are erroneously referred to as assessment. The first, assessment, is an information feedback process to guide individual students, faculty members, programs, and schools in improving their effectiveness. Assessment instruments are designed to answer a wide range of self-evaluative questions related to one larger question: how well are institutions of higher education accomplishing their mission of developing competent teachers?

Increase Accountability

A theme commonly associated with assessment is "assessment for accountability." When you think about it, it all just amounts to a regulatory process, designed to assure institutional conformity to specified norms. Look at your situation as a pre-service teacher for a minute. In every minute of your day, you are bombarded with information from a ton of sources: classes, lab work, textbooks, discussions, and student presentations. Your primary task in learning revolves around information. Moreover, there is a whole lot of it today. Those who advocate accountability, especially legislatures, appear to view colleges as mere factories and higher education as a production process (Astin, 1993). The question before them is: What are colleges and teacher preparation programs supposed to turn out? Are teacher education programs, then, supposed to produce a commodity called a teacher? If the teacher then is the "commodity" just as in factories, how do we determine the quality? We find ourselves faced by two radically complex problems. The first is a determination of what colleges ought to produce and the second is how that product is measured.

Consensus about methods of capturing student learning is an important area that has continued to receive a lot of attention. Various performance measures are implemented. Teacher education programs along with licensing agencies engage themselves in implementing assessment programs. The question that is of interest in assessment discussions is: do current assessment methods and combinations of these provide useful and accurate measures of student achievement—standardized tests, performances, licensure exams, locally designed case studies, portfolios, focus groups, interviews, surveys? More responsive and reliable assessments call for multiple sources of evidence collected over time and in multiple contexts. Tasks providing only one genre of performance data are equally inadequate. Two principles underpin this criterion. First, if assessments are to support learning and provide the information necessary for sound decisions, they must be designed so that the evidence they gather is based on adequate samples of thinking and behavior. Second, an isolated sample of performance is insufficient to form judgments about learning, teaching, program development, or pre-service teacher competence.

Shift from Traditional Assessment Procedures

Now that we have attempted to define performance assessment and identified ways in which performance is portrayed, we must specify the methods for managing the results. The last two decades have seen a shift from traditional assessment procedures to authentic measures. Spinelli (2002) who has recently reviewed publications of the National Research Council states:

> According to the National Research Council . . . greater emphasis should be placed on "assessing what is most highly valued" (as opposed to what is easily measured); "assessing rich, well-structured knowledge" (as opposed to discrete knowledge); "assessing scientific understanding and reasoning" (as opposed to only knowledge); "assessing to learn what students do understand" (as opposed to what they do not know); "assessing achievement and opportunity to learn" (instead of only achievement); and "engaging students in ongoing assessment of their work and that of others" (as opposed to end-of-term assessments given by teachers)(pp. 444-5).

Traditional assessment approaches that include the use of standardized test have been increasingly criticized. Eggen and Kauchak's (2001) review of literature concludes that traditional assessments are viewed as:

❖ Focusing on low level knowledge and discrete, disconnected content skills
❖ Objective formats, such a multiple-choice, don't measure learners' ability to apply understanding in the real world;
❖ They measure only outcomes, providing no insight into the processes learners use to arrive at their conclusions (p. 617)

Today, a defined shift toward inclusion of more authentic measure in assessment is clearly evident. This shift has transformed educators to see assessment differently from the old definition that perceived it as a process of developing, implementing, and interpreting tests (Zarrilo, 2000). On the contrary, authentic assessments as a process has the characteristics listed in Figure 4.1.

Figure 4.1: Characteristics of Effective Assessment

---

* ❖ Data are gathered from tasks that require complex, high level thinking, often through inquiry and problem solving.
* ❖ The ultimate goal is to assess students' performance on tasks that correspond to the types of things people do in the "real" world, rather than to make judgments based on tests that people take only in school.
* ❖ Data used for evaluation can come from everyday assignments students complete, if the teacher plans a wide range of challenging activities.
* ❖ The process is ongoing and longitudinal, with data gathered, analyzed, and shared throughout the school year.
* ❖ The products that students create, or records of them, are stored in portfolio.
* ❖ Students show what they know and can do in a variety of ways
* ❖ The process places greater responsibility on the student in gathering and analyzing data

---

Source: Modified adaptation from Zarrillo, James. (2000). *Teaching elementary social studies: principles and applications.* Upper Saddle River, N.J.: Merrill. (p. 162).

Wiggins (1993) defines performance assessment as an assessment of a task that simultaneously requires the use of knowledge, skills, and values that are recognized as important in the domain of study and is qualitatively consistent with tasks in which members of discipline-based communities might conceivably engage. These tasks vary in scope, content, method and presentation. Tests, as we know them, provide only a limited dimension of a narrow aspect of learning (Takona, 1999), and are generally poor predictors of how individuals perform in other settings. Studies on popular standardized tests indicate, for example, that

SAT only predicts the performance of students for the first semester in college and that such prediction is only accurate half the time (Gibbins and Bickel, 1991). Falk (2000) shares a story from one of her students who became a certified scuba diver. In her criticism that lends support to the notion that written test inaccurately reflected the performance of the test taker, she quotes her student saying:

> Though I had earned a perfect score on the quiz asking me what I would do if my air were to run out, when I actually experienced this situation—my instructor snuck up behind me (in the deep end) and turned off my air supply—I was not prepared for the anxiety I felt and did all the wrong things. I shot up to the surface and gasped for air, despite the fact that I knew this would have seriously injured my body had we been in deeper water (p. 12).

An adequate assessment of performance requires specified criteria. Performance standards often referred to as performance outcomes are defined levels of achievement students must attain to be certified at a particular degree of proficiency. The degree of proficiency is identified by the knowledge, skills and dispositions the students are able to demonstrate. The portfolio assessments of the National Board for Professional Teaching Standards (NBPTS), and Interstate New Teacher Assessment and Support Consortium (INTASC), as well as those used in many teacher education programs, are organized to meet a set of performance standard. Robust assessments of knowledge and skill can include written analyses, observation data (e.g., data based on a supervisor's, cooperating teacher's, or principal's observation), and performance samples such as videotapes, samples of student work from the student teacher's classroom, and samples of communications with families that may be gathered in field experiences assignments.

Instructors often base their decisions of using one kind of assessment method over another on how well a method aligns with what and how students have learned and how well a method measures what it purports to measure. For example, many teacher education programs require that you gain passing scores on the praxis such as PPST. Standardized tests such as the PPST may measure how well the pre-service teacher has learned information, but it may not demonstrate how well that individual can solve problems using that information. In that case, the use of multiple methods of assessment contributes to a comprehensive interpretation of achievement. Maybe you or someone that you know performs well on multiple-choice questions but not well on writing assignments that require the application be learned.

Often, many of the traditional standardized tests and instructor constructed exams tend to fall short of providing an effective measure of many important learning outcomes. Figure 4.2 provides a parallel contrast between characteristics of high-stakes assessment and a set of characteristics for assessment development. Much of what is commonly practiced in colleges of education is a combination of high-stakes assessment (such as the Praxis I & II Series) and assessments for development (such as portfolio development, oral interviews, and field experiences evaluations). Greeno (1997) as cited in Driscoll (2000) states that "when students take tests they show how well they can participate in the kind of interaction that the tests afford" (p. 8). What we know as traditional tests fail to measure the degree to one is able to effectively participate in the social practices and interactions, say, in a teaching learning setting. It, therefore, falls short of measuring the true outcomes when place in that environment. Most people find it far more applicable and effective to be assessed in a real life context (Herrington and Oliver, 2000). This does not mean that it is true all time and in every single discipline area. For example, faculty from a specific department may find it appropriate to believe that standardized test results enable them to understand how well students learn, while faculty members in from another department might not depend on standardized tests, believing, instead, that results of a locally designed essay or use of a portfolio provides an approximation of student abilities.

Some institutions use standardized assessment methods that focus on academic outcomes. Others use capstone projects to assess how well preservice teachers integrate content within their major area of study. Single test score obtained in experiences where the pre-service teachers are required to use a #2 pencil to fill the bubbles are limited and may lead to an erroneous interpretation. Moreover, such experiences do not adequately engage pre-service teachers in challenging tasks. Of course, they have their place within the assessment system of a teacher education program. However, they tend to encourage temporary learning and often encourage the learning of isolated information. This would be said of the Praxis Series examinations, which are a requirement by many teacher-licensing agencies. The truth of the matter is that the aggregate grades simply do not measure the kind of performance levels that pre-service teachers attain, nor do they come close to measuring the impact of academic

Figure 4.2 Comparisons of Characteristics between High-Stakes and Development Assessments

High-Stakes Assessments	Assessments for Development
Aspects of the standards are selected, based on both what is judged to be important and what can be measured most effectively	A wide range of aspects of the standards can be addressed both because there is time to do so but also because multiple modes of assessment over time can be applied
The assessment takes place under prescribed conditions	Conditions can vary from candidate to candidate and for the same candidate over time
The prompts and modes of response are standardized, having been developed through a rigorous process of development, pilot testing, and field testing	The prompts and modes of response need not be standardized; faculty continuously develop assessments to meet the needs of candidates and refine them as they learn from their uses
Prompts and modes may need to be "secure"	An assessment can take place over time and can be revised
The assessment is a one-time event	The assessment process is "cumulative," with the body of work developing ever-richer picture of the candidate's performance
The assessment is "summative," with a cut score that determines whether the candidate is certified or licensed	Faculty work with candidates to develop a community of professional judgment through which they share understanding and apply criteria; this community of professional judgment is the source of reliability of judgment
Cut scores are determined through a process for which assessors are trained and care is taken to ensure the reliability of assessors	Feedback is a central means for improving candidate performance
No detailed feedback is provided to the candidate	Self-assessment is a critical process for candidate learning

Source: Adopted from Lissitz, Robert and Schaffer, William, (2002*). Assessment in educational reform: Both means and ends.* Boston, MA: Allyn and Bacon. Pp. 73-74.

program on pre-service teachers. Wiggin (1990), a widely known advocate of authentic assessments, contents that:

> What most defenders of traditional tests fail to see is the format, not the content of the test that is harmful to learning; demonstrations of the technical validity of standardized tests should not be the issue in the assessment reform debate. Students come to believe that learning is cramming; teachers come to believe that tests are after-the-fact, imposed nuisances composed of contrived questions—irrelevant to their intent and success. Both parties are led to believe that right answers matter more than habits of mind and the justification of one's approach and results (p.2).

Purpose of Assessment

Because educational practice concerns itself with the attainment of a given set of desired ends, a determination of reaching those ends is done through assessment. Like evaluation, assessment in education has different purposes. Here we will discuss five primary purposes of assessment. These include: diagnose student knowledge before instruction; identify student interest; direct instruction; guide learning; and determine learning gains.

Diagnose Student Knowledge before Instruction

Knowledge of what a learner already knows is extremely valuable for a teacher because it forms a springboard for future learning. It is extremely difficult to provide effective instruction without this kind of information. Information about what students already know can be collected informally or formally. The bottom line here is that it is through assessment.

Identify Student Interest

As you prepare for the teaching profession, it is imperative to remember that good teaching often depends on one's ability as a teacher to ascertain the interests and abilities of the learner and capitalize on them. You will come to learn that effective learning comes about by tapping into the learner's special interests as a means of reinforcing learning. There are specific tests capable of identify student interest. A most common standardized tests used for this purpose is the Strong Vocational Interest Blank (SVIB) developed by Strong in the late 1930s. The SVIB is a 400-

item multiple-choice test measuring vocational preferences scored for various occupations and professions.

Direct Instruction

Assessment of student learning is a central part of teaching. Almost two decades ago, Darling-Hammond (1994) argued that the diagnosis of student learning needs and the adaptation of instruction to those needs is an essential part of effective teaching. Assessment information gives the teacher knowledge about her effectiveness in reaching the desired outcomes. If the desired outcomes are not reached, re-teaching may become necessary. Table 4.1 shows the close relationship between instruction and assessment.

Guide Learning

Assessment is of value to teachers in making instructional decisions. It is also of value to learners because it supports and guides judgment in what is important to learn, how it is learned, and how much is learned. For this to happen, assessment must be consistent, specific, and timely. A student's process, progress or product may be assessed. Rather than reducing student's work to a composite score or a value represented by number or letter grade, instructors often work hard to provide a clear and non-judgmental multi-dimensional picture that communicates attained competencies and identified challenges. In any case, learners thrive better within a structure of supportive feedback.

Determine Learning Gains

Sound assessment is a process and not just an event. The information collected through assessment must be capable of providing useful information to accurately evaluate the effectiveness of any instructional intervention. For example, they can provide useful information regarding the extent to which instructional objectives were met or the appropriateness of the methods and materials used. This information is useful as feedback that could be vital for instructional modification if students are not learning the material. The learning outcomes for a particular course will depend on a host of variables including the special needs of students, preparation of the teacher, the philosophy of the school, objectives attained in previous courses, and so on.

Table 4.1: Relationship between Instruction and Assessment

Instruction is most effective when:	Assessment is most effective when:
Directed toward a clearly defined set of intended learning outcomes	Designed to assess a clearly defined set of intended learning outcomes
The methods and materials of instruction are congruent with the outcomes to be achieved	The nature of function of the assessments are congruent with the outcomes to be assessed
The instruction is designed to fit the characteristics and needs of the students	The assessments are designed to fit the relevant student characteristics and are fair to everyone
Instruction decisions are based on information that is meaningful, dependable, and relevant	Assessments provide information that is meaningful, dependable, and relevant
Students are periodically informed concerning their learning progress	Provision is made for giving the student early feedback of assessment results
Remediation is provided for students not achieving the intended learning	Specific learning weaknesses are revealed by the assessment results
Instructional effectiveness is periodically reviewed and the intended learning outcomes and instruction modified as needed	Assessment results provide information useful for evaluating the appropriateness of the objectives, the methods, and the material of instruction

Source: From Norman E. Gronlund, Assessment of Student Achievement, 6/e 1998 by Pearson Education. Reprinted by permission of the publisher.

Assessing pre-service teachers' learning over time—known as formative assessment—provides valuable information about how well students are progressing towards an institution's or program's expectations. In addition, interpretations of student achievement can be linked to the kinds of learning experiences that do or do not promote valued outcomes. Interpreting pre-service teachers' performance over time and sharing assessment results with those individuals enables them to understand their strengths and weaknesses and to reflect on how they need to improve over the course of their remaining studies. Assessing student learning at the end of a program or course of study—known as summative assessment—provides information about patterns of student achievement. Without summative assessment data, instructors are denied opportunity to improve students' learning and achievement. And, without giving opportunities to students to reflect upon their performance they will be unable demonstrate or make the necessary improvements. Using both formative and summative assessment methods provides an institution or program with rich understanding of how and what you as a developing teacher learn. Information collected from assessments result, for example, to the introduction of new instructional strategies that effectively address diverse learning styles or development of pre-service teachers' learning in a given discipline. Results help answer questions about which kind of pedagogues or educational experiences foster disciplinary behaviors and modes of inquiry. When, for example, do those preparing to be teachers act like teachers? On the other hand, indicators can be drawn to ascertain that pre-service teachers are on track in their development as professionals.

What is Performance Assessment?

What is performance assessment anyway? A simplistic definition perceives performance assessment as that kind of assessment which requires students to apply their knowledge and skills from several areas in order to complete a task or perform a learning target. Care needs to be taken here to avoid the common misconception that any performance requires a performance assessment. That is not true. What is true is that any performance assessment requires a performance activity.

An earlier definition provided by Wiggins (1989) perceives performance assessment as an assessment of "performance of exemplary tasks that are authentic evidence of personal and intellectual growth" (p. 42). Performance assessment is defined by the United States Office of Technology (OTA) as "testing methods that require students to create an answer or product that demonstrates their knowledge or skills" and can take many forms including conducting experiments, writing an extended essay, or doing mathematical computations (OTA, 1992). Performance assessment emphasizes a hands-on approach to testing with the purpose to know if students can use knowledge in a meaningful way. Performance assessment is best understood as a continuum of assessment formats ranging from the simplest student-constructed responses to comprehensive demonstrations or collections of work (e.g. portfolios) over time. Regardless of format, common features of performance assessments involve (a) students' construction rather than selection of a response, (b) direct observation of student behavior on tasks resembling those commonly required for functioning in the world outside of school, and (c) illumination of students' learning and thinking processes along with their answers (OTA, 1992). Performance assessment has been advanced primarily for purposes of accountability and instructional intervention, rather than diagnostic or classification purposes.

The term "performance" emphasizes a student's active generation of a response to a task and highlights the fact that the response is observable, either directly or indirectly, via a tangible and permanent product. Performance assessment is sometimes called alternative assessment or authentic assessment and is a form of testing that requires students to perform a task rather than select an answer from a ready-made list. The term alternative assessment was coined to distinguish it from what it was not: it is not a standardized traditional paper-and-pencil testing. There are even now distinctions within performance assessment, a distinction that refers to the fact that some assessments are meaningful in an academic context whereas others have meaning and value in the context of the real world, hence they are called "authentic." The authentic portion of an authentic assessment, from a philosophical point of view, is the characteristic of the examination that presents to students tasks that are "directly educationally meaningful" instead of "indirectly meaningful" (Nitko, 2001, p. 235).

Performance assessment is commonly associated with authentic assessment (see Figure 4.3). Performance assessments are generally valued for testing pre-service teachers' deep understanding of concepts and inquiry strategies, for making students' thinking visible. Performance assessment requires a demonstration of knowledge, skills, and dispositions by doing or as Rudner & Boston (1994) characterized as "creating a product." Authentic assessment occurs when learners given opportunity to engaged in a task. This type of assessment requires information from a variety of sources. Tests are considered as one source of information about how well and in what ways students are able to do what instructors want them to do. Rather than choosing from several multiple-choice options, you might be placed in a situation where you are supposed to demonstrate your knowledge and skills in activities that culminate with a documentable product such a written summary of a research, writing that focuses on a targeted goal. The targeted goal may be the development of a character analysis, debating a character's motive, dramatizing a favorite story, drawing and writing about a story, an individual or group presentation project and so on. Authentic assessment is based on the constructivist theory of learning that holds that learning is a constructive process in which the learner develops representations of knowledge and develops understandings of meaning based on personal experience. Eisner (1993), a constructivist, holds that authentic assessment gives focus to learner involvement. The involvement, be it a project or other form of activity, and the observed performance should reveal how well the learner goes about solving the problems (process) and what kind of solution the learner reaches. This approach often allows more than one "correct" solution. Rather than relying on test results, or any other assessment products as the sole criterion of academic achievement, instructors may often choose to maintain systematic records evaluating and noting learning activities.

Figure 4.3: Commonly Used Terms

Performance Assessment	Assessment requiring students to demonstrate their achievement of understanding and skills by actually performing tasks or set of tasks (e.g. writing a story, giving a speech, conducting an experiment, operating a machine, etc)
Alternative Assessment	A title for performance assessment that emphasizes that these assessment methods provide an alternative to traditional paper-and-pencil testing
Authentic Assessment	A title for performance assessment that stresses the importance of focusing on the application of understandings and skills to real problems in "real world" contextual settings

Source: Norman E. Gronlund, (1998). *Assessment of Student Achievement*. Boston, MA: Allyn and Bacon.

Learning is not and never should be linear. Rather, you go over things several times, each time in greater depth, and with the benefit of some familiarity with all the other things which affect it. In educational jargon, this has come to be known as a "spiral curriculum." In this case, there is connectedness between what you know right now and what you will come to know in the future. Furthermore, there is connectedness between what you know and what you can do. Authentic assessment empowers students to show what they know and are able to do through performance tasks. These tasks, like most real-life tasks, do not have a single correct answer. Consequently, evaluating authentic assessments depends upon human judgment rather than computerized or standardized scoring. Observation is a major source of information about how well and in what ways students are able to articulate content knowledge.

The term authentic, therefore, refers to the nature of the task and context in which an assessment occurs. Educators use the term authentic assessment to define the practice of realistic student involvement in evaluation of their own achievements. Authentic assessments are performance-based, realistic, and instructionally appropriate (Pett, 1990). Authentic assessment utilizes *performance samples*—learning activities that encourage students to use higher-order thinking skills. The authenticity dimension of assessment has become a rather salient issue for two reasons. First, most educators assume that the more realistic or authentic a task is, the more interesting it is to the learners. Thus, your motivation to engage in and perform a task is perceived to be much higher for tasks you might deem relevant than for tasks where relevance to "real world" problems or issues are difficult to see. Real-world contexts are needed if learning is to be constructed and transferred beyond the classroom. Furthermore, a pre-service teacher who is motivated to learn and grow must embody skills and ability to interpret information and relate it to prior knowledge. This being so, it only makes sense that assessments must demonstrate whether pre-service teachers can or cannot use , in an appropriate way, the knowledge, skills and strategies they have learned. Second, for educators espousing an outcomes oriented approach to education, much of the assessment focus must be directed toward complex sets of skills and conditions.

You may have figured out by now that we approach learning from a position that is responsive to engaging learners in their own learning. From that position, we recognize and value the fact that learners are constructors of meaning. They are active participants in the process of learning. Inherent to this approach, we believe, learning experiences where the learner understands both what they must learn and why they must learn it. In that case, we regard authentic experiences as well as presumed authentic assessments as appropriate measures of learning. Authentic assessment may take many and varied forms. But in all cases authentic assessments engages learners in applying knowledge and skills in ways that are meaningful and reflective of real-life. Moreover, authentic assessment shifts the focus from, "Do you know it?" to "How well can you use what you know?" Box 4.2 lists several guidelines suggested by Wiggins (1989) that are related to performance assessment.

Box 4.2

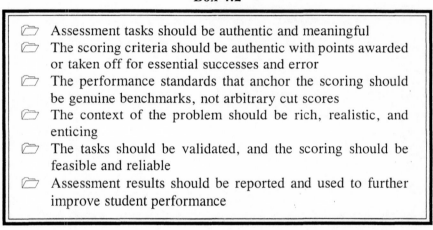

An assessment process is valued as a part of the whole learning experience. It is relevant and important to each learner. Relevant and real-world assessments facilitate and guide both the learner and instructor in monitoring learning and assessing it against specified criteria. In so doing, they are empowered to make formed decisions. Information drawn from assessment supports the instructor in identifying learners' needs, plan instructions, and assess progress. In so doing the instructor's action will provide you, as a learner, a defined direction in your pursuit to construct knowledge and apply that knowledge to complex thinking engagement. The instructor is, therefore, afforded the opportunity to uses information gathered from this form of evaluation to guide a variety of instructional decisions and actions.

The process of becoming a teacher is not a mere completing a sequence of courses and field experiences leading to graduation. Rather, it is a process of becoming competent in the knowledge, skills, and dispositions and results in the development of an effective teacher. As you begin to assimilate this posture and change in perception it becomes apparent that the difference between becoming a teacher and becoming an effective teacher is certainly worlds apart. When you develop to be such a practitioner you will be characterized by the ability to successfully motivate your students to achieve high levels of learning.

What are Formative and Summative Assessments?

Formative assessment is the process of assessing learning as it occurs. The results of a formative assessment are used as feedback to inform instructional decisions. Both pre-service teachers and their instructors need to know how learning is proceeding. Feedback may operate to improve your learning as well the instructor's approach to teaching. In cases where a portfolio undergoes formative assessment, your instructor or your advisor often does such assessment in an informal way. The outcome of the assessment may not "count". In effect, the examiner may require that the learner continues to receive instruction or work to support the refinement of the portfolio. Assessment for feedback to the students taken regularly throughout the course is called *formative*. Using assessment for formative purposes allows skills to be noted, reflected on and developed in a continuous manner. It calls for *considerations*. These considerations, for example, may call for re-teaching or change of strategies used to reach the desired goal. Assessment at the end of a course work, sometimes by averaging the formative assessment to provide a grade, is called *summative*. While it is neither uncommon nor good practice, one exam at the end of the course is unlikely to provide adequate feedback or a defensible basis to form a decision on final credentialing for the student. It needs to be appreciated that a single type of assessment of the students' work is definitely not adequate to make a reliable judgment of the overall quality of their work. Most of the time instructors are compelled to plan for frequent assessment points to be confident that the results they obtain are reliable without drowning students.

When summative assessment is used, its purpose is intended to determine how well the pre-service teachers learned what was intended. It calls for *consequences* and the results are final. For example, a lack of mastery of what is to be learned requires "punishment" which may be the form of not being allowed to continue in the program. When the portfolio is used for summative assessment, the results are used to inform all stakeholders of the product of your learning. When the results of the portfolio are used to determine your eligibility for admission to the teacher education program or to student teaching, then the portfolio is used as a summative assessment.

Summary of Key Points

In this Chapter, we have introduced several key concepts in assessment while making a sharp distinction between them and the meanings often assigned. While the terms assessment, testing, evaluation and measurement are frequently used interchangeably, each of them has a different focus, meaning, and emphasis. In this chapter, we have made a distinction between these terms and placed emphasis on performance assessment while showing that as a pre-service teacher you play a significant role in the assessment of your learning and growth.

References

Alverno College. (1996). *Ability-based learning program: teacher education*. Milwaukee, WI: Alverno College Institute.

Astin, A.W. (1993). *Assessment for excellence*. New York, New York: Collier Macmillan.

Darling-Hammond (1984).Beyond the commission report: The coming crisis in teaching. *Phi Delta Kappan*. 73 (3), 220-225.

Diez, Mary E., and Hass, Jacqueline. (1997). No more piecemeal reform: Using performance-based approaches to rethink teacher education. *Action in Teacher Education*. 19 (2), 17-26.

Driscoll, M. (2000). *Psychology of learning for instruction*, (2nd ed.). Boston, MA: Allyn and Bacon.

Eggen, P. & Kauchak, D. (2001). *Educational psychology: Windows on classrooms*. (5th Edition). Upper Saddle River, NJ: Merrill.

Eisner, E. W. (1994). Educational reform and the ecology of schooling. In A. C. Ornstein & L. S. *Behar* (Eds.), *Contemporary issues in curriculum*. Boston, Mass: Allyn & Bacon.

Falk, Beverly (2000). *The heart of the matter: Using standards and assessment to learn*. Portsmouth, NH: Heinemann.

Gibbins, N., & Bickel, R. (1991). Comparing public and private high schools using three SAT data sheets. *The Urban Review*. 23. 101-115.

Gronlund, N. E. (1998). *Assessment of student achievement*. (6th ed.). Boston: Allyn & Bacon.

Herrington, J., and Oliver, R. (2000). An instructional design framework for authentic learning environments. *Educational Technology Research and Development*. 48(3), 23-48.

Jonassen, David H. (2000). *Computers as mindtools*. Upper Saddle River, New Jersey: Merrill.

Linn, R., & Gronlund, N.E. (2000). *Measurement and assessment in teaching*. Englewood Cliffs, NJ: Prentice Hall.

Lissitz, Robert & Schafer, William. (2002). *Assessment in educational reform: both means and ends*. Boston, MA: Allyn and Bacon.

Nitko, Anthony J. (2001). *Educational assessment of students*. (3rd ed.). Upper Saddle River, New Jersey: Merrill Prince Hall.

Office of Technology Assessment, U. S. Congress (1992, February). *Testing in American schools: Asking the right questions (OTA-SET-519)*. Washington, DC: U.S. Government Printing Office.

Rudner, L.M., & Boston, C. (1994). Performance assessment. *The ERIC Review,* 3(1), 2-12.

Pett, J. (1990). What is authentic evaluation? Common questions and answers. *Fair Test Examiner*. 4: 8-9.

USDOE. (1998). Goals *2000: Reforming education to improve student achievement* http://www.ed.gov/pubs/g2kreforming/g2ch1.html

Spinelli, Cathleen G. (2002). *Classroom assessment for students with special needs in inclusive settings*. Upper Saddle River, NJ: Prentice Hall

Takona, J. P. (2001). *Perspective on grade assignment at east Africa's state universities*. Clearinghouse Report No: TM033172. (ERIC Document Reproduction Service No. ED455312).

Takona, J. (1999). *Distribution of undergraduate Examination questions among the specified levels: A case of an African university*. Clearinghouse Research Report No HE033165. (ERIC Document Reproduction Service No. 444429).

Wiggins, G. (1989). A true test: toward more authentic and equitable assessment. *Phi Delta Kappan*. 70 (10), 703-713.

Wiggins, G. (1990, June). *The truth may make you free, but the test may keep you imprisoned: Toward assessment worthy of the liberal arts.* Paper presented at the fifth AAHE conference on assessment in higher education, Washington, DC.

Wiggins, G. (1993). *Assessing student performance: Exploring the purpose and limits of testing.* San Francisco, CA: Jossey-Bass Publishers.

Zarrillo, James. (2000). *Teaching elementary social studies: principles and applications.* Upper Saddle River, NJ: Merrill.

Chapter 5

Purpose of Pre-service Teacher Portfolios

Orientation

Earlier chapters have, principally, set the stage. We have traced the current approach to assessment to a dynamic school reform movement spanning over two decades. We have noted that virtually every agenda implemented has required assessment as a driving force intended for accountability. This chapter explores several fundamental purposes of a pre-service teacher portfolio which includes its ability to allow you to take responsibility of your learning; promote partnership in assessment, encourage self-reflection, promote ownership of learning, encourages critical thinking, and is a key component of the licensing process and program assessment.

Focus Questions

☞ What is the difference between the following terms: Assessment, measurement, evaluation, testing, and measuring?

☞ How do you become responsible for your own learning, thinking, and destiny?

☞ Why is authentic assessment becoming a preferred way of assessing students?

☞ What kind of assessment are Praxis series examinations?

When appropriately developed, a portfolio encourages engagement in think critically about the professional choice and offers new methods of assessing that choice. Moreover, engaging in portfolio development affords opportunities to discuss your development and growth with peers, advisors, cooperating teachers, your PreK-12 students and others. Fundamentally, a pre-service teacher portfolio is similar to an artist's portfolio. It incorporates a sampling of the breadth and depth of an artist's work in order to showcase to the viewer the unique abilities, strengths and styles. The idea of an artist's portfolio is certainly familiar to most people. Commonly, an artist's portfolio is a collection of the best, authentic examples of the artist's own expression. Unlike an artist's portfolio, however, the main body of a pre-service teacher portfolio guides and informs the reader, through a sampling of learning and development documents, of the degree of one's achievement.

Portfolios have been used for a variety of purposes and at all levels of education. In some cases, a portfolio has been used to provide a physical evidence of student achievement. At other times, portfolios have been used for documentation in performance reviews for the teacher as well as provide rich ground for program reviews. This chapter will also examine the portfolio under its definition as a collection of authentic, learner-specific artifacts that give evidence of one's growth and development as a teacher. The portfolio is also recognized as a tough that ought to reflect academic and professional developmental stages of a pre-service teacher over time in an individualized process. Typically, a pre-service teacher portfolio is an elaborate collection of materials that highlight and summarize the character as it regards professional growth and development of the pre-service teacher.

Defining a Portfolio

A portfolio has been variously defined. While in the business world a portfolio customarily refers to investment variety, in the world of education, it typically refers to a selection of contributions which show that the student has worked at, understood, and integrated a specific curriculum related to a particular discipline. The portfolio has generally been defined as ". . . a systematic and organized collection of evidence used by the teacher and student to monitor growth of the student's knowledge, skills, and attitudes in a specific subject area" (Blake, et al., 1995).

Qualifications have been added to the definition: ". . . the collection must include student participation in selecting contents, the criteria for selection, the criteria for judging merit, and evidence of student self-reflection (Borko, et al., 1996).

A contemporary view of the portfolio envisions ". . . a purposeful, collaborative, self-reflective collection of student work generated during the process of instruction" (DeBruin-Parecki, et al., 1997). True, it includes a collection of student work but as Arter and Spandel (1992) have expressed, a portfolio is a "purposeful collection of student work that tells the story of the student's effort, progress, or achievement in given areas. The key word in Arter and Spandel definition is "purposeful." We will expand on these definitions by adding that the portfolio development process is not a scavenger hunt that results in the creation of a scrapbook of learning memorabilia. Rather, it is a structured, responsive, and a purposeful goal-driven activity that engages reflective capacities of a pre-service teacher to isolate growth and development within learning incidences against preset criteria. These incidences may be planned or unplanned. The types of products collected are cumulative, connected and representative of tasks completed over time. When placed in a systematically organized portfolio, these products provide a "motion picture" of learning progress versus the "snapshots" (Ziomek, 1997) that each provides standing in isolation. Furthermore, learning is *developmental*, a cumulative process *involving the whole person*, relating past and present, integrating the new with the old, starting from but transcending personal concerns and interests. It is, certainly noticeable from these definitions that a portfolio is obviously more than a folder of mere curricula products. Examine Figure 5.1 to see a comparison between portfolios and student folders. In contrast, some teacher education programs find better meaning in a definition that is more in line with that of Wade & Yarbrough (1996) which asserts that "a portfolio is the collection, selection, and organization of teacher education students' work over time that shows evidence of self-reflection and learning" (p. 65). We might add here that this collection displays both your accomplishments as a developing teacher and the rationale behind your choice for the teaching profession. Further, it is designed to highlight not only what you are doing in your preparation for the teaching profession, but gives you a venue to explain why you chose to do certain things, and how your understanding of teaching is evolving.

Figure 5.1: Comparison of Portfolio and Student Folders

Portfolio	Student Folder
Student work is purposefully selected to match instructional objectives	Student work is whatever the student produces and is not necessarily tied to instructional objectives
Students' progress in mastering a process, such as critical thinking, problem solving, strategizing, and planning, is one of the criteria for judging items.	Products generally reveal completion of a task or product and not the process of working on the task
The students select content	The teacher generally controls content
The teacher uses selection guidelines and shares them with students	If the teacher has selection guidelines, students usually do not know them
Criteria for judging items are set in advance and often are shared with students	Criteria for judging usually are not set in advance and are not shared with students
Students' self-reflection is presented through some means such as a journal	There is no evidence of self-reflection

Source: From Ward, A. W. and Murray-Ward, M. (1999). *Assessment in the classroom.* Belmont, CA: Wadsworth Publishing Company, p. 193.

Philosophically, a pre-service teacher portfolio has several distinguishing features:

* Authentic tasks and work samples are collected to provide evidence of a pre-service teacher's learning and professional growth
* Pre-service teachers take ownership and responsibility for their own professional development and growth
* Portfolios promote involvement and collaboration with others
* Pre-service teachers are empowered to make judgments about progress from multiple measures gathered over time.

A primary focus of the portfolio development process is to observe and document performance in an organized and a continuous way and evaluate the level of progress toward the mastery of specified goals. Moreover, portfolio development is all about personalizing one's preparation for the profession. It is about acquisition of tools need to gauge professional growth and development. It is about using data to make better and informed decisions. Developing a portfolio can get you there, but it is not an easy task. It requires soul searching—reflection.

How can you leverage your current coursework and experiences to demonstrate your capacity of acquired knowledge and skills that characterize a developing professional? How do you do this within the context of defined competencies, standards, performance outcomes, principles, and other criteria delineated by your teacher education program, institution, professional organization? In evaluating your performance as a pre-service teacher, valuable information can be gathered through your work samples and reflections.

A pre-service teacher portfolio consists of the following three major components:

Attestation Documents

Attestations documents may include materials that you have generated yourself (a philosophy of education, academic transcripts, and scores on standardize tests such as the Praxis Series).

Material from Others

Materials from others who have observed your development and growth (professors, cooperating teachers, your academic advisor, even your peers) or those you have facilitated (students).

Material from Self

These include material from courses (term papers, graded examinations, lab reports, etc.) as well as other experiences that you have completed (lesson plans, personal website pages, reflective journals, student work samples collected during your student teaching assignment, etc.).

The portfolio is an appropriate place to organize your goals, thoughts and tenets relating to teaching and learning. It has great potentials to enable you to think in meaningful ways about your decisions and experiences as a developing teacher in addition to providing a systematic way of gauging your progress toward the teaching profession. Furthermore, a portfolio encourages you to relate your development and practice to the learning process and the educational context in which it takes place.

A portfolio is a means of presenting yourself and your work in a succinct and effective way. The term "portfolio" refers both to an ongoing process of assessment and documentation of the product of that process at different stages. Portfolios are multifaceted as they reflect the complex nature of learning and professional growth. The entire artifact collection should represent you as an individual and a developing professional. Because portfolio artifacts are collected over time, they can serve as a record of growth and progress. The portfolio you develop as a pre-service teacher is likely to evolve into a professional presentation that you will continue to update and use throughout your working years. It is likely that you will change jobs, even professions, numerous times in the years ahead. Because a portfolio contains a broad repertoire of performance evidence collected over time, it has the potential to paint a rich developmental view of learning and professional growth. Additionally, a review of artifacts contained in the portfolio provides a panoramic view, to your instructors, of your growth as an aspiring teacher and of the teacher education program. These three aspects are important because your development is only as good as the teacher program itself. To some reasonable degree, the products in a portfolio reflect the quality of learning. Of course, this should not be excuse for developing a lousy portfolio. In that regard, therefore, a portfolio is useful as an evaluation tool of your learning as well as of the teacher education program itself.

A portfolio offers an opportunity to present your individuality and achievement in visual form while allowing you to display your best work as a demonstration of growth in ability and performance. Unlike other forms of assessment, which obviously are intended to set one apart from the crowd or seek to identify one position within a crowd, a portfolio provides tangible proof of your accomplishments and gains. When appropriately developed, a portfolio strives to exhibit abilities in a prospective teacher often desired by your instructors, licensing agencies, and prospective employers. In developing a portfolio, you commit yourself to an avenue that proffers occasion to demonstrate reflective thinking strategies and professional growth and development over time. In addition, it enables you to relay your personal attitudes toward teaching and learning. By selectively collecting work and personal documents of achievement, you are building a visual representation of your growth and development. When your knowledge, skills, and dispositions are supported by tangible and visual representations, your instructors and others to gain a deeper and clearer picture of where you have been, where you are now, and where you are going in your growth and development as an aspiring teacher. Evidence of goals you set, heights you reach, and continued growth and development are all reflected within a single consummate product. With confidence, we can therefore define a portfolio in a simple, yet serious way, as a consummate product that tells a story about you.

As you become engaged in the development process of your portfolio, which by all descriptions is a consummate product, your awareness of strengths and weaknesses increases. In addition, you become particularly aware of strategies and principles that are critical to effective instruction and the teaching profession in general. Such awareness is necessary to provide a better picture of shortcomings to work on as well as strengths to nurture.

Portfolio content may be classified into three specific categories in terms of their purpose: (1) evidence of professional development and achievement; (2) concrete evidence of attaining stated competencies and; (3) reflections on that evidence. The evidence begins with attestation documents. These may include artifacts that speak of your growth, attainment, and plans for the future. Moreover, these documentations extend to include a variety of activities which have had an impact on your professional development as pre-service teacher, such as records of professional examinations, teaching certificate programs, academic transcripts, videotapes of your lectures and classrooms, etc. The inclusion of these other components adds depth to your presentation of professional development. Most importantly, the meaningful aspect of the portfolio lies in your written reflective statements about the evidence of your professional development and attainment of stated competencies. These reflective statements must be evident in your reflection abstract pages as well as in your summary reflection essay.

In engaging in the development of a portfolio, opportunities avail themselves to allow for reflective activities. While such sessions engage you in thinking about your own professional development and growth, you will find yourself deliberating over your choice of a teaching profession and how you are going to teach. Notice here that we are talking about your choice of profession—teaching—and your objectives for achieving that goal. Reflecting on these issues is a difficult task and is best tackled with others. If this then is an accurate assumption, the pre-service teacher is, therefore, able to shifts emphasis away from content accumulation to its usefulness and to its use. What have I learned? How much of it have I learned? What makes me think that I have learned? These are difficult questions and that is why pre-service teacher portfolios are the product of collaboration with colleagues, mentors, and others. The process of developing your portfolio may prove to be more difficult than originally expected. Therefore, constant and honest feedback is key to producing a successful product. Combined input from these constituencies helps in clarifying and refining your personal statements and reflective descriptions.

Why a Pre-service Teacher Portfolio

Pre-service teachers are individuals seeking to enter a profession that requires highly qualified (US Department of Education, 2002) professionals who must show evidence of that qualification in tangible and physical products. The bottom line here is that they must take more control over their professional development activities. Focus on increased accountability translates into expectations of improved standards of teaching, which will result in better service to classrooms. Beyond that, the diversity of needs and interests within the teaching profession necessitates an equal diversity of development activities that the pre-service teacher can be involved.

The reasons for promoting the use of a pre-service teacher portfolio are numerous. We will not seek to state all of them here. However, four will receive mention: The first, promotion of the use of portfolio is based on their wide recognition as a tool for self-evaluation and self-reflection. Preparation for the teaching profession requires a pointed examination of self and an inquiry into a range of questions you must ask yourself that may include the following:

❖   What are my current experiences and associations with schools and learning sites? As a learner? As a pre-service teacher? As a community member? How much do I know about the way schools work? Do I have insight into the concerns of school staff, students, and parents? What is it that drives their day? Do I have a positive attitude about the various constituents of a school setting?

❖ What are my beliefs about education, school settings, learning environment, teaching, and children? How do I feel about the education system today? What have I read about education today? Is it positive or negative? How do I view teaching? What do I believe about how children learn? What do I think children need most to be successful learners? What do I need to effectively impact the learning of my students? How can I best assist the learners?

❖ What do I know about tutoring or literacy? Have I ever taught someone (my sibling, a neighbor, my child, etc) to read? Have you ever tutored as part of a service project? What do you do in "everyday life" that you can bring to this work?

❖ What beliefs or characteristics do I hold or have that will help or hinder my preparation for the teaching profession? Looking at my responses to the first five questions, are there any answers that speak to this question? What are my concerns or fears relative to the teaching profession? Am I flexible? Have I previously worked in a diverse setting?

As you examine yourself in this manner you will discover that the resulting outcome, really, leads to opportunities in capturing and improving learning. The second is the self-reflective process initiated by the portfolio. Typically, this sets the stage for a habit of continuing professional examination that would lead to development. Examples of question that come to play would seek answers to questions such as: What strategies had you used to learn the material in this course? Which were most effective? Why? What risks did you take in this course? What would you change about it? What problems did you encounter in this program? How did you solve them? What one question about this program is uppermost on your mind?

What would you like to learn further about this subject? In what area would you like to continue to strengthen your knowledge or skills? What personal reward do you expect to obtain from the teaching profession? What is my attraction to and personal interest in the teaching profession? Do you have a sense of mission? Why do I want to prepare for this profession?

Do you have a clear understanding of what is a major requisite to successfully impact learners? Do you have a clear understanding of the mission associated to the teaching profession? How compatible is the general mission of the teaching profession to my own personal mission? How is it different? What knowledge, skills and dispositions have you attained and need to pursue to be all you need to be in the teaching profession?

The third reason for promoting a portfolio as an effective tool for self-evaluation is its potential as a conduit to enhancing collegial discussion. Fourthly, the pre-service teacher portfolio can prove to be a very effective tool when seeking employment and can improve likelihood of being hired. Finally, for those in the teaching profession already, the development of a portfolio results in the improvement of instruction.

Today's Classroom Environments

What are we trying to accomplish in education? Ideally, everything that occurs in the classroom must contribute to a realization of those goals that society accepts as the proper objectives of education. Further, everything that goes on in the classroom must pass the test of making a positive contribution toward the attainment of the targeted goals of education. Classrooms today, whether at the university or PreK-12 grades, are beginning to look and sound different. Soon, we would be able to say gone are the days when quiet rows of learners filled the room. Soon we will be able to say, gone are the days when learners were treated as passive receptacles—they were lectured to and they dutifully took notes, responded only when they were called upon, memorized material, regurgitated it on examinations and soon forgot. Many colleges are continuously working toward changing the old feeling of isolation. Isolation had always been a characteristic of academia—you study alone, you bring to the classroom your own work, and you do a test without the support of others. These and many other activities that go on in the classroom are done in isolation. Today, many of these activities are often challenged and replaced by current emphasis on active cooperation, open communication and partnership. In environments that encourage these activities, learners are regarded as co-creators of curriculum. Students are now encouraged to work together with their professors, in pairs, small groups and as a whole group to solve problems, delve deeply into content and refine their skills. Drawing from their previous experiences, students generate questions for study and investigation. As partners, they work together to examine information, debate and clarify positions. They review each others work and offer suggestions for improvement, as well as congratulate each other on a job well done. Such change has the potential of capturing the intellectual excitement of the subject matter.

As classroom environments change so do the roles of teachers. Today's teachers are viewed as facilitators of learning rather than disseminators of knowledge. They are partners in teaching, learning, assessment and evaluation. Recognition of this relationship has replaced the old vertical dimension that once dominated the classroom with a more responsive horizontal partnership. This partnership is pivotal in assuring your development as a self-directing autonomous professional, which is the ultimate goal of your teacher preparation.

Assessment and testing have also changed. A concern of interest to many an instructor is the question: have students learned what I want them to learn? Stated another way, what responses will be accepted by instructors as evidence that students can make the associations? Obviously, instructors make judgments by observing students to collect perceptible evidence—evidence that demonstrates what students know and are able to do. If this is what instructors want, then it should be obvious that they can only depend upon students to demonstrate what they know and can do.

Pre-service Teachers as Assessors

Who says that college instructors are the sole assessors of your learning? One of the most important features of portfolio development is the involvement that it creates in the developer. Given time and support, you can develop the capacity to evaluate yourself. You are the only one who is the expert of yourself. It is only you who knows yourself best. There are certain things that you cherish and believe in. Moreover, research has yet to reveal to us a test that can bring about all that you know, believe and feel. Even the best test or closest system of evaluation may not reveal adequate dimensions that have been impacted. Portfolios are extremely valid measures of literacy. An approach to validity, known as consequential validity, maintains that a major determinant of the validity of an assessment measure is the consequence that the measure has upon the student, the instruction, and the curriculum (Linn, Baker, & Dunbar, 1991).

A well-designed portfolio represents important contextualized learning that requires complex thinking and expressive skills. Traditional tests are insensitive to local curriculum and instruction and of assessing not only student achievement but also aptitude. Performance-based assessments function as tools in determining whether or not instruction is consistent and balanced across areas. One of the most important elements in the teaching-learning transaction is feedback. When appropriately used, feedback becomes a springboard to learning a skill. A portfolio can become a vehicle to provide an equitable and sensitive portrait of what a pre-service teacher knows and is able to do. In so doing, the portfolio encourages both pre-service teachers and their instructors with credible evidence of learning achievement, and informs policy and practice at every level of the teacher education program.

A basic premise of this text is that a portfolio captures the complexities of learning in ways other forms of evaluation cannot. In Shulman's (1998) words, portfolios

> . . . are messy to construct, difficult to score, and vulnerable to misrepresentation. But in ways no other assessment method can, portfolios provide a connection to the contexts and personal histories that characterize real teaching and make it possible to document the unfolding of both teaching and learning over time (p.24).

Within the theories of learning, retrieval of information is an important phase of information processing. This phase, though a rudimentary level in the learning process has come to be known as the recall phase (Bloom, et al., 1956). If we have learned something, we must be able to recall it when appropriate cues are supplied. The cues are used to search the mind for the required information. Moreover, providing the appropriate cues or reminders is also an important part of instruction and learning. Further, the retrieval of old information may bring about the encoding of new information. The new information becomes meaningful as a result of associating it with other existing information. When a portfolio is used appropriately, it does just this—it sends you back to retrieve old information and make it available for new information. In that activity, you gain a re-enforcement of old learning and an opportunity to assimilate new learning.

Taking Responsibility of Learning

If this then is the current arrangement in the classroom, can you, as a learner, take responsibility of your learning and convince your instructors that you are performing at a level that is reasonably expected from you? How can instructors tell if you are learning and are able to perform at a satisfactory level of educational achievement? How can instructors tell if you are meeting performance outcomes that are defined in your institutional conceptual framework? These questions are difficult to answer and have bothered instructors, the public and politicians. Portfolios foster an inquiry approach and help shift ownership and responsibility of learning to the learner (Graves and Sustein, 1992).

The concept of using a portfolio originated from the arts and occupations where creativity is a necessary skill. This portfolio is often developed for purposes that may include a response to an employment opportunity. Employers seeking to hire persons in jobs related to art, advertising, and journalism often require a portfolio. However, a portfolio can also help document achievements and skills in any field including teacher education. In developing a pre-service teacher portfolio you engage in evaluating yourself and your career decisions. In so doing, you place yourself in a better position to explore careers which match your interests, in addition to comparing your skill level to the level needed for your chosen career. Your active participation and involvement is essential in your preparation as a teacher because it is your learning that is under discussion. A portfolio has become an acceptable form of assessment. When we talk about a portfolio, what do we exactly mean? An understanding of its meaning and purpose is important before engaging yourself in its development. A portfolio is a mirror and a window at the same time. As a mirror, the portfolio enables you to reflect on your growth and see it. As a window, the portfolio allows others to look in and see you.

Partnership in Assessment

A portfolio places a responsibility for monitoring growth and development for the teaching profession in the hands of the pre-service teacher. Its use represents a shift of initiative, from evaluation being what happens to the pre-service teacher to assessment being a shared responsibility. A portfolio invites pre-service teachers to participate in the evaluation of their own professional development and growth.

It is possible that you too, like most learners at all levels, see assessment as a procedure that is done to you with regard to your class work by someone else. Beyond "percent correct," assigned letter grades, and grammatical or arithmetic errors, you might have little knowledge of what is involved in evaluating your learning. This perception is, in itself, a barrier to learning. With the new partnership that portfolios in learning and assessment bring between you as a learner and your instructor as a facilitator, it is certain to bring about an opportunity for better learning. When an individual enjoys both the freedom to make mistakes and protection against penalty for failure, his questioning activities are certain to be more numerous and more bold, therefore, chances for enjoying frequent and consistent success are enhanced. This is an integral part of learning. Portfolios can provide you with structure for developing and understanding criteria for good efforts, in coming to see the criteria to your development and growth as a future teacher. There is substantial evidence that portfolios inform pre-service teachers of their professional growth and development, faculty, as well as others, of the effectiveness of the program. The results can be used to improve learning for the pre-service teachers and instruction for faculty, which are both major dimensions of good assessment (Gomez, Grau, & Block, 1991).

A priceless quality of the portfolio development activity is its potential to involve pre-service teachers in setting standards for effective preparation for teaching. A portfolio can prompt practice that is more reflective and improvement. Moreover, portfolios development fosters a culture of professional development and a new discourse about it. Whether used for formative or summative purposes, teaching portfolios can introduce more compelling, authentic evidence about portfolio development.

As an assessment instrument, the portfolio gives the pre-service teachers a sense of control over the evaluation process. In addition, teacher preparation that encourages pre-service teachers to submit portfolios will need to have discussions about what, if any, documents will be required and what will be left up to you to decide, how detailed the portfolio product can (or should) be, and how much reflection is required.

Self-reflection and Assessment

Pre-service teachers provide a fertile testing ground for the use of portfolios as an instigator of reflective thinking. Reflective thinking is widely touted as the most critical quality a soon to be teacher can develop (Zeichner & Tabachnick, 1991; Schon, 1987). With this in mind, teacher education programs are adopting portfolios, which are seen as an authentic means of assessing the development of their soon to be teachers (NCATE, 1999; Borko, Michalec, Timmons, & Siddle, 1996; Krause, 1996; McLaughlin & Vogt, 1996; Wilcox, 1996). Practicing teachers are also being targeted for portfolio assessment. With the current emphases on employing teachers who consistently strive to better their instructional methods, school districts are scrambling to find ways to assist teachers in understanding the value of self assessment in the hope that this will lead to improved instruction. The use of teacher portfolios as part of a teacher evaluation process may provide a useful means to accomplish this goal (Lyons, 1998; NBPTS, 1996).

An effective approach to developing a good portfolio involves reflection. A good teacher preparation program is one that engages prospective teachers to be reflective. Developing such a character is a responsibility of both the program and the pre-service teacher. A serious prospective teacher must gain from her own experiences, and to gain from those experiences, one must reflect on them. Only by questioning your learning and development can you hope to improve them.

These reflections must be deliberate, frequent, systematic, consistent, and thorough. They may include a reflective statement that can cover topics such as professional development and learning, your assumptions about the roles of students and teachers, and goals the instructor expects prospective teachers to achieve. No matter what particular experiences you have had in your teacher preparation program, these experiences are and must be a major source of strength in becoming an accomplished teacher, because they are the only place to start developing your own commitment and skills related to the teaching profession. You might ask: how could setbacks be a source of strength in my becoming a promising teacher? This is illustrated well by the story of Lakisha Moore.

Lakisha was admitted to the teacher education program during her last semester as a sophomore. Since her admission, a lot has changed in her life. She has lived with her grandmother who she calls "Moomi." Moomi raised her after she was orphaned. They both get along well but

"Moomi" is 87 and will be moving into a retirement center within the next few months. Lakisha's life will drastically change and her preparation for it has forced her to work four nights a week and a Saturday. All this is in addition to going to choir practice on Tuesday night, the only evening during the week that she does not work. This has affected her grades as well as her attempt to pass the Praxis II series examination last fall. Lakisha might ask herself: how could I succeed in my teacher preparation program? She will look at her present situation and might need to consider how to manage her other time.

The key word here is manage. To manage herself, she needs to be reflective. Lakisha has decided to keep a reflective journal where she logs her daily activities and strategies; she puts herself in a position to manage her pursuit for the teaching profession. If she so chooses, she can include these reflections in her portfolio in whole or as excerpts.

The process of collecting documents also requires reflection, which results in the selection of some items over others, reviewing past work, and so forth. As a result, the portfolio is well suited to helping the pre-service teacher examine his/her goals for teaching and student learning, and compare those goals to the reality of his/her praxis.

If you are at an advanced stage of your teacher education program or even a practicing teacher, you will quickly realize that portfolios have increasingly become important tools for self-reflection. Their importance is inherent within character of being complex and rich source to display collected evidence. A portfolio may house one's ongoing articulations about important teaching learning principles and practices—for example, matching student outcomes to teacher and curriculum-set goals as well as extensive self-reflections focused on improved teaching. Many pre-service teachers who invest and place value in their portfolio assessments share the process while completing field experiences with their students thus enriching their classroom evaluation methods, empowering their students to participate in their own assessment and promote reflective thinking in themselves and their students.

As a pre-service teacher, you gain a sense of effective preparation and become aware of opportunities from a variety of sources to improve your preparation. These opportunities may include instructor's feedback, self-perception, discussion with peers, and so on. By constructing a portfolio, you afford yourself an opportunity to systematically look at the various sources of data about your progress in the preparation for the teaching profession. As you discover your abilities, you thereby place yourself in a position to make informed decisions about your career choice, your strengths, and awareness of areas you may wish to build as well as problems in your growth and development you wish to address. The reflection and improvement process can be enhanced further when you work together with peers as you develop your portfolio. Peers can offer support and advice, exchange new ideas and solutions to problems, and broaden your views as a developing teacher. Moreover, such exchanges help create a learning community that is based on a concrete, discipline-specific context.

Further Learning

As you advance through the teacher preparation program, you will become exposed to various philosophies and approaches to teaching and learning. Those who adhere to the constructivist philosophy believe that individuals learn better by constructing meaning through interacting with and interpreting their environments (Brown, 1998). The meaning of what is taught when coupled with life experiences and contexts supports and enhances learning. Learning is anchored in the context of real-life situations and problems. This has often been referred to as contextualized learning. In many ways, contextualized learning is nothing new. It is based on the proposition that people learn more effectively when they focus on something that they are interested in, that they already know something about, and that affords them the opportunity to use what they already know to figure out new things. Developing a portfolio affords you an opportunity for connected learning experiences. These learning experiences are capable of providing some form of scaffolding to develop as learners (Eggen and Kauchak, 2001). This scaffold consists of specific content and processes bringing that content together to contribute to the development of an educated and productive citizen. A portfolio offers a rich source of insight and data to instructors so as to make informed decisions in the refinement of curricula. They encourage a more public, professional view of teaching, together with a more explicit understanding of how teaching is assessed and valued on campus.

Promotes Ownership of Learning

An important purpose of engaging in the portfolio development process is the opportunity it provides to gain a sense of active participation in or ownership of learning. When you think about your preparation as a teacher, questions such as what do I have power and control over? How can I get more control of my learning? Can I determine my own agenda and gauge my own influence on my preparation? Who else is involved in this preparation and do I have a say in it? You have a right to be a significant contributor to your learning. Portfolio development provides an opportunity to engage in the ownership of your learning. With this power in your hand, you place yourself in control of decisions that effect changes in your own professional growth and, possibly, that of others. As you engage in the development of a portfolio, you are involving yourself in an activity that results in the quantification of your learning in meaningful ways. Your learning is enhanced when it is represented in tangible products and when you monitor and take an inventory of your learning as demonstrated by tasks that are embedded in real-world activities.

Enhances Critical Thinking

Developing a colorful portfolio is not an end in itself. We need to be reminded constantly that besides it use as an effective assessment tool, a primary purpose for constructing a portfolio is to enhance the academic performance and the development of critical thinking abilities. The processes of thinking as problem solving, strategic reasoning and decision-making are deliberately developed rather than innate. You can extend your critical thinking to be more conscious, more reflective, more flexible, more efficient, and more transferable. Critical thinking is learning to think for yourself and to develop your own independent opinions backed by sound reasoning and support. It is learning to drop the role of passive student and to assume the role of a self-reliant thinker and researcher. Thinking critically in a learning context however, connotes a positive process to challenge your thinking or the thinking of others. The term "critical" is often used in a negative context. Critical thinking simply means to question, make sense of, or analyze. Nickerson (1987) characterizes a good critical thinker in terms of knowledge, abilities, attitudes, and habitual ways of behaving. Some of Nickerson's views of characteristics of such a thinker are illustrated in Figure 5.2.

Figure 5.2: Characteristics of a Critical Thinker

❖ Uses evidence skillfully and impartially

❖ Organizes thoughts and articulates them concisely and co-herently

❖ Distinguishes between logically valid and invalid inferences

❖ Suspends judgment in the absence of sufficient evidence to support a decision

❖ Understands the difference between reasoning and rational-izing

❖ Attempts to anticipate the probable consequences of alterna-tive actions

❖ Sees similarities and analogies that are not superficially ap-parent

❖ Can learn independently and has an abiding interest in doing so

❖ Applies problem-solving techniques in domains other than those in which learned

❖ Can structure informally represented problems in such a way that formal techniques, such as mathematics, can be used to solve them

❖ Can strip a verbal argument of irrelevancies and phrase it in its essential terms

❖ Habitually questions one's own views and attempts to under-stand both the assumptions that are critical to those views and the implications of the views

❖ Is sensitive to the difference between the validity of a belief and the intensity with which it is held

❖ Is aware of the fact that one's understanding is always lim-ited, often much more so than would be apparent to one with a non-inquiring attitude

❖ Recognizes the fallibility of one's own opinions, the prob-ability of bias in those opinions, and the danger of weighting evidence according to personal preferences

Source: Adapted from Nickerson, Raymond. (1987). *Reflective reasoning.* Hinsdale. NJ: Lawrence Erlbaum Associates.

Critical thinking skills support one decision and belief about an issue, how to defend that belief and how to evaluate the beliefs of others. This form of thinking empowers the mind. It is for this reason that employers like graduates who can think critically. By thinking critically, you stand the best chance to arrive at reasonable beliefs.

Component in the Licensing Process

A large number of entities including teacher education programs, school districts, state boards of education, and national professional organizations support the use of portfolios by pre-service and practicing teachers. Portfolios are neither uniformly defined nor consistent in purpose. There is also a clear difference between portfolios designed for pre-service teachers and those designed for classroom teachers. A pre-service teacher portfolio is dominated by artifacts developed by the pre-service teacher while a classroom teacher portfolio contains, predominantly, student work samples. Often these differences in philosophy, assessment, and purpose may not allow for continuity between portfolios begun in teacher education programs and those teachers start as they launch their professional careers.

In addition, some school districts require recent teacher education program completers to submit a portfolio as part of an application process. Information contained in the portfolio ought to be potentially capable of indicating your readiness and potential for the teaching profession. For the most part, the requirements vary widely among school districts. Some require just a list of courses taught and length or a reflective statement on teaching, and some ask for specific items. The earlier in your professional development that you begin to thinking about your portfolio, the more chance you will have to retrieve the documents you find most representative of your accomplishments. Aside from its value for the job market, a portfolio often represents the first time that you, as a beginning teacher, have had the opportunity to reflect on your career choice, which you may quickly find to be both challenging and rewarding.

Most performance-based teacher education programs develop their own conceptual frameworks that set guidance and elaborate a chosen philosophical or practical approach to the preparation of teachers. The conceptual framework, which most often is in a written document, presents a set of beliefs, assumptions, and values about human beings, learning, education, and relationships that support and give direction to efforts in educating future teachers (see an example of a conceptual framework in Appendix A).

Fundamental Assessment Component

A pre-service teacher portfolio has become a standard required component of most teacher education programs. In most cases, teacher preparation programs require leveled portfolios. At LeMoyne-Owen College, for example, pre-service teachers are required to develop portfolios that are assessed at four separate intervals of the teacher education program. A *PreCandidate Portfolio* is required for admission to the teacher education program. This portfolio responds to institutional benchmark competencies. A *Level I Portfolio* is required after the completion of a set of foundational courses in the profession education core courses and addresses performance outcomes gained. *Level II Portfolio* is required after the completion of a majority of upper level courses except clinical practice. The final portfolio, *Level III Portfolio* is completed during the clinical practice—student teaching and internship—semester and is used as a tool for promoting reflective practice. This portfolio process is, therefore, a systematic engagement in assessment used throughout the pre-service teacher's program.

Clearly, the portfolio process enables you to gear up toward the development of long-term reflection and growth and provide a place to demonstrate your progress toward chosen goals. Such goals may be either self and/or other selected goals. Reasonable purposes for these types of portfolios are state in Figure 5.2.

A pre-service teacher portfolio is often developed through out the duration of teacher education program and is not limited to one course or one teaching experience. Although distinct guidelines and grading rubrics may exist, opportunities are often provided for pre-service teachers to select much of what is included. These guidelines often support the design and evaluation schemes of the portfolio and allow pre-service teachers to become reflective and responsible for their own learning and progress as well as provide them with opportunities to understand and practice the process of portfolio development and assessment.

A portfolio provides a pre-service teacher opportunity to develop reflective capacities which result in outcomes that connect easily with the development of professional and effective teaching practice and provide

Figure 5.2: Purpose of a Pre-service Teacher Portfolio

❖ Provide opportunities for you to make your own selection and choice to document growth and development
❖ Provide a place to highlight exemplary practices
❖ Provide a means for authentic learning and evaluation
❖ Furnish evidence of self-reflection
❖ Provide you with opportunities to document and reflect on your learning and teaching,
❖ Allow you to assemble and reassemble a multidimensional representation of interlapping examples of your learning
❖ Assist you in your self-discovery, organization, and accountability
❖ Encourage your ownership of and responsibility for your own learning
❖ Offer students a place for future reminiscence after beginning classroom teaching

---

Source: Adaptation from Guillaume, A. M., & Yopp, H. K., (1995). Professional portfolios for student teachers. *Teacher education quarterly,* 22(1), 93-101; McLaughlin, M & Vogt, M. E. (1996). Portfolios in teacher education: Technical or transformational. In N. Lyons (Ed.), *With portfolio in hand: Validating the new teacher professionalism* (pp. 123-142). New York: Teacher College Press.

a smooth transition for continued authorship of classroom teacher portfolios. As Wenzlaff and Cummings (1996) have stated: "gathering data for a portfolio should not end with graduation from a teacher education program; rather, it should mark the beginning of an individual's professional development program" (p.111). There is, therefore, some substance to the idea that teachers who value the reflective process and have strong desires to improve their practice use portfolios to serve authentic purposes by focusing on the decisions that shaped their actions in response to challenging classroom situations (Wolf, D., Bixley, J., Glenn, J., & Gardner, H., 1991).

Summary of Key Points

This chapter began with a contemporary view of the portfolio which envisions it as ". . . a systematic and organized collection of evidence used by the teacher and student to monitor growth of the student's knowledge, skills, and attitudes in a specific subject area" (Blake, J., et al, 1995) and provide a panoramic view to your instructors of your learning and growth. A pre-service teacher portfolio is similar to an artist's portfolio whose primary purpose is to sample the breadth and depth of his works in order to display to the viewer a spectrum of abilities, strengths and styles. Unlike the artists' portfolio however, the main body of your portfolio guides and informs the reader through this sampling.

In addition this Chapter has explored several fundamental purposes of a portfolio which include the ability to allow you to take responsibility of your learning; promote partnership in assessment; encourage self-reflection, promotes ownership of learning, encourages critical thinking and is an important component of the licensing process. The products in your portfolio often reflect the quality of your learning.

Your portfolio affords to you an opportunity to display your best work as a demonstration of your growth in ability and performance. As you develop your portfolio, you commit yourself to an avenue that enables you to demonstrate reflective thinking strategies and show professional growth over time in diverse educational situations and settings. In addition, it enables you to relay your personal attitudes toward teaching and learning. Your awareness of strategies and principles that are critical to your learning and the teaching profession that you aspire, also come across boldly in a successful portfolio.

We have noted that a successful portfolio contains at least three basic elements: evidence of professional development and achievement, concrete evidence of attaining defined competencies, and reflections on that evidence. In developing the portfolio, the key questions that require special attention are: what makes you want to choose the teaching profession? What progress are you making towards gaining the necessary skills need? And, how are you going to teach? Many school districts require recent teacher education program completers to submit their portfolios as part of an application process. Information contained in the portfolio is commonly used as a proof of teaching experience and potential.

References

Arter, J.A. & Spandel, V. (1992). Using portfolios of student work in instruction an assessment. *Educational measurement: Issues and practice*, 11(1), 36-44.

Blake, J., Bachman, J., Frys, M., Holbert, P., Ivan, T., & Sellitto, P. (1995). A portfolio based assessment model for teachers: Encouraging professional growth. *NASSP Bulletin*, 79 (573), 37-46.

Bloom, B. S., Englehart, M.D., Furst, E., Hill, W.H., & Krathwohl, D. R., (Eds). (1956). *Taxonomy of educational objectives: The classification of educational goals. Handbook I: Cognitive domain.* New York: David McKay.

Borko, H., Michalec, P., Timmons, M., & Siddle, J. (April, 1996). *Student teaching portfolios: A tool for promoting reflective practice.* Paper Presented At The Annual Meeting of the American Educational Research Association, New York City, NY.

Debruin-Parecki, A., Boraz, M., Shaw, E., Yeager, E., Visscher, S., & Lehan, M. (March, 1997). *Preservice teachers and the development of their self-initiated professional portfolios.* Paper Presented at The Annual Meeting Of The Michigan Reading Conference, Grand Rapids, MI.

Gomez, M.L., Grau, M.E., & Block, M.N. (1991). Reassessing portfolio assessment: Rhetoric and reality. *Language Arts*, 68, 620-628.

Sunstein, B. (1992). *Portfolio portraits.* Portsmouth, NA: Heinemann.

Guillaume, A. M., & Yopp, H. K. (1995). Professional portfolios for student teachers. *Teacher Education Quarterly,* 22 (1), 93-101.

Krause, S. (1996). Portfolios in teacher education: Effects of instruction on preservice teachers' early comprehension of the portfolio process. *Journal of teacher education*, 47, (2), 130-138.

Linn, R., Baker, E., & Dunbar, S. (1991). Complex performance-based assessment: Expectations and validation criteria. *Educational Researcher*, 20, 15-21.

Lyons, N. (1998). Portfolio possibilities: Validating a new teacher professionalism. In N. Lyons (Ed.), *With Portfolio in Hand: Validating the New Teacher Professionalism.* New York: Teachers College Press.

Mclaughlin, M. & Vogt, M. E. (1996). *Portfolios in teacher education.* Newark: DE: IRA.

National Board for Professional Teaching Standards (1996). *What teachers should know and be able to do.* Detroit, MI: NBPTS.

National Council for the Accreditation of Teacher Education (March, 1999). *NCATE 2000 Standards revision* [On-Line]: http://www.ncate.org/specfoc/2000stds.pdf.

Nickerson, Raymond. (1987). *Reflective reasoning.* Hinsdale. NJ: Lawrence Erlbaurn Assoc.

Schon, D. (1987). *The reflective practitioner: How professionals think in action*. New York: Basic Books.

Shulman, L. (1998). Teacher Portfolios: A Theoretical activity. In N. Lyons (Ed.), *With portfolio in hand: Validating the new teacher professionalism* (Pp.23-37). New York: Teachers College Press.

Snyder, J., Lippincott, A. & Bower, D. (1998). Portfolios in teacher education: Technical or transformational. In N. Lyons (Ed.), *With Portfolio in hand: Validating the new teacher professionalism* (Pp.123-142). New York: Teachers College Press.

U.S. Department of Education. (2002). No Child Left Behind. On-line document: *http://www.nochildleftbehind.gov/next/overview/index.html*

Wade, R. C., & Yarbrough, D. B. (1996). Portfolios: A tool for reflective thinking in teacher education? *Teaching & Teacher Education*, 12 (1) 63-79.

Ward, A. W., & Murray-Ward, M. (2000). *Assessment in the classroom*. Belmont, CA: Wadsworth Publishing Company.

Wenslaff, T. & Cummings, K. (1996). The portfolio as a metaphor for teacher reflection. *Contemporary Education,* 67 (2), 109-112.

Wilcox, B. (1996). Smart portfolios for teachers in training. *Journal of Adolescent and Adult Literacy*, 40 (3), 172-179.

Wolf, D., Bixley, J., Glenn, J., & Gardner, H. (1991). To use their minds well: Investigating new forms of student assessments. In G. Grand (Ed.). *Review of research in education*, 17, 31-74). Washington, DC: AERA.

Zeichner & Tabachnick (Eds.). (1991). *Issues and practices in inquiry-oriented teacher education*. London: Falmer Press.

Ziomek, R. (1997, March). *The concurrent validity of ACT's Passport Portfolio Program: Initial validity results*. Paper presented at the annual meeting of the National Educational Research Association, Chicago, IL.

Chapter 6

Conceptualizing Professional Development and Growth

Orientation

Where is the beef? In the early 1980's, a small elderly woman could be seen nightly in a popular ad campaign for Wendy's hamburgers. She'd walk into a competitor's restaurant, order a hamburger and with an irritated look in her eye cry out, "Where's the beef?" This textbook has examined how we got to where we are—performance based assessment. We have looked at the various reform reports of the early 1980's when public demand called for evidence. We have made an observation that these reports have made a tremendous impact on curriculum and instruction, including assessment. Of course, somebody is going to say that pre-service teachers may be viewed as instruments for achieving the intentions of curriculum developers. This statement is radically strong, yet very true. The role of a pre-service teacher may be compared to that of a performing musician who is limited by the number of composers. The musician may present his own interpretation of a composition and not be expected to rewrite it. This chapter is about documenting professional development and growth. The key to attaining this is your understanding of competence statements. Does this sound simple? A statement of the obvious? If you answered, "yes," you are right. However, it also requires that you have available to you a means of meeting them. In other words, understanding where you need to go and how to get there.

Focus Questions

- 📂 What role does a pre-service teacher play in documenting his or her own learning?
- 📂 What is reflective thinking?
- 📂 What is the difference between reactive thinking and reflective thinking?
- 📂 What steps must one take to write a successful journal?

Concept of Competence and Attainment

More often than not, learning is regarded as the acquisition of knowledge by going to school or college, taking and completing courses, and validating the process with a diploma or degree which is backed by a transcript. This, in fact, is not what education is all about. Rather, education is a process of growth and development which takes place as the learner works at it under, both, favorable or unfavorable conditions. The number of courses, the overall GPA, or the fancy degree does not say enough about what you know and can do. Their primary function, however, is to validate the process and not necessarily the product. Stepping to the plate and showing your learning with tangible evidence of what and how much you know and can do is more definitive. Of course, placing yourself in such a vulnerable position is hard and painful. It will take effort and an attitude willing to confront fear and exposure. But what if you cannot prove it? This is where fear comes in. Eleanor Roosevelt once said "the answer to fear is not cowering and to hide; it is not to surrender feebly without contest. The answer is to stand and face it boldly, look at it, analyze it, and, in the end, act." A thought-provoking discovery that is likely is the realization not knowing it all. A portfolio is meant just for that—it is a tool that attempts to indicate concretely what your academic gains are. True, it is humiliating after you take an inventory of your knowledge, skills, and disposition and still find yourself wanting.

A mere accumulation of a body of knowledge does not make one educated. Rather, the change of disposition, perception, abilities and acquisition of skills to think independently and clearly are rudimentary to being educated. What about knowledge, you might ask? Knowledge is a means to this end and not an end in itself. However, as instructors or others engage in the process of gauging your mastery of information, focus is targeted on three basic areas—knowledge, skills, and dispositions. These three areas are examined on the context of performance. A common feature, which comes as no surprise to you, is that within the performance-based learning environment growth and development are gauged against defined terms of competencies. It is possible that your institution refers to these competencies as standards or performance outcomes. These competencies always have a stated level or target guiding their attainment. Some of the time, these competencies are not only stated but are also explicated in rubric form. The emphasis on competencies leads to an increased demand for demonstration of the competence. An individual who is described as competent is one who can continually evidence the ability to apply a repertoire of the selected knowledge, skills, and dispositions within a given context.

Gauging Competence and Attainment

Reflective Thinking

What exactly are we saying when we talk about reflection? Essentially, when we talk about reflection we don't mean recollection and, neither do we mean remembering. Rather, it is that kind of "thinking that extracts meaning from experience as a mechanism to propel development" (Guillaume & Yopp, 1995, p.96) or "the ability to think about what one does and why. Reflection influences how one grows as a professional by influencing how successfully one is able to learn from one's experiences" (Richert, 1990, p. 525).

Ross and Bondy (1996) defined reflection as "a way of thinking about educational matters and involves the ability to make rational choices and to assume responsibility for those choices" (p. 65). More recently, Evans and Policella (2000) have characterized reflective thinking as "an activity that requires teacher to be introspective, open-minded, and willing to make rational choices and assume responsibility for those choices" (p. 62).

Reflective thinking is not the same as reactive thinking. These two types of thinking are different. What is the difference between "reactive thinking" and "reflective thinking?" Reflective thinking is what produces real insight, valid opinions, and original ideas. Of course, it is not to say that reactive thinking is bad. To a certain extent, we need to have both kinds of thinking to function as rational beings and to use them appropriately. In his thought provoking work*: Silicon snakes: Second thoughts through the information highway*, Stoll (1996) presents a good example of the two kinds of thinking when he writes:

> One way of thinking is simply to react to what is happening. It is how our minds work in traffic: that car is too close; I'd better slow down. A ball rolls into the street and I skid to a halt. I'm part of the action. This kind of reactive thought is trained by experience. Pilots are great at it, as are pinball wizards and Nintendo addicts. It's what makes computer games fun; computers are great at teaching this kind of thinking. But there's another kind of thinking, call it "head scratching" or "reflection" or "cogitation." It's where we get new ideas, create hypotheses, and figure out solutions. This is hard and slower—we don't get the zowie feedback that Nintendo provides. Computers don't help us much with this kind of thinking—at their best, they can give us a playing field for thought, but they lack insight. Reading helps, as does writing. Analytical criticism helps. Teachers help a lot (p. 14).

Instructors in many teacher preparation colleges are finding reactive thinking as being far too common. All too often, teacher preparation programs change programs to reflect institutional, state or professional standards. While many of these changes and requirements appear to be absurd, they are intended to provide better preparation for prospective teachers. For example, your teacher preparation program may require passing a portfolio development as a prerequisite to advance in the program. Typically, most pre-service teachers immediately slide into "reactive thinking." Is not this too familiar—"I know of a friend of mine who did student teaching without a portfolio requirement"? This statement is made after "reactive thinking" certainly not after "reflective thinking." Our culture is drenched with "reactive thinking" while "reflective thinking" is taking the prominent position of being scarce.

Jonassen (1994) connects the learner's use of cognitive tools to a generative processing of information where new and meaningful knowledge is constructed following periods of reflection. According to Jonassen, reflective thinking is ". . . a careful, deliberate kind of thinking that helps us make sense out of what we have experienced and what we know" (p. 2). In essence, interest in reflection is usually marked by an implicit belief that ". . . knowledge is personally constructed, socially mediated and inherently situated" (Clarke, 1995, p.243).

Reflective practice acknowledges that central to learning is a process of mindful decision making (Seifert, 1999; Zumwalt, 1989). The act of reflection provides you with a vehicle to examine your daily life as a learner, to consider the various messages your instructors have transmitted to you, and to respond with choices that are more mindful. The concept of mindfulness infers that you critically ask yourself "why?" before, during and after decision-making. Reflective practice, as a mindful process, makes it possible to examine the thinking that precedes decision making (Schon, 1983, 1987), and thinking that occurs during decision making including thinking that examines previous actions (Killion & Todnem, 1991).

Reflective Journaling

Many teacher education programs require that pre-service teachers keep a journal of their introspection, feelings, and reactions to any aspect of the teaching experience. They reflect upon it and make decisions about changing what they are doing as a result. Dewey (1933) refers to reflective action as the "active, persistent and careful consideration of any belief or supposed form of knowledge in light of the grounds that support it and the consequences to which it tends" (p. 9). Dewey promoted reflection as an enactment of self-awareness and exercising preparedness for future possibilities. According to Dewey, reflective thinking "converts action that is merely appetitive, blind, and impulsive into intelligent action (1933, p. 17). A well developed portfolio utilizes Dewey's concept of reflective action as its organizing principle. As emphasized repeatedly in earlier chapters, the development of your pre-service teacher portfolio goes beyond a grade and is intended to help you become more aware of yourself. It is a process of self-assessment that helps promote professional growth through analytical and critical evaluation regarding your development process.

Any form of taking stock of your academic and professional development and growth is valuable in your learning. Journal keeping is a tool of choice that many teacher education programs encourage to support teacher candidate engagement in reflective activities as a source of learning about teaching. Reflection is effective only when its results are evident in tangible products. A requirement for most field experiences assignments in today's teacher preparation programs is keeping a reflective journal. This journal is a log of your experiences as a developing teacher.

The journal will also provide you with a place to record activities that tie into your learning plan. It should include thoughts about your learning and development responsibilities; new skills and accomplishments that you acquire; critical incidents that occur, and your thoughts and feelings. Reflective journal writing is a useful way of keeping track of what you are learning and instills in you a desire to learn more. As Sarason (1995) describes this desire:

> If when . . . motivated to learn more about self and the world, then I would say that schooling has achieved its overarching purpose. . . . [T]he student more you know, the more your need to know. . . . To want to continue to explore, to find answers to personally meaningful questions, issues, possibilities are the most important purpose of schooling (p. 135).

Journal writing is not a new idea. It has been around for a long time and may even have existed before the invention of paper as types of journals were found in the Egyptian tombs and the ruins of Pompeii. Many famous people including Leornardo da Vinci, Anne Frank, Fyodor Dostoyevski (Steiner and Phillips, 1991) all kept diaries. The motive for keeping a journal is centered on the idea that writing is a means of reflection, and that reflection on experience leads to meaningful learning. Simply put, thinking intensely about (reflecting upon) the things that happen during your preparation for teaching will help you become better teachers. Such reflection allows you to isolate your positive teaching experiences, to analyze what made them positive, and to repeat them. Likewise, negative teaching experiences will be isolated, analyzed and eliminated or avoided.

Reflective journaling is not a superficial observation and description of actions and activities that occur during your practicum as in the example below:

> Wednesday afternoon, I went to Booker T. Washington High School for my Field Experiences assignment as scheduled and completed the 2 hours and 30 minutes requirements for EDUC 254.

Rather, reflective journaling is a tool capable of clearing a mental fog and finding clarity in your observations, and reorienting your focus and approach to what you are engaged in. It involves the use of a logbook, a pen, and your brain. Its primary purpose is to help you turn experience into learning, learning into insight; insight into creative ideas; and ideas into actions that bring more meaning and purpose into your preparation as teacher. This appears to be very complicated. That is not necessarily true. In reality, it has only a few easy steps as illustrated in Box 6.1. How long does this take to complete? It all depends on how far you can soar. If, one day, you feel you are an eagle, the sky is the limit; if your feelings make you feel like a tweety bird then it can be completed within a few minutes. In other words, the question of time is irrelevant. What is important is the product of your journaling is what is important. If you spend less time, the reflection in your journaling may end up being shallow.

Box 6.1

☞ Quiet your mind
☞ Capture your experience
☞ Reflect and discover
☞ Set your goals

Here is how it works. Let us assume you are currently involved in your field experiences or any other project—it could be a Chemistry lab project, or a research project in history. Decide upon the focus of your reflection observation. With a journal pad and pen nearby, you are ready to begin the four easy steps.

Step 1: Quiet your mind. Take a moment to find quietness. You might want to look for a place where there is no other chatter going on either around you on in your head.

Step 2: Capture your experience. First, begin free writing whatever comes to mind as you revisit the experience you wish to reflect upon. Write your thoughts exactly as they come into your mind, without censoring. You may edit later, if you wish—the point is not to stop the flow of your thoughts. A journal is your own personal manuscript, detailing your struggles and triumphs as you experience them. Without worrying about spelling or syntax, capture any impressions that come, paying special attention to any spontaneous images and feelings. One piece of caution is in order here: do not use your journal as a work log in which you itemize and record events, tasks, and statistics. Rather, use your observation skills to tap into your own emotions and your senses. Your writing will become more interesting, and your experiences gain an enhancement as well. Concentrate on recapturing each idea on paper in vivid detail. Look at it from this point of view. If you are undertaking courses that require field experiences, you will find it easiest to maintain the journal by jotting down notes at the end of each day you complete your field experiences assignment. You might want to begin each entry with a brief factual account of what occurred that day. What did you learn? What were your responsibilities? What are you learning about the teaching profession? What are you learning about the classroom environment?

Next, write about your perceptions of what transpired that day. Describe your feelings and questions raised as a result of engaging in various activities. What was the most difficult part of the day? What was the most satisfying thing that happened? Were your initial expectations met? Have you met anyone who is especially interesting? Next, look at how this experience influences your preparation and involvement in the teaching profession. Is this experience making your course work more meaningful? Has your interest in teaching as a profession of choice enhance? Is the experience causing you to review your educational and career goals? These questions, and similar ones, will guide you in beginning and keeping a reflective journal.

The reflective journal process is meant to enhance your learning experiences. Use it in a beneficial way to you. Your teacher education program or specific instructors may require additional writing assignments using information that you have collected in your journal. You may also find that the journal is useful in classroom discussions and presentations. If you are experiencing difficulty keeping a journal, discuss it with your instructor who can provide suggestions and assistance that you might need.

Step 3: Reflect and Discover. Review what you have written, looking for the nuggets again. Your purpose in this step is to reflect on a select set of experiences you wish to remember, ponder and perhaps write more about them. Again, do not engage yourself in sentence structure as long as it makes meaning to you. It does not need to be pretty and academic. Let the typographical errors slide—in other words, be yourself. In your narrative, try to discover the key information as you include any striking observations. Underline or highlight each one. If at all possible, read your words aloud to yourself. You may find it helpful to begin looking at your experiences differently and discover insights you might have overlooked. As a product of reflective and analytical activity, your journal allows you to grapple with problems and frustration as well as identify specific accomplishments and breakthroughs as you undergo your preparation for the teaching profession.

Step 4: Set your Goals. Just as experience, or what you find yourself engaged in, does not naturally become learning and your discoveries do not become insights until you have reflected upon them, neither matter much until you do something about them. The journal is your means of charting your growth and development, both academically and personally. Determine a path forward by making a to-do-list in response to this final unfinished sentence: "And now I will . . ."

There are varied and different styles of writing and occasion that call for keeping a journal. Some instructors require that you keep an ongoing reflective journal for the course. Such a journal might include thinking in-depth about the class discussion, the term paper, or any other reactions that might be a part of the course. This is especially common in institutions where technology is prevalent and the student is allocated web space on the college web server or activities and participation in chat rooms and listserv facilities. Whether it is a digital or the traditional flat copy journal, it has great potential to significantly improve the quality of your learning. True, many students hate the assignment at first. Nevertheless, they get used to it after a while and it just becomes second nature as they come to see it as an avenue to "upload" their opinions, challenges, frustrations, and successes. Journal keeping thus becomes a clear demonstration of a commitment to learning—not just in intention but also in practice. You might already have a format that is prescribed by your institution. If your institution does not have one, there is a general agreement about what reflective journals should record. A few examples of activities that may be included in a reflective journal are illustrated in Box 6.2.

Box 6.2

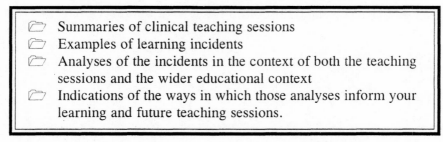

In writing a journal, it is important to make frequent entries and as near as possible to the incidents you are recording so that all traces of information—teaching context, an account of the incident, and implications for future teaching—are adequately and accurately documented. Moreover, use the journal time to scan through previous entries to detect if general themes are forming. If such an indication is revealed, this may also warrant a separate focus—particularly if the outcome of a similar incident has been influenced by the analyses in a previous journal entry.

Such a theme might form a basis of your journal as it is likely to suggest key themes, which may be problem areas, aspects about which you realize you know little and feel you should know more, or simply areas of interest to you. Having settled on a theme or a set of themes, you may use excerpts from the journal to exemplify that theme and providing an analysis to demonstrate your ability to link together other aspects of the course.

An effective reflective journal serves two purposes. First, it is useful way of monitoring and reviewing your learning and progress as a pre-service teacher. Secondly, it provides a rich source of evidence to document your attainment of defined performance outcomes for your portfolio. In a more general sense, it offers you insight into yourself as a learner. This insight will be helpful in many different situations, not just in your preparation for the teaching profession.

Some types of journal writing are "free form" with few or no stipulations on format or content. However, the reflective journal is a bit more "systematic" as its format leads one through a series of questions designed to promote description, reflection, and action. Journal writing is a very personal activity, and there is no "right" way to go about it. You will find yourself developing you own style once you start.

As a valuable skill, reflection represents a process that can help you learn about yourselves as a person and about your development as a teacher. This knowledge is an avenue to help you assess and improve your own learning. As you become aware of your own thoughts and behaviors, you become better prepared to respond in ways that will improve your learning and preparation for the teaching profession. Thus, reflective journaling for a portfolio asks you, in the context of your teacher preparation, to look at your own professional development critically, as well as your experience of the process. Begin by spending time looking through your program of study, rethinking your philosophy of education, field experiences material, and re-reading your course material. The best reflective journal is one that is critical and honest and reveals your ability to evaluate yourself fairly and candidly. Beyond this, your journaling will succeed insofar as it demonstrates sound logic, clarity, and development.

When used appropriately, reflective journaling support efforts in making a personal sense of your development within diverse set of experiences. This is particularly important when learning is to be incorporated into every day practice. It might just appear simple to say that a reflective journal assists the reflective process. Schon (1987) writes about reflection-in-action. He describes reflection as a process of learning by doing with the help of a coach. This is after all the way we all learned to talk as infants. As mature practitioners, we are able to exploit the process more fully. To maximize our learning we can question and challenge the coach, ask for clarification and together build new understandings. In this way, we learn to be reflective with our partner. Brookfield's (1995), *Becoming a critically reflective teacher,* describes the process of hunting out our assumptions and critically examining them. As you engage yourself in reflective thinking, look for the assumptions that underpin your practice and then play devils advocate and develop a contrary argument. You now have two sides of an argument to evaluate. This is engaging in personal critical reflection. Reflective journal writing is becoming a common practice in teacher education as a means of causing teachers to focus on the context and experiences of their own teaching and learning. Journaling is a way to express ourselves. We write down events and our reaction to them. Journaling brings out deep feelings that may otherwise never get expressed.

Through your teacher education program you will be required to engage in field experiences and clinical practice. Field experiences provide a fertile ground to engage in and develop your reflection abilities. Chambers & Stacey (1999) observed that the most successful teacher education students are those who, early in their studies, can make connections between their current learning experiences and future applications when they are in the field. A reflective journal is intended to provide an opportunity to capture in an organized fashion your observations, questions, and reactions to things you experience during your field placement. The journal is a place meant for you to document experiences that you deem important and find interesting in your development endeavor; pose questions to yourself on things you find problematic; try to make connections between things you are observing in the field, and ideas you are reading about; work out ideas that you find perplexing; comment on your own personal feelings in reaction to events and ideas; and speculate on the meaning of these experiences and what you have learned from them.

Consider for a moment that learning is an engagement that touches emotions. In that case, it simply means that learning is an emotional activity. A good learner, therefore, is one who engages in reflection activities on his or her own feelings and perceptions of the feelings of others. This is a very important aspect in professional development. As you prepare yourself to become a teacher you must carefully attend to your own feelings as well as how those feeling relate to those of your students', their parents', colleagues' and administrators'. Of course the feelings of your students have to be considered always, but developing a keen awareness of your own feelings is also critical—for your effectiveness, growth, and of course survival within the teaching profession.

To be reflective, of course, is not an easy task. The act of reflection is a form of jogging the mind. Jogging the mind requires the use of words to express emotions. We don't always fell like jogging the mind. We do not want to sit down and write or even have the need to "say" something. Reflecting is hard and painful. Exercising the brain is just as hard (if not harder) than exercising the body. But just like routine body exercise, you need to be a measure of discipline and must force yourself to do it. Reflective journaling helps you note, connect and interpret your own learning. It is a useful tool that enables you to map, interpret and question your own development into becoming a teacher. Guidelines that shape the form and contents of the reflective journal have been given by Posner, 1992 and Pultorak, 1993) and are summarized in Figure 6.3.

Figure 6.1:
Guidelines for Developing an Effective Reflective Journal

---

1. Keep a journal during each practicum and each student teaching experience.

2. Write two entries per week in the journal.

3. Write an entry which is composed of three parts:
    *   *Description* of an experience (Answer the following questions: What happened? What did I do? What did the students do?).
    *   *Reflection* upon the experiences (Answer the following questions: What does it mean? What informed my decision? How did I come to be that way?).
    *   *Decisions, conclusions, or actions* on how subsequent teaching will change because of the experience and reflection (Answer the following question: How can I enhance my learning? How can I maintain the positive and avoid the negative?).

4. The first entry of each week should be a description of and reflection upon a positive experience.

5. In the second entry each week, describe and reflect upon either a positive or negative experience.

In principle, you will need to equip yourself with a notebook or a log file to make records. It does not need to be an expensive pad. You can acquire one at a very inexpensive price at Wal-Mart or a similar department store. Of course, we have said that it should not be expensive. However, we suggest that you choose something that is of a quality that reflects the importance of this sort of work and yet sturdy enough to withstand the ravages of time. Keep it in a safe place. We hope that self-reflection will become a lifetime habit that will stimulate your future growth and development. Because it is entirely private and personal, no teacher education program has a way of directly assessing you in this area. As you become more aware of your abilities and shortfalls ask yourself the probing question, 'what do I need?' and consider the various forms of support and help available. This, certainly, is a big step toward becoming a better manager of your destiny! The uses of a reflective journal help you monitor your progress and become aware of that progress and needs. It leads on very naturally to exploring how to satisfy them. In it, you record your experiences, thoughts, feelings, reactions, observations etc. From time to time, review what you have written and reflect on it. Do not try to analyze it. Rather, sit with it. Digest it and see what happens. Particularly notice the recurring patterns, the situations that always give rise to the same reactions. When you notice certain peculiarities, ask yourself: What is going on here? Hold on to the question, reflect on the events, and see what comes to you. Because this journal is private and personal you might decide to use only excerpts for the portfolio. The more use you make of it, the greater value it becomes to you in your personal and professional development. To get the most benefit from your reflection activities, you need to:

- ❖ Write regularly
- ❖ Be honest
- ❖ Deal with feelings as well as events
- ❖ Look back and look forward from time to time
- ❖ Think about what all this means to your learning

Process of Self-Assessment

Research (Frazier & Paulson, 1992; Lamme & Hysmith, 1991; Tierney, Carter, & Desai, 1991) has provided convincing evidence that any learner can and does improve in his ability to assess his own strengths and weaknesses and monitor progress towards meeting specific goals. This research describes how learners improve in their awareness of what they know, what they are learning, areas that need improvement, and so forth. Pre-service teachers learn how to interact effectively with their course content, instructors, PreK-12 teachers and students, and parents to gain an even fuller picture of their own achievements and progress.

An effective method of gauging one's path toward mastery of defined competencies is though self-assessment and documentation using defensible products. Self-assessment is the process of gathering information about you as a basis for making an informed decision. This decision may be personal or career oriented. This process may include taking an inventory of your skills, preferences, interests, aptitudes, abilities, and personal traits. It involves identifying your strengths and weaknesses. It is figuring out who you are, what you want, and analyzing what you have done and what you can do.

It is important to understand that self-assessment is a necessary step toward documenting your growth and learning because provides a means of determining the direction in which you will focus your efforts. For some, this may be an easy step. For most people it is a difficult process. It can be challenging because it depends upon your ability to be completely honest with yourself. It takes time and discipline to become proficient in your self-assessment. However, you will need to work on it and allow it to become a continual process. Your vision of what you want and what is expected of you as a pre-service teacher and as a prospective teacher should be constantly adapting to your changing growth in knowledge, interests, and skills as well as to the world's changing opportunities.

In practice, self-assessment can be either informal, meaning that you can assess yourself as you go about your daily activities or it can be formal, meaning that you purposely sit down and become engaged in and actively focus on self assessment. Developing a portfolio truly engages you in that process as you figure out what you are expected to collect, select, reflect, and display. Early in the school year, you might be pressed to consider: What would I like to re-read or share with my instructor, friends, or employer? What makes a particular piece of writing, or an approach to a mathematical problem, or a write-up of a science project a good product? In developing a portfolio of selected pieces and explaining the basis for their choices, you generate criteria for good work. Of course instructor and peer input is of great value in focusing on this goal. Those criteria become a good starting point for self-assessment. Box 6.3 lists a number of reasons why self-assessment is important.

Box 6.3

- ☐ Only you know yourself
- ☐ You have the right to contribute to your own assessment. You can play a vital role in the collection of information about your own growth and development
- ☐ Instructors have a lot of time constraints placed on them and should be prepared to transfer to pre-service teachers as many evaluation tasks as possible
- ☐ It makes you more aware of your learning process

Research has consistently shown the benefit afforded to you by an awareness of processes and strategies involved in writing, solving a problem, researching a topic, analyzing information, or describing your own observations. Without instruction focused on the processes and strategies that underlie effective performance of these types of work, most students will not learn them or will learn them only minimally. Without curriculum-specific experience in using these processes and strategies, even fewer students will carry them forward into new and appropriate contexts. A portfolios can serve as a vehicle for enhancing an awareness of strategies for thinking and successfully engaging yourself in such activities that encourage thinking skills.

Summary of Key Points

This chapter has examined the concept of competence as well as an effective way of gauging it. Central to the concept of competence and attainment is the process of mindful decision-making. As a mindful process, reflective practice makes it possible to examine the thinking that precedes decision-making and thinking that occurs during decision-making, and thinking that examines previous actions. We have stated that reflective thinking is not the same as reactive thinking.

In addition, journal keeping and portfolio development are two inevitable requirements in many teacher preparation programs. These two activities force you to engage in focused reflective thinking. This chapter expounded on the notion that the motive for keeping a journal is centered on the idea that writing is a means of reflection, and that reflection on experience leads to meaningful learning. If you are a teacher, such reflection will allow you to isolate your positive teaching experiences, to analyze what made them positive, and to repeat them. The reflective journal helps you become aware of your own progress and needs and provides an evaluation tool capable of monitoring that progress and those needs. In it, record your experiences, thoughts, feelings, reactions, observations etc. while considering it as an entirely private and personal document.

Developing a portfolio allows you to discover the degree of mastery of a defined set of knowledge, skills, and dispositions, as well as afford you an opportunity to ask of yourself sensible questions about your thoughts and tenets regarding to issues in teaching and learning. In addition, it provides you a channel and a need to engage in self-assessment. Self-assessment is defined in the chapter as the process of gathering information about you as a basis for making an informed decision and may include taking stock of your skills, preferences, interests, aptitudes, abilities, and personal traits.

References

Brookfield, S. D. (1995). *On becoming a critically reflective teacher*. Jossey-Bass, San Francisco.

Chambers, D.P. & Stacey, K. (1999). *Authentic tasks for authentic learning: Modes of interactivity in multimedia for undergraduate teacher education*. Paper presented in the 10th Annual Conference of Society for Information Technology & Technology Teacher Education International Conference (San Antonio, TX, February- March, 1999).

Clarke, Anthony. (1995). Professional development in practicum settings: Reflective practice under scrutiny. *Teaching and Teacher Education*. 11(3):243-261.

Dewey, J. (1933). *How we think. A relation of reflective thinking to the educative process*. Chicago: Henry Regnery.

Evans, J.F. & Pollicella, E. (2000). Changing and growing as teachers and learners: A shared journey. *Teacher Education Quarterly*, 27(3), 55-70.

Frazier, D.M., & Paulson, F.L. (1992, May). How portfolios motivate reluctant writers. *Educational leadership,* 49(8), 62-65.

Guillaume, A. M., & Yopp, H. K. (1995). Professional portfolios for student teachers. *Teacher education quarterly,* 22 (1), 93-101.

Jonassen, D. (1994). Technology as cognitive tools: Learners as designers, [Website]. ITForum. Available: http://itech1.coe.uga.edu/itforum/paper1.html [2002, March 2].

Killion, J., & Todnem, G. (1991). A process for personal theory building. *Educational leadership*, 48(6), 14-16.

Lamme, L.L., & Hysmith, C. (1991). One school's adventure into portfolio assessment. *Language arts,* 68, 629-640.

Posner, G. (1992). *Field Experiences: A guide to reflective thinking*. New York, N.Y.: Longman Publishing Company.

Pultorak, E.G. (1993). Facilitating reflective thoughts in novice teachers. *Journal of Teacher Education*. 44 (4), 288-295.

Richert, A. E. (1990). Teaching students to reflect: A consideration of program structure. *Journal of curriculum studies,* 22, (6), 509-527.

Ross, D., & Bondy, E. (1996). The continuing reform of a university teacher education program: A case study. In K. Zeichner, S. Melnick, & M. L. Gomez (Eds.). *Currents of reform in pre-service teacher education.* New York: Teacher College Press.

Sarason, S. (1995). School change: *The personal development of a point of view.* New York. Teacher College Press.

Schon, D. (1987). *The reflective practitioner: How professionals think in action.* New York: Basic Books.

Schon, D.A. (1983). *Educating the reflective practitioner: Toward a new design for teaching and learning in the professions.* San Francisco: Jossey-Bass.

Seifert, K. L. (1999). *Reflective thinking and professional development.* Boston: Houghton Mifflin.

Steiner, B. & Phillips, K. (1991). *Journal keeping with young people.* Englewood, CO.: Teacher Ideas Press.

Stoll, C. (1996). *Silicon snake oil: Second thoughts on the information highway.* New York, N.Y.: Doubleday.

Tierney, R.J., Carter, M.A., & Desai, L.E. (1991). *Portfolio assessment in the reading-writing classroom.* Norwood, MA: Christopher-Gordon Publishers.

Zumwalt, K. (1989). Beginning professional teacher: The need for a curricular vision of teaching. In M. C. Reynolds (Ed.). *Knowledge base for the beginning teacher.* New York: Pergamon Press.

Chapter 7

Stages in Developing an Exemplary Portfolio

Orientation

With a likely probability that a *typical* portfolio does not exist, the process described in this chapter is, by definition, generic. The process explored in this chapter, albeit briefly has no dependency on any particular teacher education program or mandates. As such, some details that may be of value and importance to your teacher education program may have been left out for clarity. It is intended to provide practical and supportive strategies for developing a meaningful and successful portfolio. It is important to remember that the portfolio development process is not a panacea—simply following it will not necessarily guarantee success any more than knowing the recipe for your mother's famous homemade cornbread will guarantee a faithful reproduction of the original. Our discussion in this chapter, in general, concentrates on the various components and, to some degree, the mechanics of developing a successful portfolio. After reading this chapter, you should be able to articulate the various stages involved in the development of a pre-service teacher portfolio. We encourage you to supplement your reading of this text with hands-on performance activities. Additionally, as you read through this chapter, look for answers to the five focus questions listed below.

Focus Questions

- What are the four stages in portfolio development?
- How would you describe the portfolio development process?
- What are the various components of the portfolio development process?
- What kinds of products are appropriate for your portfolio and how do you determine their appropriateness?
- Which relationships are beneficial to the portfolio development process?

It is time to address the procedure for getting down to the development of your portfolio. "What should I include in my portfolio?" Frankly, that is a reasonable question to ask. The most reasonable answer to the question is, "it depends". It depends upon you as a pre-service teacher. It depends upon what it is that you want to evidence. It depends upon the purpose of the portfolio. Your institution might require that you to develop a portfolio to meet a particular benchmark within a program. It depends on your audience. Much of the time, the audience is your instructors. Other times the audience is a licensing agency. It depends on the guidelines provided for the development of the portfolio. Most entities, be they a teacher education program or employer, require a portfolio. It is common to have established guidelines set forth for the development of your portfolio. However, it is noteworthy to state that portfolios, in general, are less restrictive because of their very purpose—to evidence mastery. If any single word epitomizes unrestrictiveness, it is choice.

Whose Work is it Anyway?

Any teacher education program seeking to foster mastery certainly gives pre-service teachers an opportunity for making their case within an environment that allows free choices. This choice includes the collection, reflection, reduction, and display of tangible evidence to back a claim on mastery. In essence, this activity offers opportunities to stretch yourself in a direction you most care about, and to learn from your successes and as well as your failures. That is all there is to the portfolio development. You could liken the portfolio development process to a Nintendo game.

You repeatedly make mistakes in a Nintendo game. You learn from mistakes and self-correct them. As you consciously make choices, you become more attuned, on every level, to the opportunities and possibilities. Moreover, you do not give up. Rather, you need return and try again. As you consider it from this perspective, you become more resilient and are able to take risks, capitalized on the outcome of those risks, and base your judgment on successes and risks as you target on achieving a stated goal. This is, exactly, what makes portfolio a powerful learning tool.

Portfolio Development Cycle (PDC)

You have heard of the story of the Chinese bamboo tree—the bamboo farmer plants the bamboo seed, tends it for six years and does not see a sprout. To the untrained eye, the extensive labor of the farmer is in vain. The farmer knows that at some point in the sixth year it will sprout out and will rapidly grow into a 70-foot healthy bamboo stock—commonly known as the "Tree of Heaven." The moral of this story is simple—it takes time to see the gains of an important work. We are all living in the age of "now". We want everything instantaneously—our coffee, Internet access, you name it. However, the development of a portfolio takes time, diligence, and patience. In general, when people talk about a portfolio, they focus primarily on the content and the aesthetic aspects. Of course, such ideas sound intuitive and attractive. However, content and beautification is only one part of the overall process. How do you begin the development of your portfolio? What steps and guidelines do you need to follow to develop a portfolio?

We have already begun to understand that a portfolio is a representative of the various aspects of your learning and growth. This means looking beyond the most obvious part of your courses and course activities to include the meaning of those activities based on the overall goal of your growth and development. Products of your work should demonstrate these qualities any of a number of activities. These may include a given sequence of courses, field experiences assignments, or activities in your fraternity, in your church or in the chapter of your professional organization. Nevertheless, you need to be reminded again that mere completion of teacher education courses is important. However, such accomplishment does not fully reflect your growth and development as a prospective teacher. An attractive GPA on a transcript may not say much.

We all know of students who are capable of memorizing a thick textbook and do well on the multiple-choice questions. On the other hand, an unattractive GPA is not necessarily an accurate measure of your capacity. The C grade can mean anything. It can mean you just had a bad day. It can mean that you are not good with tricky questions. And, that does not necessarily mean you are also not good in course content. It can also mean that the instructor gave you the C out of sympathy when your actual grade was far less. Developing a portfolio is an on-going process and, in reality, a very dynamic one. Figure 7.1 presents the four stage cyclical process of portfolio development. The portfolio development cycle (PDC) includes collection, reflection, reduction, and display.

Figure 7.1 Four Stages of the Portfolio Development Cycle

Collection

"Well, I'll start on my portfolio when the spirit moves me." Forget it! There are two guiding principles. The first is collecting products for your portfolio is not a scavenger hunt. Rather, it is an orchestrated engagement with defined goals and purpose to provide a defendable longitudinal record of your progress. The second principle is that time is always the greatest enemy of portfolio development. Portfolio development requires planning ahead of time and keeping every bit of work as potential artifacts. Such work samples might include written work such as reports, term papers, graded tests and assignments, lesson/unit plans, artwork, lists of professional books and articles you have read; lists of conferences you have attended and sample materials from those conferences, letters from parents, notes from pupils, tape recordings of your teaching, and so forth. By now you may have come to realize that the development of a portfolio encourages you to become a true pack rat yet a connoisseur of classroom and out of classroom products. The more carefully you organize your possible artifacts, the less overwhelmed you will feel when inundated by the additional task of actual development of the portfolio.

You have come to learn in this text that the portfolio development process is (and must be) an ongoing project. It is a process that must begin soon after you set foot on your college campus. The rudimentary stage in portfolio development is the collection of information. This means that developing a paper trail, is indeed, necessary. Your collection of artifacts should be a conscious engagement rather than a haphazard collection of learning products. Moreover, to successfully develop a rich and meaningful portfolio, start out by keeping everything from each class and a good inventory list of your material. You will be surprised how many pre-service teachers become devastated because they are unable to find that term paper, that graded test and that other project that was completed in the previous class.

Creating an exemplary portfolio starts with compiling a set of quality artifacts that exhibit development and achievement while highlighting the diversity of such experiences. Its primary purpose is simple—material to be placed in the portfolio should be diverse, creative and planned ahead of time. In so doing, you are starting off to your best advantage. Most people do much more than they are aware of, and collecting data several semesters later is simply not accurate enough. In addition, most pre-service teachers have a tendency to discard their learning products before becoming aware of their importance as key elements to a portfolio. If this is the case for you, then you will definitely have a challenging time finding your artifacts.

There is a need to quickly learn the importance of keeping all your papers, creative work, membership cards and letters to or from professional societies, and letters or evaluations from clinical experience supervisors or individuals, and the list goes on, in a safe container. A good starting point in developing your portfolio, is sorting through your accumulated curriculum and extra material. This activity must be approached with an eye towards addressing your mastery or path toward mastery of standards required of you.

What to place in the portfolio should be determined by four key questions:

- ❖ What is your absolute best work that demonstrates the degree of your mastery of a given competency?
- ❖ What work best shows the diversity of your preparation as a teacher?
- ❖ What honors or awards have you received?
- ❖ Is there any related non-course work experience, which should be mentioned in a separate area?

As you gather artifacts for your portfolio, consider two factors. First, the relationship of the artifact to the pre-stated performance outcomes needs to be clarified. A common pitfall in portfolio development is confronting the unquestioned unfamiliarity of a performance outcome. Do you remember the fable of the Fuzzy at the beginning of Chapter 3? You might want to flip back and look at it once more. Had the Fuzzy known the true profile of the "goodest" of men he would still have his four legs on him. Too often, pre-service teachers approach the development of their portfolios without the faintest idea of the statements they seek to address. Before you begin developing a meaningful portfolio, you need to have a good understanding of performance statements set before you.

Second, consider the appropriateness of the artifact. Remember that your intention in developing a portfolio is to evidence academic and professional growth and development which is attained as a result of gaining mastery of defined competencies. Of course, your instructors will not expect a portfolio that exhibits "A" paper in its entirety. You might not be an A student, just an average student. In this case, you might want to collect both your worst and your best products to show your gains and improvements. Keeping up with al of the papers can be overwhelming. A way to avoid mountains of "possible" artifacts is using a log sheet. Figure 7.2 presents an artifact analysis form that is specific to one teacher education program. This form can be used by pre-service teachers as a guide through Stage I (Collection) of the Cycle in preparation for Stage 2 (Reflection) and Stage 3 (Reduction).

Figure 7.2 Sample Pre-Candidate Portfolio Artifact Analysis Form

Pre-Candidate Portfolio Artifact Analysis Form

Directions: Begin by identifying artifacts that appropriately address each of the ten College competencies. Identify several artifacts for each competency and reflect and narrow them to two or three that best demonstrate your mastery of the competency. Next, clearly identify the physical location or source of your artifact (i.e. COSI 118 notebook, Yellow Scrapbook with my Certificates). Knowledge of the location will ease their retrieval when you begin to assemble your portfolio. After collecting artifacts for the various competencies, review, reflect on, and evaluate what you have gathered. Think about the appropriateness and adequacy of each artifact in addressing the competency statement. It is not uncommon to discover the need to want to switch artifacts from one category to another. This activity should be done over a period of time. Rating is the last stage in the analysis process. You will probably re-evaluate your artifacts several additional times before completing your portfolio. Based on your review, rate each artifact as follows:

DI = Definitely Include   M = Maybe Include
CFAS=Consider for Another Performance Outcome   DNI=Do not Include

Competency Statement	Name of Artifact	Location/Source	Rating
1. Think creatively, critically, logically, and analytically using both quantitative and qualitative methods for solving problems	1. _____ 2. _____ 3. _____	1. _____ 2. _____ 3. _____	1. _____ 2. _____ 3. _____
2. Communicate effectively (listen, speak, read, and write) on formal and informal levels	1. _____ 2. _____ 3. _____	1. _____ 2. _____ 3. _____	1. _____ 2. _____ 3. _____
3. Distinguish, clarify, and refine personal values for the attainment of richer self-perception and relate those values to the value system of others	1. _____ 2. _____ 3. _____	1. _____ 2. _____ 3. _____	1. _____ 2. _____ 3. _____
4. Appreciate, understand, and know the foundations of the Afrocentric perspective	1. _____ 2. _____ 3. _____	1. _____ 2. _____ 3. _____	1. _____ 2. _____ 3. _____

Figure 7.2 Sample Pre-Candidate Portfolio Artifact Analysis Form (cont.)

Pre-Candidate Portfolio Artifact Analysis Form

Competency Statement	Name of Artifact	Location/Source	Rating
5. Appreciate, understand, and know the foundations of diverse cultures in the context of a global community	1. _____ 2. _____ 3. _____	1. _____ 2. _____ 3. _____	1. _____ 2. _____ 3. _____
6. Appreciate, understand, know and pursue the principles, methods and subject matter that underlie the major discipline(s)	1. _____ 2. _____ 3. _____	1. _____ 2. _____ 3. _____	1. _____ 2. _____ 3. _____
7. Accept social responsibility and provide service to humankind	1. _____ 2. _____ 3. _____	1. _____ 2. _____ 3. _____	1. _____ 2. _____ 3. _____
8. Maintain levels of literacy that allow them to understand the impact of science and technology on individuals, society, and the environment.	1. _____ 2. _____ 3. _____	1. _____ 2. _____ 3. _____	1. _____ 2. _____ 3. _____
9. Attain motivational, personal management, interpersonal skills, professional development and research experience, as well as resourcefulness that will form the basis for a career and/or further educational experiences.	1. _____ 2. _____ 3. _____	1. _____ 2. _____ 3. _____	1. _____ 2. _____ 3. _____
10. Attain critical skills, frame of reference, and understanding needed to appreciate and discriminate between artistic achievements.	1. _____ 2. _____ 3. _____	1. _____ 2. _____ 3. _____	1. _____ 2. _____ 3. _____

Reflection

When appropriately used the portfolio process can be an effective means of self-examination. Suppose that, at the end of the semester, you found out that you are lacking in a specific area. Knowledge of this nature could form an agenda to bring to your academic advisor or instructor. By way of interaction and taking stock of your current skills you will be able to map out a plan to develop that area. This is the true strength of developing a portfolio. The portfolio brings forth your strengths and your weakness. Knowing your strengths enables you to capitalize on it and work toward enhancing it. At the same time, you get to discover your weaknesses. There is nothing quite as humbling as weaknesses. Rather than focusing on a weakness, you need to see it as an opportunity for growth. It is a natural human tendency not to see or even accept the existence of a weakness. An eagle eye towards filling in those perceived weaknesses in the examination of a portfolio is required and must be done. By doing so, the portfolio then becomes a means by which the preservice teacher set long-term goals and take control of the process of educating oneself.

The second phase incorporates an interactive exercise where you engage yourself in looking at the artifacts and reflecting on them from the standpoint of the performance outcomes. Without reflection, leaping into the dark in the next stage becomes likely. Having engaged yourself in a reflection activity, you gain informed advice that allows you to validate the artifacts in question allowing your passage to the next stage of the PDC. A committing to act of reflection provides a meaningful way of validating artifacts as you engage your thoughts and feelings into a personal analysis of your progress toward becoming a prepared and highly qualified teacher. This on-going process of reflection and validation is an attribute of a focused and promising portfolio product.

Determine which competencies or performance indicators your portfolio will demonstrate (the purpose) as you relate them to the primary audience for the portfolio. Set up the portfolio demonstrating the performance indicators of the specific standards that have been selected. This could be done in the reflective abstract sheet. In principle, reflection abstracts must demonstrate and examine evidence of self-reflection and self-assessment. An important component of your reflective abstract page is the rationale. The rationale is a reflective narrative that explains how you think you attained the standard. To be reflective entails being able to step back from the immediacy of the situation and examine your knowledge, skills, beliefs, attitudes, values and behavior in a dispassionate manner. The reflection abstracts provide insight into your perspective concerning the artifacts presented as evidence of meeting stated objectives. When we take these reflections and set goals for future learning, the portfolio becomes a lifelong learning tool. For each performance indicator, write a statement about what you still need to learn while setting some reasonable goals so that you can work toward achieving this standard in a reasonable period.

Reflection is perhaps the most important step in the portfolio process and sets the portfolio apart from a mere scrapbook or a general storage file. It is here that you explain why you choose a particular artifact, how it compares with other artifacts, what particular skills and knowledge were used to produce it, and where you can improve as a learner. The importance of this step lies in having to take an active role in the assessment process. In developing your rationale, you will probably observe more directly the quality of your own achievement and, with sincerity, detail where improvements are needed.

Reduction

A third major component of the PDC is the reduction stage. The reduction stage allows for the identification of artifacts that demonstrate mastery of a competence. Artifact reduction refers to the process of focusing, selecting, abstracting and transforming documents to meet the standard. This stage in the portfolio development can become problematic if you have not done a good job in your reflection.

As you engage yourself in the document reduction process, you need to be cognizant of the fact that artifacts may have the potential to demonstrate your mastery of more than one competence. Remind yourself, over and over, that your portfolio serves a dual purpose. It serves as a self and collaborative assessment and evaluation tool as well as a catalyst for self-reflective skills. Such an assessment implies a limited audience at least during the initial stages of development. The audience may be limited to only you and possibly your peers. You are your own primary audience. It is important that the artifacts that you choose for inclusion should be meaningful first to you as a prospective teacher.

Have you ever heard of the common cliché "working smarter not harder?" That is the approach you need to take as you work on your portfolio. How do you work smarter instead of harder? Reduction requires that you look at the performance outcomes that you intend to document a relative level of attainment. You will need to gain an understanding of specific requirements and use that understanding in your *reduction* process. A way to categorize possible items for inclusion is to divide them into three categories based on the source of the item: materials from oneself (e.g., reflective statements, term papers, graded assignments and homework, quizzes and examinations), materials from others (e.g., student comments, evaluations made by student teaching supervisor), and products of your field experiences activities (student work samples that may include essays and creative work, a record of students grades). Some of these sources may be more appropriate for certain aspects of learning than for others.

Two main challenges are likely at the *reduction stage*. The first concerns choice and quantity. Remember that a portfolio contains works that are representative as opposed to being comprehensive. The second concerns the selection of artifacts that represent your learning and attainment in a convincing way. Let us look at each challenge separately. With regard to the choice and quantity, each artifact that you choose for inclusion should represent at a significant aspect of you and/or your learning. Bear in mind, at the same time, that your development, as a professional teacher is a complex process. Therefore, it is not possible to represent all aspects. In general, your primary focus should be on representing goals and your growth toward those goals and later, achievements.

Second, finding artifacts that demonstrate your mastery of performance outcomes can be a major hurdle, especially if your collection is expansive. This is also true if your collection is thin and limited. In either case, your primary objective is to find artifacts that evidence your mastery of performance outcomes. Select artifacts that provide sufficient evidence of your progress toward selected performance outcomes. Your artifact should be meaningful not only to you, but also to others including your peers and your instructors. Item chosen must be those that adequately address a performance outcome. Breaking a large goal down into several smaller parts is a useful way to adequately address a performance outcome. True, you should always seek to include your best work in the portfolio.

Your friends Michael and Amber have both developed attractive portfolios and their artifacts all show A's. True, your friends are smart and you consider yourself smart too and you have worked so hard for the grades that you have. You achieved a GPA of 2.50 required for admission by your teacher education program. College does not come naturally for you and you are constantly working hard to keep that GPA and remain in the program. Your portfolio contains artifacts that are mostly C+'s and a couple B's. What are you going to do about that? Aren't you only evidencing average performance? You need to recognize that knowledge and skill development is incremental. Until your perception takes such an orientation, your portfolio development effort will always be a painful task and you will always lack a feeling of success and satisfaction.

In tandem with the kind of artifacts to include in the portfolio is the number of artifacts deemed adequate. Again, just as you have come to know that there is not a *typical* portfolio, there is also no such thing as a set number of artifacts. What is more important than the number of artifacts to include in the portfolio is the range of their diversity. Useful evidence takes many forms, and needs to be carefully selected and presented. However, care must be taken in presenting artifacts while guarding against loosing sight of the purpose while providing clarity and ease in reading and understanding the rationale behind each piece.

A good portfolio is one that has variety. Ultimately, however, your claims about your preparation will be most convincing to readers when they are supported by documentation from a variety of sources. This documentation may include coursework, community service activities and other extra-curriculum engagements. Some have also chosen to include products such as letters from their students (unsolicited letters are preferable to solicited) or from peers, instructors regarding their teaching. Try to consider incorporating into the portfolio evidence of your academic growth and development through products such as lab books and assignments notebooks. These types of product are likely to demonstrate your improvement throughout a particular course. With the increasing availability and use of multi-media styles and technologies, might even consider including video footage from actual classes and classroom activities in your field experiences assignments.

Artifacts selected at this stage are your *active artifacts* in the sense that you have identified them as possible items of inclusion. Your artifact selection activity at this point has already begun focusing on the competencies and their various components. You have begun to capture the artifacts' relative potential to address a performance outcome. As you involve yourself in the reduction process, you should quickly learn that creating a portfolio is both a reflexive as well as reflective process. In that case, be ready to rewrite your rationale statements several more times while completing other sections of the portfolio. Rationales give a voice to your artifacts and, effectively, cause you to rethink your approach to documenting your learning.

In narrowing the number of artifacts you have gathered the following list of suggestions is designed to increase your options and support your efforts.

- Review your collection carefully while being mindful of the need to collect variety in terms of kind, setting, and time.
- Review the competency statements to make sure your have a clear understanding of their meaning
- Identify peers who are currently developing their portfolios and seek their assistance
- Network with peers and faculty to support your effort in understanding the competency statements

Available artifacts not selected are your *dormant artifacts*. These artifacts may not immediately appear to address a performance outcome. Be sure not to discard your dormant artifacts. As you grow professionally, your perceptions change. The paper you once thought to be wonderfully creative may seem outdated or not trendy in two years down the road, while the dry pedantic paper that you once rejected and piled among your dormant artifacts may seem more articulate and mature as time progresses. This stresses a factor in portfolio development—the portfolio process is an ongoing examination of your experience. If this then is the case, it therefore follows that the examination of artifacts is as important as any reasonable way of assuring your knowledge and skills. Moreover, the selection process enables you to communicate your philosophy of education either through the type of artifacts selected or through the reflective pieces you write in support of each artifact. The selection process is a dialogue as shown in Figure 7.2.

Display

The final stage of the portfolio development cycle is artifact display. We define display as an organized parade of selected artifacts in a visually appealing manner to demonstrate mastery of a performance outcome and permit a comprehensive review by a review panel.

Figure 7.2: A Self-Reflection Exercise in Selecting Artifacts

---

- Select an artifact for your portfolio
- Mentally review the activity and reflect upon the process and product
- Reflect on the greatest value of this activity or experience. Connect that value to one of the standards
- Write a rationale about your selection. Be sure to explain the following and include it in your portfolio with the artifact:
- Why I chose this piece
- What I learned and the competence I gained
- What are my future goals

Source: Dorothy M. Campbell, et al. (2000). *Portfolio and Performance Assessment in Teacher Education*. Boston, MA. Allyn and Bacon

When you fail to recognize and act on your portfolio project based on the four stages, you will lack a firm and secure platform to document your mastery of given competencies. Any or all of these come to play in your decision of the content of your portfolio. While it is important that you maintain the flexibility of your portfolio, it is also necessary to ensure some degree of consistency in order to make its evaluation fairer and more reliable. Faculty in your institution might establish consensus on required portfolio content and format including page limit, design and focus, or the depth and opportunities for reflection. Certainly, that is true. Faculty do not need to worry about format and can concentrate instead on the content. In general a portfolio should include three basic sections: Attestation Documents, Evidence Documents and, Reflection Summary Essay.

What to include in your portfolio must be determined by four key questions presented in Box 7.2.

As we have already discussed, it is unusual for you to have complete control over what goes into your portfolio. Your institution more often than not will dictate the content. However, if you have a choice of layout, consider visibility: Can you clearly see the argument of your learning, growth and development? Can the audience clearly see the argument of your learning and growth? The guiding principle here is visibility—to see and be seen. In a very unique way, a pre-service teacher portfolio is an argument; it is developed around the claims you wish to make about

Box 7.2

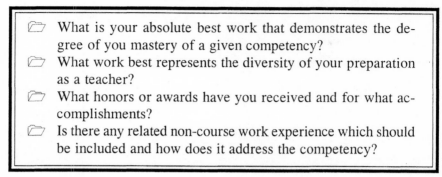

What is your absolute best work that demonstrates the degree of you mastery of a given competency?

What work best represents the diversity of your preparation as a teacher?

What honors or awards have you received and for what accomplishments?

Is there any related non-course work experience which should be included and how does it address the competency?

yourself as a developing teacher. A way to highlight these claims in your portfolio is to present them in your philosophy of education. Ideally, your philosophy of education needs to explicate two primary questions. The first concerns the most significant claims of what you make about your learning and development as an aspiring teacher? The second one relates to why you believe that these claims are significant?

No doubt about it —portfolio development is a very expensive enterprise. It requires budgeting and planning in terms of time, stationeries, and other supplies. A standard portfolio requires a three ring binder. Before purchasing the binder, check with your teacher preparation program if there are standard requirements related to the size, color, and other type of binder. Some teacher education programs require certain colors for certain portfolio levels in addition to the size. If your program does not have specific requirements, we recommend a 2-inch three-ring binder with a clear cover and inside pockets. And suggest that you avoid the extra expense of purchasing document insert shields which are not only expensive but are annoying to examiners who will have to remove your artifacts from the plastic pockets for examination and for the purpose making comments. In addition, you need not spend a fortune on paper. You might want to include color-coded section dividers.

With regard to the content of your portfolio, assign a number to each page. Unless your institution requires that the page number be placed elsewhere on the page, we recommend that you number the pages in Arabic numerals in the lower right-hand corner of the page. Number the pages consecutively from the first page following your table of contents through the last page in your portfolio. If cost is not prohibitive you might want to write your page numbers on dot-stickers. This will resolve the problem of certain artifacts in your portfolio such as term papers that were originally numbered.

The entire artifact collection must represent you as an individual and a developing professional. Further, since artifacts are collected over time, they must serve as record of growth and progress. A review of your portfolio must therefore contain a repertoire of performance over time and must paint a richer developmental portrait of your learning, professional development and growth.

Who is Out There to Help?

Developing a portfolio calls for individual accountability. Nonetheless, an effective portfolio is never developed in isolation. Alas! Development of an exemplary portfolio must occur within an environment that is friendly and supportive. Inclusion of portfolios in the repertoire of assessment strategies has led to new teaching/learning relationships require interdependence. These relationships may involve instructors, peers, counselors, and members of the community. This appears to be a contradiction to what we stated early and that is the portfolio development begins in isolation and the only audience is you. It is still true, yet there is a range of people whose input and advice can be useful in your development of the portfolio. These include your instructors, your peers and your counselors

Relationship with Instructors

When most people think of an instructor-student relationship, they never perceive of a teacher-student support relationship. Rather, you are focusing on a relationship that is more disciplined and controlled. This relationship is one that is often a vertical—a top-down structure. Often, the instructor calls the shot and expects a response. The instructor draws the rules with little or no input from students. The student is penalized when the rules are broken. Nothing happens to the instructor if the graded homework that he promised to return by the beginning of the next class is collecting dust and still sitting ungraded for another week. This definition must change. It must change to include *instructor's support* that focuses more on the role of the instructor to support your learning. You will need to get used to such a paradigm. Of course, it is hard to get used to it unless you begin defining an instructor as a facilitator of learning. This definition rejects the traditional position of an instructor as a dispenser of knowledge and empowers the learner. In this book, we choose to define empowerment as a term meaning the degree to which the students feel that they count and that learning is seen as a transaction. Any transaction is a two-way activity. As an empowered pre-service teacher, begin to gain a feeling that someone is listening to you, and that you play a vital part in your assessment and destiny. Research (Gomez, Grau, and Block, 1991) has shown that students who develop portfolios grow in their understanding of themselves as learners when they see the need and seek guidance and support from their instructors.

Partnership with instructors can help you gain insight in your accomplishments and attainment of competencies. Instructors are a rich source of input and guidance the self-reflective process needed to enrich and develop a successful portfolio. Don't hold back from directing question to your instructors. Instructors are there to help you. However, they will not do the work for you. Your instructors are valuable resource in making decisions on appropriate artifacts to meet a particular standard or competency. They can also help by giving ideas and suggestions when you "don't have a clue" about what you can use to demonstrate a competency. Instructors can also assist you by giving you feedback on your writing. It's okay and advisable to draft reflective abstracts or the reflection summary essay, have your instructor review it before finalizing it. This will help to ensure that you are on the right track as errors are corrected before you submit your final document. Remember excellence is no accident. If you want an excellent portfolio then you must put time, thought, reflection and hard work into it. Remember, your portfolio is a reflection of you and potential for some, it will be their first introduction to you, as a pre-service teacher. Therefore, it is important that you make a good impression because your first impression is often the one that has the most lasting impression. Use your instructor as a resource for guidance and support. If you see your instructor as partners in the portfolio development process, and you both do your part effectively, you should develop a product that you both are proud of.

Student life—and here we mean learning—is probably the most isolating profession one can have. If you are a student—not a fraternity type but a studious student—you will spend the bulk of your time separated from your peers. Efforts in bringing students together, though not a new concept are gaining momentum. Many college classrooms encourage collaborative learning, group work, learning communities and so on. Perhaps the greatest allies in portfolio development are your peers. Portfolio development calls for the establishment of stronger peer relationships. All along your schooling career, it has always been you against them. Reflection is often not best carried out alone. You will need a partner if your reflection activities are to become meaningful.

Partnership is based the assumption that conflict and competition should be avoided. As Adler (1992) says "competing is based on the belief that conflict is a struggle, collaboration assumes that conflict is a natural part of life and that working with other people will produce the best possible solution" (p. 125). Collaboration is extremely important to successful portfolio development. The partnership with peers is not a panacea and not intended to ease your task in developing the portfolio or to be in a company of sympathetic partners who will agree with you when you say, "where do instructors expect me to keep all the lousy papers in the dorm?" Rather, you need that peer support which is capable of actively supporting your learning. Seek out pre-service teachers who are currently working on their portfolio.

Unlike most activities that go on in school, the act of developing a portfolio promotes non-competition, self-correction, and confirmation of your success within the guard and safety of a community of other learners. Interaction and collaboration with other is an essential component of the portfolio process. Interaction and collaboration provides a scaffold. The term "scaffolding" is often used to refer to that kind of support, in which teachers or other competent individuals perform tasks support learning. Construction workers use scaffolds to support a building while it is being constructed. Peers provide support and assist each other to perform a task or activity beyond one's actual abilities. Scaffolding can help you avoid lowering your expectations.

Collaboration enhances comprehension of the process which is critical to learning. We all need to realize that true learning occurs in an atmosphere that is free of competition. Notice the direction that a portfolio predisposes you toward. It is capable of placing you in a non-competitive atmosphere that creates the trust that is necessary for learning through collaborating and cooperating with others. Peers can actively support your engagement in the portfolio development process by helping critique your work. Good writers rarely write something and it is great the first time. It usually takes writing and re-writing a document several times in order to get it just right and achieve excellence. Excellence should be the goal that you are striving for not only in your portfolio, but in everything you do. Sometimes after you have labored over writing something, it is often difficult to pick out typos and other subtle mistakes. Because of the closeness that you have with your work it is easy to get to the point where "you can't see the forest for the trees." This is a good time to ask a peer to give an objective critique of your work. As partners, your peers can provide an essential mirror to facilitate your reflection by giving you a different perspective. Supportive peers are more than mere rubber stamps of work. They ought to be honest evaluators. Your want suggestions from them on strengthening your work; what needs to be added, what ought to be eliminated and what must be changed. As you select evaluators from your peers make sure that they have an awareness of the requirements. A good way to help them help you is by giving them a description of what is expected, the kind of document to be included and any other guidelines provided for the portfolio process. Your peer should use these guidelines to objectively review your document and determine the thoroughness and completes of your portfolio. When you think about it, you realize that portfolio development is also all about networking.

The portfolio development process offers opportunities for networking. Networking gives you the advantage to discuss and share ideas, problems, and issues with other who have or have had similar concerns. Portfolio veterans are often of great help. A veteran will most likely be flattered if you ask for ideas and help.

Counselor

While it is important to get advice about any factors you consider as problematic in your effort to document your growth and development, meeting with your academic advisor or the members of a possible assessment panel can also provide an opportunity to influence your reflection efforts. By gaining an understanding of how different people see your portfolio and see you as a developing teacher, you gain a fuller, more balanced view of your total self. You might need to ask others questions about yourself. This requires that you also listen to comments you receive. The perception of others, even if incorrect, says something about who you are. For a moment, examine the reason why people perceive you in a certain way may add to your self-understanding or your strengths as well as more about areas in which you need improvement. Asking someone to criticize your work and using the comments you receive appropriately calls for a mix of self-confidence and objectivity. The risk in sharing your portfolio with others may seem monumental. And this is so because you are placing yourself on the batting plate and exposing your weaknesses to others. Nevertheless, compare that risk with submitting the portfolio to your teacher education portfolio review process and receive a failing grade.

Summary of Key Points

Our discussion in this chapter has centered on the mechanics of developing a successful portfolio. At this point, you should be able to articulate the various stages involved in the development of a pre-service teacher portfolio. The question: "What should I include in my portfolio?" as we have seen, depends upon the purpose of your portfolio and your requirements. However, in all cases you develop your portfolio with the mindset of you being your own audience before envisioning your instructors as an audience. Is the documentation of your learning and growth visible to your audience? A pre-service teacher portfolio is an argument. You must therefore develop it around those qualities, strengths and attainment statements you wish to make about yourself as a developing teacher. We have already defined a portfolio as a representative of the various aspects of your learning and that developing a portfolio is an on-going process and in reality a very dynamic one.

Collecting products for your portfolio is not a scavenger hunt. Rather, it is a purposeful engagement that calls for a collection of work samples to isolate tangible evidence of your progress in becoming a highly qualified teacher. The more carefully you organize possible artifacts, the less overwhelmed you will feel when inundated by the additional task of actual assembling the portfolio. The first stage of the portfolio development cycle is the collection of information. This paper trail may include: outstanding papers, projects, evaluations, creative work (slides, musical scores, etc.), videotapes of class presentations or of your field experiences activities, letters from faculty or employers, lesson plans, etc. Your collection of artifacts should consciously represent the full range of your work rather than a haphazard collection. Creating an effective portfolio starts with compiling a set of artifacts such as term papers, graded quizzes and tests, photos, publications, lesson plans and student work that represent those competencies you wish to promote to others.

The second stage is, perhaps, the most pivotal to the portfolio development project. As an on-going process, the reflection stage is one that purports to validate experiences to provide a focused portfolio product. The portfolio needs to be examined with an eagle eye towards filling in those perceived weaknesses. Make sure that it adequately and accurately demonstrates mastery of specific standards. Reflective abstract sheets must demonstrate self-reflection and self-assessment. As you engage yourself in reflection and setting goals for immediate future goals, a portfolio becomes a lifelong learning tool. We have acknowledged that reflection is perhaps the most important step in the portfolio process.

The third stage consists of the artifact reduction process. Following your reflection on each standard, identify artifacts or experiences that adequately demonstrate a mastery of required performance competencies. Your selections are your *active artifacts* and those that may not appear immediately to adequately evidence your mastery of a competence are your *dormant artifacts*.

The final stage is artifact display. When you fail to recognize and act on your portfolio development project based on the first three stages, you will lack a secure platform for action. In general a portfolio should include three basic sections: Attestation Documents, Evidence Documents and, Reflection Summary Essay.

From this discussion, it is obvious that portfolio development is not a scavenger hunt that results in the creation of a scrapbook. The portfolio must therefore contain a carefully selected repertoire of performances evidence collected over time to paint a rich developmental portrait of learning and professional development and growth.

References

Adler, R.B. (1992). *Communicating at Work: Principles and practices fro business and the professions*. New York: McGraw-Hill, Inc.

Campbell, D. M, Melenyzer, B. J., Nettles, D. H., & Wyman, R. M. (2000). *Portfolio and performance assessment in teacher education*. Boston, MA: Allyn and Bacon.

Gomez, M.L., Grau, M.E., & Block, M.N. (1991). Reassessing portfolio assessment: Rhetoric and reality. *Language Arts*, 68, 620-628.

Chapter 8

Content of a Portfolio

Orientation

This chapter provides a discussion on the content of a pre-service teacher portfolio while acknowledging that there is no single or right way to "do" a pre-service teacher portfolio. However, as you advance through your teacher education program, you will be confronted by standardized ways to compile your portfolio. These may be related to the layout, which may include the cover page, title page, and table of contents and the approach that you give to the development of your philosophy of education.

An important part of planning for your portfolio is to realize that artifact format must suit the requirements of your teacher education program. Two other subjects of consideration concern the format and adequacy of your artifacts. Two important questions will emerge: Can the selected artifact fit into your portfolio? What is the number of artifacts that would be considered as adequate for the portfolio? This chapter will also introduce you to the reflective aspect of a portfolio and will discuss the place of a rationale in developing your portfolio. We will also look at the role of a reflection summary essay.

Focus Questions

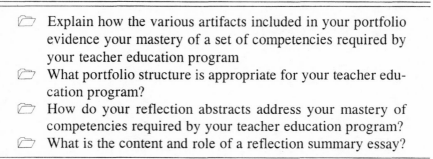

Explain how the various artifacts included in your portfolio evidence your mastery of a set of competencies required by your teacher education program

What portfolio structure is appropriate for your teacher education program?

How do your reflection abstracts address your mastery of competencies required by your teacher education program?

What is the content and role of a reflection summary essay?

There is no single or right way to *do* a pre-service teacher portfolio. That is a not a very encouraging statement and definitely, spells out much confusion. Such confusion is likely to come about when you begin to realize that portfolio is a means to an end and not an end in itself.

The selection of portfolio content and inclusion emerges from the scope and kind of information requested by your teacher education program. Depending on your institution, portfolio content can be assigned or chosen. Portfolios used in teacher education programs often stress best work, and are evaluated by strict assessment schemes designed by professors to meet program requirements. It is often not clear whose purpose they are serving—the pre-service teacher or the instructor's. The portfolio that you develop in a teacher education program may contain a purposeful collections of artifacts linked to program outcomes used and viewed by your program as perfect barometers demonstrating what you have learned over a period of time, say a semester. Your institution may have a required list of what to include along with guidelines for writing accompanying reflection abstracts. In addition, you might also have pre selected assessment criteria, most often in the form of a rubric to guide you through the development process. Often, contents are dictated and demand standardized means of evidence collection.

As you advance through your teacher education program, it is likely that you will be confronted by various standardized ways of developing your portfolio. In most cases, you lack the right to personal selection of portfolio contents. In other cases you are given only limited choice of what you may include in predetermined categories. You are not alone. Many pre-service teachers find this to be rather unsatisfactory, as their ideas for categories and how to define them are quite different from those required by their programs. This is well and good. Instructors understand that the purpose of a portfolio is to develop "self-analytical teachers who are vitally interested in directing their own goal as educators" (Guillaume & Yopp, 1995, p. 94). Instructors mean well, however, when they provide a structured way of developing a portfolio. Their intention is to provide guidance and assure consistency. Here we will discuss a number of common components of a structured portfolio.

Cover Page

A cover page is not and should not be confused with a title page. If your portfolio is housed in a three-ringed binder, a cover page goes on the outside of the binder. This page can be personalized and more rightly so if a portfolio is defined as a window to your learning. A number of questions might be brought into consideration when writing your reflective abstract sheets. Does the reflective abstract sheet page whet my appetite to want to read the portfolio? What might be changed to make the cover more interesting? Is the picture on the cover page a good choice? Is it clear and of appropriate size? What might be improved? The portfolio cover is your personal space where you get to make a statement about yourself and your portfolio. However, this also requires that you have your audience in mind. For example in the selection of typefaces and fonts, you need to keep in mind that some are easier to read than others. And a whole lot of them are flatly annoying to the eye.

Title Page

This is the first page that must appear in the portfolio. A portfolio title page contains four main elements:

Complete Title

Make sure the title is consistent with the type of portfolio you are developing. If your institution does not specify the details of the title of your portfolio, make sure that you write a title that is informative without being either too narrow or too extensive. An example of a narrow title may be "Portfolio."

Your Name

Remember that the title part of your portfolio should be designed in the most formal manner. For that reason, nicknames and other none formal name should be avoided and only full legal name must be given.

Program of Study

Include the name of your program of study—for example, Early Childhood Education, Middle Grades Education, Special Education, etc. Of course this is only possible if you have formally declared your program of study.

Name of Your Institution

This includes the full name of the broader institution as well as of your teacher education department.

Date

As an aspiring professional, it is virtually important that you get into the habit of dating every document that you create. A number of ways can be used in dating your documents. You may, for example decide to date the portfolio by semester that you submitted or by the actual calendar date.

Make sure that the portfolio title page is of a quality that has an aesthetic appeal, yet simple and dignified. Every line needs to be centered. Remember to leave a larger margin at the left of the page to allow binding or punching holes for a multiple-ring binder.

Table of Content

What might a potential table of content look like? This question could be addressed better when you have a clear understanding of the primary purpose of the table of content. The table of contents should serve as a map through your portfolio. It should provide enough information to direct your audience through your work. It is here that you will need to think of its role as a tour guide. In assuming that role, the table of content should provide enough activities for your "clients" yet allow freedom to explore side trips according to their interests and needs. Your table of contents should include both major and minor items and the pages in which these items begin. Unless your teacher education program has a prescribed format, a good rule of thumb is to use the American Psychological Association (APA, 2001) format as presented in Box 8.1:

Box 8.1

```
I
     A
          1.
          2.
     B
          1.
          2.
          3.
II
     A
          1.
          2.
               a.
               b.
```

Attestation Documents

Attestation documents are intended to demonstrate your professional commitment and qualifications.

Philosophy of Education Statement

The lynchpin of a well-developed portfolio is the philosophy of education statement. Writing a philosophy of education essay takes time and thought. Before investing a lot of energy, think about what you belief, what you want to accomplish, and what it will take you to reach your goal. Look at your philosophy statement as you would an abstract to a scholarly article. It is advisable that you write your philosophy of education, preferably in its entirety, before you begin developing the portfolio. This can be a way to approach your portfolio development project as you would your term paper. In writing your term paper, begin by writing your abstract first, as a way to give focus to the main points, knowing very well that may have to go back and reevaluate and may be rewrite it in a concise manner.

An effective portfolio includes a statement on your belief of education. Such a belief is then your philosophy of education. A well articulated philosophy can form a valuable basis that lays out the portfolio's theme or thesis. In his book, *The skillful teacher* (1990), Stephen Brookfield points out that the development of a philosophy of education can be used for four purposes:

Personal purpose: ". . . a distinctive organizing vision—a clear picture of why you are doing what you are doing that you can call up at points of crisis—is crucial to your personal sanity and morale." (p. 16)

Political purpose: ". . . a sense that your position is grounded in a well-developed and carefully conceived philosophy of practice. . . . You are more likely to gain a measure of respect for your thoughtfulness and commitment, which is important both for your self-esteem and for your political survival." (p. 17)

Professional purpose: ". . . a commitment to a shared rationale for college teaching is important for the development of a collective identity and, hence, for the development of professional strengths among teachers." (pp. 17-18)

Pedagogical purpose: "Teaching is about making some kind of dent in the world so that the world is different than it was before you practiced your craft. Knowing clearly what kind of dent you want to make in the world means that you must continually ask yourself the most fundamental evaluative questions of all—What effect am I having on students and on their learning?" (pp. 18-19)

The term "philosophy" ought not to cause anxiety and intimidation assuming that that your philosophy of education essay is a document requiring complex terminology and written at a high level in formal language. In contrast, a philosophy of education statement must be simple and capable of maintaining readability with content coming out of your own background. Did we say background? Undoubtedly, you can find it from your own background. Look at the excerpt from DaShawn's philosophy statement in Box 8.2

Box 8.2

Excerpts from DaShawn's Philosophy Statement

. . . I grew up in a housing project in South Memphis where I spent my first twenty-one years of life. That includes the fifteen years that I spent in my PreK-12 education. There were few, if any, positive black male role models there. Well, I have been away from my neighborhood for five years now. I've had several short-term jobs including my most recent one working for FedEx at the airport. Many of these jobs were satisfying. Deep within me, I owe it to my neighborhood. And I would like to give something back. After I get my degree, I am going back to my neighborhood because I believe those kids there, and especially males, need a role model.

A well written philosophy of education could anchor a portfolio and provide the scaffolding for the evidence that follows. This should be a concise and cogent expression of your beliefs, attitudes, and feelings regarding learning and teaching. In it, you might also want to comment on your goals, both long and short-term. These may be educational, professional, or personal goals. In that case, much of the actual content of the portfolio should be the logical extension of the principles, beliefs and goals that you discussed in your philosophy of education. As you conceptualize and develop your philosophy of education you are, in essence, building a foundation for your portfolio. Many students struggle to express themselves (so do professors—writing never gets easier), and that is quite natural. Good writing requires rewriting, rewriting and rewriting again. Maintaining the readability of a philosophy of education means that you ought to expect to write more than two drafts. Once a satisfactory draft of your philosophy is complete put it aside for a day or two. This will give you a cooling-off period and will enable you to examine it from a new perspective. In rereading your draft, you may discover glaring mistakes in the logic of your presentation or ideas that are not clearly developed. Another viable approach is to have a friend read it aloud to you or tape record the reading and then listen carefully to how it sounds. Another strategy that might work better for you is to visualize yourself before the evaluation team to discuss your philosophy of education. Try to envision what a member of that team would say about your approaches to learning and teaching. As you engage yourself in such visualization, you gain distance from your work and examine it from a more objective and critical perspective.

A clearly articulated philosophy of education answers a number of questions:

- ❖ What do you view learning to be?
- ❖ How does one learn and what is the role of the teacher?
- ❖ What do you expect your students to be able to do intellectually because of taking the course?
- ❖ How will you help them acquire those abilities?

Statements in your philosophy of education may be used to highlight particular sections within the portfolio (e.g., "The basis of my teaching is firmly grounded in . . ." "For example, one can see from my philosophy of education the emphasis I place on . . ." or "On this term paper, I chose to follow the 'X' approach . . ."). It is a place to clarify your own reasoning and motivation behind your aspiration for a teaching profession, while reviewing it reflectively. Moreover, it could serve as the declaration of the goals that guide your approach to the preparation for the teaching profession.

Statements of your philosophy of education, essentially, answer the question: What are your beliefs about the teaching-learning transaction? What do you consider teaching and learning to be? What are your beliefs about assessment? Deciding on what you believe about teaching or about assessment begins with deciding on what you believe about how children learn: what your role is as a teacher and how instruction occurs in the classroom. To internalize the concept of portfolio assessment you must be clear about your views of what you want that assessment to show and how you intend to use that information to develop your portfolio.

Where do I start? Let us think about that for a moment—if your philosophy of education is an expression of your beliefs then the starting point is a decision about the conduit of that expression. To some extend you should select a way of expressing it from the stand point of what the best way to communicate it to your audience. As with any writing, attention to the audience is important. Your audience is faculty, portfolio reviewers, peers, employers, parents, and others. In this case use a not so formal style yet modest enough to strike a balance between an expression that is scholarly and that which comes from your heart. Your philosophy of education may be expressed in a number of ways, and may take as its starting point any one or more of the dimensions listed in Box 8.3.

Box 8.3

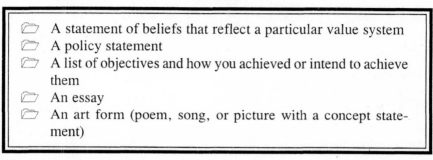

A statement of beliefs that reflect a particular value system

A policy statement

A list of objectives and how you achieved or intend to achieve them

An essay

An art form (poem, song, or picture with a concept statement)

What should you include? There is no required content or set formula for writing an educational philosophy. While not yet a practicing teacher, it is important to heed to Goodyear and Allichin (1998) suggest a number of ideas that practicing teachers might find useful to include as components in their philosophy of education. A summary of these suggestions are given in Figure 8.1.

Although these suggestions are intended for practicing teachers they could, however, serve as a guide to you in choosing what to include in your philosophy of education. Students sometimes have particular problems formulating the philosophy of education, autobiography and putting together a resume.

Engaging in the writing of a philosophy of education requires writing. Writers have different writing styles, different writing clocks, and different writing locations. Some writers prepare an overall outline and then write the narrative. Others begin to write and let the outline and concepts flow out of their writing. Some writers are able to write with support from peers, while others need time alone with their thoughts. Others brainstorm thoughts and ideas with peers and then retreat to write in a quiet environment. As a pre-service teacher ready to develop a meaningful portfolio, try to discover your style, seek compatible partners, and begin writing. In all cases, the following suggested principles are given to help you write a clear and coherent philosophy of education essay.

Figure 8.1:
Possible Content of a Philosophy of Education Document

AREAS OF INCLUSION	POSSIBLE QUESTION TO ANSWER
Integration of responsibilities	How do you integrate the different dimensions of scholarship?
Expertise	What do you know about your major/or teaching and how have you learned it?
Relationships	How do you create and maintain positive relationships with students?
	Have you and your students developed links with the community?
	If so, do you now have certain beliefs related to collaboration that influence your philosophy of education?
Learning Environment	What do you do to create a supportive, learning environment?
Values Imparted	What values do you convey to your students? Methods, Strategies, and Innovation Have you used a particular approach, technique or strategy that works especially well in your subject area? If so, how does the strategy match your philosophical assumptions about learning and the goals of teaching?
Outcome	Beyond mastery of certain facts, what should students gain from your course (e.g., thinking skills, attitudes, values, and technical skills)? What are your most important learning goals? Can you give some specific examples?
	In what way have you met your personal expectations for growth and change? How have you made a difference in the lives of your students?

1. **Organize the content of your philosophy so it flows logically and sequentially**. The sequence of the content of your essay needs to be orderly, logical and purposeful.

2. **A philosophy of education essay is not a mystery novel**. Write concisely, persuasively, and clearly focused paragraphs. Think carefully about making your beliefs and points simple. Use topic sentences and topic paragraphs. Each paragraph should focus on one idea, a collection of paragraphs on one topic. A topic sentence, often the first sentence in a paragraph, tells the reader the main idea that is presented in the paragraph. Subsequent sentences within the paragraph expand or modify the idea. Clearly organized paragraphs make a philosophy of education essay easy to read and easy to understand.

3. **Use active rather than passive verbs**. A majority of your verbs must be active verbs such as prepare lesson plans . . . , select materials . . . , test for understanding . . . , teach my class . . . manage my class. . . .

4. **Use consistent format, style, and terminology**. Your attention should bear clarity and simplicity. Make sure that you essay is free of spelling and typographical error.

A sample critique sheet for your philosophy, autobiography and resume can be found in the appendix of this book. Feel free to copy it and have several of your peers critique your work. Following critiques from peers review the suggestions and reflect on their comments. Incorporate the relevant comments and suggestions and correct any typos or grammatical errors which you may have. Then you are ready to submit the document to your instructor for further feedback and suggestions. Don't feel discouraged if after you submit the document to your instructor, that change is still needed. Fear of failure is can be inhibiting in a portfolio process. And, fear can thwart your efforts. Palmer (1998) in his book: *The courage to teach: Exploring the inner landscape of a teacher's life* recognizes that the deepest fear of a teacher is

The fear of having a live encounter with alien "otherness" whether the other is a student, a colleague, a subject, or self dissenting voice within. We fear encounters in which the other is free to be itself, to speak its own truth, to tell us what we may not wish to hear. We want those encounters on our won terms, so that we can control the outcomes, so that they will not threaten our view of the world and self. (p. 37)

This Remember you are striving for excellence. The more feedback you have, the better your document will be when you submit your final draft in your portfolio.

Resume

A resume is often the first documents one gets in order when deciding to look for a job. Today, a resume is used for various purposes in educational programs. In teacher education, a resume is a vital component in the admission process as well as a portfolio artifact. There are no hard-and-fast rules on what make a wonderful resume. To take a position on what a good resume ought to be is to take a nose dive into the mayhem of semantics—what is acceptable and what is not? What is adequate and what is inadequate? A resume is adequate when it provides a fair summary of its owner. That is what a resume is intended to do. "Resume" is a French word for *summary*. It has often been debated if a one-page resume is sufficient to provide enough information for a reasonable decision.

A resume is a short summary of education, skills, accomplishments, and experience often prepared by the applicant for a position. A resume is not an autobiography. Rather, it is a short designed sketch of personal, educational, and experiences for whatever positions you are applying. It is not intended to say everything about you. However, it should interest the reader in wanting to talk to you as an individual. Beyond that, it must give focus on your qualifications and achievements. Although the format of a resume may be standard, it is still your responsibility to work on the content and writing style for the resume. No one else can really do that for you.

We recommend that you have both a one-page *summary resume* and an *expanded resume*. There are occasions when either, or both are appropriate. A well-written *summary resume* precludes the necessity to construct a lengthy cover letter. On the other hand, unless you have considerable experience, you don't need two pages.

Traditionally, there are three types of resumes: chronological, functional and combination. The chronological, also known as the classic format, is unique in that it lists all jobs and educational background in the order of most recent first and works its way back to the earlier work and education. On the other hand, functional resumes stress skills over jobs. A functional resume, however, is often ambiguous as to what skill was learned at what point and on which job. Functional resumes were popularized a couple decades ago. These may not be as effective as they once were thought. This type of resume may carry the perception of a "problem" work history. The combination resume, as the name suggests, borrows from both formats. This approach is very popular since it offers the most opportunities to do effective marketing of your skills. A combination resume makes use of bullets to provide a summary of key information to attract the reader's interest. These bullets are often done at the very top and features information that is mentioned elsewhere in the resume.

No matter which type of resume one chooses to write, there are standard practices that need to be followed. A good resume requires a considerable investment of time to develop. Such a great investment is necessary because of the various components and types of information it contains. The preparation of a successful resume requires that know how to review, summarize, and present your experiences and achievements on paper. A resume is developed and designed. It cannot simply be typed. Much more planning and formatting are needed in the preparation of an acceptable resume. Of course, handwriting and typewriters are out. In that case, therefore, learning a word processing program will work to your advantage. Many word processors come with resume templates and wizards that make the creation of the document easier. You must, however, bear in mind that the effectiveness of your resume depends on the effort put into it. Moreover, without sufficient planning, the development of a resume can be a frustrating task and especially if you jump into it without much thought. As you begin developing your resume, start by breaking it down into sections. Begin writing the sections with which you are most comfortable or find the easiest to deal with first. Outline your achievements briefly and succinctly. Even though the outline of the resume is structured following a particular order, you do not need to write each section in the sequence in which it will finally be presented. Writing the section with which you are most comfortable provides an immediate feeling of accomplishment. Keep in mind, however, that writing a resume—just like any other kind of writing—is best done one step at a time. While the inclusion of a resume in the portfolio has a purpose that is other than employment, it should include all the relevant information! The major sections of a resume are summarized in Box 8.4.

Box 8.4

> 📁 Identifying Information
> 📁 Objectives
> 📁 Education
> 📁 Related Courses
> 📁 Experiences
> 📁 Skills
> 📁 Honors
> 📁 References

Identifying Information

You will need to include your identifying information such as your name, e-mail address, mailing or permanent address and telephone numbers including area codes.

Objective

A statement of your objective(s) is one of the most important parts of a resume. A resume that goes into your pre-service teacher portfolio must have a defined objective statement. These objectives will certainly be different from those written for a job opportunity. You might not be looking for a job at this point. What you might be looking for is either admission to the teacher education program or admission to student teaching. In either case, your objectives will need to be tailored to that particular purpose. However, if you are at an advanced stage of your teacher education program you may wish to include within your objective career objectives. If you have a specific position in mind, you may wish to write brief objectives. Try to tailor your objectives to suit the circumstance. In all cases, the objective statement must be brief, clearly stated and consistent with the goals and accomplishments outlined in the body of the resume

Education

This category is particularly important because the assessment of your portfolio pivots on your education. Start with the highest degree level and work backwards. Include the university's name, the degree program, major, minor, and concentration, and date of graduation. Include your GPA if it is 3.0 or higher. If your GPA is below 3.0, you may want to identify only your major GPA.

Related Courses

This section includes a summary of course work both within the major and outside the major. This works well usually when they relate in any way to the objective. You might also include your course related field experiences.

Experiences

This is the heart of the resume and, of course, it is the largest section of the document. However, do not feel overly concerned if this ends up not to be the largest section of your resume—remember you are just a college student. Of course, take comfort in knowing that your resume is not intended for employment at this point. Notice here that we have labeled this as experiences. Experiences may include full-time or part-time employment, summer jobs, volunteer work, and internships and cooperative education. List the employer's name, your job title, city and state. List related skills, responsibilities, and results of your actions. Use action words to describe your experience and accomplishments. Box 8.5 presents examples of some of the actions words that you can use:

Box 8.5

Assembled	Demonstrated	Hired	Organized	Resolved
Assessed	Designed	Implemented	Originated	Reviewed
Assisted	Developed	Improved	Performed	Selected
Audited	Devised	Informed	Planned	Separated
Budgeted	Discovered	Interpreted	Prevented	Set up
Calculated	Edited Drafted	Interviewed	Produced	Simplified
Centralized	Eliminated	Maintained	Programmed	Solved
Collaborated	Established	Managed	Promoted	Surveyed
Composed	Evaluated	Marketed	Provide	Staffed
Conducted	Expanded	Minimized	Publicized	Supervise
Constructed	Explained	Motivated	Recruited	Taught
Contracted	Forecasted	Negotiated	Reorganized	Tested
Converted	Formed	Obtained	Reported	Trained
Coordinated	Founded	Operated	Researched	

Order your experiences in a chronological manner, starting with the most recent and working back. Occasionally, a more functional approach is better, but the chronological approach remains quite common. Include the job title and company name for each position you held along with years of service at each. Often the beginning and ending year for each position is adequate, but the months are sometimes specified as well. For each position, enumerate your responsibilities and accomplishments. Remember to use all relevant keywords.

Skills

This section will focus your resume on qualifications important to your potential success as a prospective teacher. Include computer, foreign language, and transferable skills.

Honors

Here you will want to list any honors, which indicate your strong academic abilities—honor societies, scholarships, awards, and dean's list.

References

Remember here that you are developing a pre-service teacher portfolio and your audience is your professors. Because your resume is submitted to your professors, do not end with the usual AUR (available upon request) or FUR (furnished upon request). Rather, you should include the names and contacts of your references. The list of references must include their titles, departments they are associated with, office addresses, phone numbers, with appropriate extension numbers, and email addresses. Always make sure that you have the permission from individuals before listing them as references.

Just as you would be careful in the writing of a resume to a prospective employer, the resume that goes into your portfolio should be carefully written. Errors in spelling and grammar will not be well received by your examiners and may be viewed as signs of carelessness or a broader incompetence. Do not write the way you talk! Use the spell checker in your word processing program. Use a dictionary, as needed, if you are in doubt.

Autobiographical Sketch

An autobiography is a narrative written by an individual to provide information about one's own life. It is all about that person's life! There is no prescribed or standardized format of writing an autobiographical sketch. The reason is simple—each person has a unique self. However, when writing your autobiography, we suggest that you use interesting facts to explain as much about yourself as you can. Such facts may include descriptions about what life means to you and what your outlook on the future is. The autobiography written specifically for a portfolio should include both personal and professional information. It should include events in your life that have had an effect upon the decision to become a teacher. An exemplary autobiographical sketch is one that is written in a personal voice as opposed to a lifeless series of declaration. Examples of such declarations are: "My family moved to Chicago when I was an infant. They were so poor. My childhood was miserable."

The content of an autobiography must be organized to flow logically and sequentially. The sequence of the content of the essay should be orderly as well as purposeful. Some people prefer to use a chronological style of writing, listing and describing their achievements by dates, and linking their personality to those anecdotes. This has the advantage of being an easy to follow system where the reader can quickly and easily visualize your personal development. However, it can be easy to be sidetracked using this method by focusing too much on each particular experience. It's also very easy to see any gaping holes if you have an unproductive period in your life.

Others write their autobiography from the perspective of what life means to them. Such an approach calls for a narrative on how one perceives life to be and may approach the task in response to questions similar to those listed in Box 8.6.

An effective approach to writing an autobiography is not by stating your name or where you were born. Rather, it is by pointing out where you are now. Remember that an autobiography is not meant to be a scholarly treaty. It is an honest and simple document that is personalized. You may consider including such details as what has happened to you recently. Identify something that might interest your readers—depending on who they are. In essence, write anything that's on your mind, from your heart. Let you audience become aware of the type of person you are; use facts about yourself such as: awards recently won? Where

Box 8.6

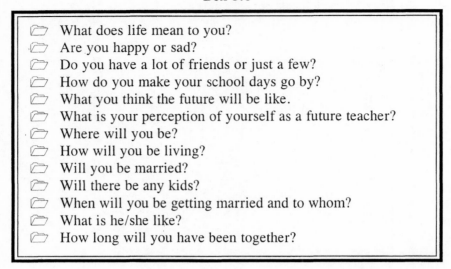

did you complete high school? Where are you in your educational career? Where did you start your college education? An important aspect of an autobiography is its potential to engage and cultivate interest from a reader. Rather, use the autobiography to highlight your personal side. Your transcripts and Praxis scores will determine your academic standing and that means that you do not need to mention them here. The exception here is that while you may not mention your PPST scores and GPA, if you receive any, you should definitely note any academic or social awards you have received. This is the opportunity to mention these.

If the autobiography is a component of your application process, then that is a good reason to use it as a selling tool. This is especially true if the application is where you have one shot. If that is the case, you have to make that single shot count. Make the autobiography neat in appearance and professional in tone. Of course, sell yourself. Because if you won't, and don't, who else do you think will? Reflect back to each time that you met someone, how the first impression forms within minutes. Be honest. Since your autobiographical essay is the "first impression" that you place in your portfolio, it is critically important that you develop a strong, concise essay that hits all of your major positive points without losing them in a sea of unimportant details.

The concluding paragraph of your autobiography is extremely important and must receive the attention it deserves. In the conclusion, reword the introduction and add a closure to bring the whole narrative together. Alternatively, you might want to conclude your autobiography with an inspirational word that might be helpful to another person. This can be a lesson that you may have learned from your experiences, a dream you may be pursuing, or may simply be a desire such as: "Yes, I will take time to smell the roses, go on family picnics and get to know my neighbors a lot more."

Once the first draft of your autobiography is complete, give yourself a short break and come back and edit, re-arrange, organize, and make changes as you see fit. Then, go through the whole work again and edit some more. Take out anything that is redundant or unnecessary. Read it as if you were your own audience. Split up long, confusing sentences into shorter, spiffier phrases. Use action verbs that show, rather than adjectives and adverbs that tell. With that said, it's obvious that the grammar and spelling of your essay should be impeccable. Try not to over-use the dictionary or thesaurus in a false attempt to sound over-educated—unless that is your usual style of writing.

When all is said and written, be sure to enlist the help of friends to read the essay and check for possible improvements in content, organization, grammar, and spelling. Of course, you control the content of the essay, however, your friends, as proofreaders, should decide on the effectiveness of your presentation and the degree of clarity to which that content is transmitted. It should be obvious by this point that the essay is not a piece of work to start working on at the last minute. Ideally, you should start months ahead, as that gives you sufficient time to brainstorm, to write it, and solicit adequate and useful feedback from others.

Cover Letter

What is a cover letter? A cover letter is all about first impressions. First impressions, whether good or bad, lasts. The cover letter is one place that faculty examines your disposition. This is why the development of your cover letter is critical to your portfolio evaluation—it is used as your first introduction to the evaluators. Your cover letter should be no longer than one page. The letter should "plant the seed" that creates interest in the reader. It should maintain an upbeat pace, by making the information exciting—it helps to use vivid language. It is important to understand that your cover letter is a personal document that encases your voice and represents you in your absence. Let your personality shine through since this is all about you and not someone else. Your teacher education program might, like most other, require that you write your cover letter as a formal application for admission to the teacher education program. If this is the case, check with your teacher education program to find out what needs to be in your cover letter. The rules for writing a good cover letter are much the same as for writing a good resume: speak to your audience, edit carefully for sense and form.

Evidence Documentation

Artifacts are authentic products of activities that serve as indicators of your skills and abilities. These products must be presented in a manner such that they are attractive and easy to understand. Commonly, teacher education programs have no restriction on where the activities were performed. Acceptable activities may have been conducted alone or with a group, inside or outside school. They do not necessarily have to be class projects or anything you have done connected to your program of study—as long as they are activities that demonstrate skills relevant to your professional goals. Artifacts are tangible evidence that indicate a pre-service teacher attainment of knowledge, skills and dispositions and the ability to apply understandings to complex tasks (Campbell, D. et al., 2000). A portfolio requires the inclusion of a variety of evidence and artifacts. The artifacts to include in the portfolio should be directly related to the performance statement in question and must provide convincing evidence of what it is you seek to prove. Artifacts can serve different purposes, and you must make careful choices about the artifacts you submit. For example, one artifact might simply show that you completed a task or project. Another artifact may reveal a depth of understanding about the featured task or project.

In a portfolio, artifacts are silent and can only speak when prompted. For this reason, every artifact needs a description. A reflective abstracts is necessary in order to do that. What are reflective abstract? The discussion that follows provides an analysis of reflective abstracts.

Reflection Abstracts

The *reflection abstracts* are one-page written descriptions that are placed in front of entries (or artifacts) in the portfolio. The importance of a reflective abstract lies on the premise that it is the first section of your documentation evidence that a reviewer will read and it often leaves a lasting impression of the content.

A reflective abstract that is inadequate, not clearly written, or is filled with grammatical or typographical errors gives the portfolio evaluation team a poor impression that may influence the evaluation of the artifact itself. This page serves the following purposes:

- ❖ Describes the nature of the entry, the context in which it was created, and the portfolio outcomes it addressed;
- ❖ Analyzes why the entry is important to the standard and the success of the teacher; and
- ❖ Reflects on how this particular entry demonstrates the achievement of the competency.

Components of a reflection abstract page are given in Box 8.7

Box 8.7

Competency #: *(restatement of the competency)*
         Interpretation:

         Evidence:
                 Artifact #_:
                         Name of Artifact:
                         Date created:
                         Source:
                         Context:
                 Rationale:

Restatement of the Competency

Here, you need to write the competency or standard statement, as is, in its entirety. Consider for example this INTASC standard:

Standard #6—Communication Skills—The teacher uses knowledge of effective verbal, nonverbal and media communication techniques to foster active inquiry, collaboration, and supportive interaction in the classroom.

Interpretation

Your portfolio can never be better than the kinds of artifacts you present. Furthermore, the artifacts included are only as good as your understanding of the competency statements. Stephen Covey (1989) in is work on human behavior has given this advice:

> Seek first to understand. Before the problem comes up, before you try to evaluate and prescribe, before you try to present your own ideas— seek to understand. . . . If we really, deeply understand each other, we open the door to creative solutions and third alternatives. Our differences are no longer stumbling blocks to communication and progress. Instead, they become the stepping stones to synergy (p. 259).

Covey's advise suits well to general understanding of most things. To engage in a meaningful portfolio development project without a clear understanding of the competency statements is a first step toward approaching the task blindly and, therefore, meet failure. Your understanding of a competency statement finds refinement as you compose an interpretation. An interpretation is a short narrative intended to provide your interpretation of the competency indicating what it means to you. This narrative could be done in two or three sentences.

Evidence

Every artifact in a portfolio needs prompting. Unlike a picture, an artifact (including a picture) does not have a voice of its own. This section of the abstract page presents evidence identifiers. These identifiers contain key information that identifies the artifact. Box 8.7 presents an example of the evidence identifier section.

Artifact Label Number

Each artifact in your portfolio must be assigned a unique identifying number. It really is up to you to decide how you will assign the number. A most logical way is to assign the number to your artifact that is associated with the competency that you are seeking to evidence. While this is up to you to decide how you want to label your artifact, you might want to consider labeling them as follows: Assuming that you have two artifacts for inclusion label the first one as

Artifact #1.1 and the second one as **Artifact #1.2.** The first digit references the competency. In this case, it is competency #1. The second digit the assigned identify. Here you have artifact 1 and 2. To maintain consistency, keep your labeling system in as simple and as logical a manner as possible.

Name of the Artifact

Here you will need to state the name of the artifact instead of its type. For example, if the artifact is a term paper, avoid naming it a "term paper." Calling it a term paper is too vague. You should, therefore, go beyond stating what it is and specifically identify it with its title (for example: *Impacts of Global Warming on Reliability of Water Resources*).

Date created

This is the date that you completed the artifact not the date that you entered it into the portfolio.

Source

Under this section you will need to briefly describe the origin of your artifact mentioning under what context it was developed. Much of the time, the context might be a course. If it is a course, give the course number and the full name of the course. The context might be field experiences, service learning or other community service activity.

Context

This section of your reflective abstract sheet provides background information about the artifact. For example, one may write: "This artifact is a letter of recognition that was awarded to me following the completion of 34 hours of community service. This is not where you provide your rationale. Rather, it is where you give a descriptive summary of the artifact. Look at the example of an evidence identifier section in Box 8.7.

Rationale

Artifacts need to be introduced and defend using meaningful and well articulated rationale statements. A rationale statement is a short essay that justifies the use of the artifact to evidence meeting the competency. The rationale statement must be written for each artifact included in your portfolio. Such a statement must be assertive and clearly provides a justification of why you chose to include the artifact in your portfolio. The writing of a rationale is not merely a matter of physical doing. Rather, it is a conscious and a highly complex mental exercise that skillfully connects artifacts to the competency statement in an accurate and most convincing manner. In other words, your rationale statement should show your reader that the artifacts display is founded on a clear understanding of the competency statement. Many pre-service teachers choose to summarize the artifact in this section. This is well and good. However, and for all practical purposes, it needs to be made clear that a rationale is neither a description nor is it a summary of the document. Rather, it is a well thought-out narrative that addresses the how and why questions of growth and development as evidenced by the artifact chosen. A rationale statement must have a reflective quality to it and must provide an analysis of the portfolio artifact. This analysis contains three parts that are described in Box 8.8. As a reflective piece, a meaningful rationale statement requires complex thinking rather than simple self-expression and regurgitation of the content already embedded in the artifact. In all cases, the rationale statement must relate specifically to what was learned in the curriculum. In addition, the rationale paragraph extends an invitation to you to interact with the competency beyond the closure of your "term paper." And, it is designed to convince your audience that you have attained a certain level of mastery.

Box 8.8

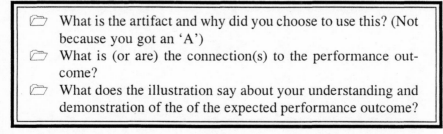

The rationale statement embraces a brief description of the context in which the artifact was created. This description tells the reader the circumstances surrounding the development of the artifact. A second property of the rationale statement is its ability to tell the reader something about what you have learned through the development of the artifact. This description may relate theory to practice.

Artifacts

The ultimate purpose of a portfolio is to document your knowledge, skills and dispositions to evidence readiness for the teaching profession. It is meant to be a personal, meaningful, and sincere product that articulates a response to mastery or path toward a mastery of defined set of competencies intended to meet high standards for thinking, and learning and teaching. To meet this purpose, the development of a portfolio will entail a great deal of initiative and thought on your part in drawing carefully selected artifacts.

Artifacts are a collection of various documents and visuals that may include term papers, lesson plans, samples of student work, videotapes, photographs, etc. This collection is organized and integrated in a logical manner to for the purpose of evidencing mastery or path toward mastery of a defined set of competencies. Artifacts as whole or their various components may be used for this purpose. Each artifact or entry is to be placed immediately after a reflective abstract. In addition, each performance outcome addressed requires the development of separate reflection abstract pages. Although we discourage the practice, it is possible for an artifact to evidence mastery of more than one performance outcome. If this is the case, you will need to write separate reflection abstract pages for each competency statement that you seek to evidence using the artifact. Furthermore, it is important to duplicate the artifact itself and place it in the appropriate location instead of directing the reader to refer to the artifact included elsewhere.

Format of Artifacts

An important part of planning for your portfolio is a realization that the format of artifacts must be appropriate and suit the requirements of your teacher education program. Before deciding on what goes into your portfolio, you will need to deal with two preliminary concerns. The foremost concern is whether the artifact addresses the competency you are out to document. The next relates to the format of the artifact—can it physically fit into your portfolio? If it does not, can it be reproduced without altering its effectiveness? Will the reader or evaluator be able to easily examine the artifact? For example, if the work is stored in a diskette or a CD, is the format compatible with the reader or evaluator's equipment? Does the reader use a Mac or a PC unit? Does the reader have access to a CD drive?

Number of Artifacts

In developing a portfolio, one is often confronted by the question on the number of artifacts must be included in the pre-service teacher portfolio. This really depends on the number of artifacts required by your teacher education program or the size of the portfolio that your institution requires. Furthermore, institutions specify the size of binder to the portfolio requirements. Many institutions will require a size that is no more than two inches. It is not uncommon for institutions to specify the requirements and provide guidelines. In either case, the number of artifacts that must be included in your portfolio must be sufficient enough to evidence mastery of a performance outcome in question. Clearly, the minimum number of artifacts to include must be sufficient enough to adequately respond to the competency in question.

Complete Captioning and Labeling

The cliché *a picture worth more than a thousand words* is probably true in some real life situation but certainly not in the portfolio world. In the portfolio, a picture is silent and has no word of its own! A picture in a portfolio requires, at the minimum, a title and a caption. The title of a photo is an effective method of giving it a word. Photo captions should answer four basic questions: who? What? Where? And when? In addition, photographs need captions. The caption informs the reader of the content of the picture. It tells the reader who the people in the photograph are—they have names, don't they? It tells the reader who is positioned on the far left. Tells the reader who is next to that person. Tells the reader what activities are capture in the picture. Moreover, if you have to include photographs and or videotapes, make sure you include labels also. Without such a description, your audience is left wondering what the photograph is all about.

Checklist of Content

A checklist is a list of items with a place to check whether or not the required item is present and perhaps to what degree. Many teacher education programs often provide a checklist to assure that the content of the portfolio is complete. Checklists can vary according to the level of specificity desired. In other cases, the very assessment of your portfolio could be done using the same checklist. An example of such a checklist is given in Figure 8.2.

Figure 8.2 Sample Portfolio Checklist

Portfolio Checklist

Last Name	First Name	Middle Initial	Candidate ID #

Date	Name of Faculty	Name of Faculty

Evidence of Teacher Candidate Performance

I. Introduction

Yes   No

_____ _____ Title Page
_____ _____ Table of Contents
_____ _____ Teacher as Facilitator of Transformative Processes Model
_____ _____ Performance Outcomes of Teacher as Facilitator of Transformative Processes
_____ _____ Autobiography
_____ _____ Resume
_____ _____ Introductory Letter
_____ _____ Transcript
_____ _____ Praxis Series Examination Score Records
_____ _____ Evidence of membership in a professional organization

II. Curriculum: Construct and Deliver Appropriate Curriculum

_____ _____ Essay: Why I Want to Teach Essay
_____ _____ Philosophy of Education
_____ _____ Samples of Written Communication in General Education
_____ _____ Significant Papers from Content Area Classes
_____ _____ Reflection Paper: Methods Courses

III. Assessment: Assess Student Learning with Variety of Assessments

_____ _____ _____
_____ _____ _____

IV. Relationships: Establish Professional and Reciprocal Relationships with others Invested in Student Learning

_____ _____ Samples of Letters, Memos to Students and Parents
_____ _____ Awards, Memberships in Professional Organizations
_____ _____ Participation in Campus Activities
_____ _____ Volunteer/Service-Learning Experiences

V. Environment: Create Positive and Caring Environments for Student Development and Learning

_____ _____ Lessons Plans
_____ _____ Unit Plans
_____ _____ Major Area Paper
_____ _____ Videotape of Field Experiences (Macro-teaching)
_____ _____ Technological Artifacts
_____ _____ Photographs
_____ _____ Progress Reports to Parents and/or Students
_____ _____ Reflection Paper: Content and Methodology (Goals/Objectives)
_____ _____ Final Reflection Paper
_____ _____ Personal Oral Interview Rating Sheet
_____ _____ Methods Field Experience Evaluation

VI. Comprehensive Evaluation

The above named teacher candidate has completed all requirements for the Pre-service Teacher Portfolio as a partial requirement for Benchmark III Evaluation and has earned a score of   4   3   2   0   (Circle one based on Portfolio Evaluation Rubric)

Date	Faculty Signature	Faculty Signature

Comments:

Guidelines for Selecting Entries

To develop a portfolio, you must reflect mindfully on what you have come to know and how you have come to know it. First consider those processes and concepts that you think you have developed most during a given period—say, a semester, block courses, clinical practice, etc. Determine which artifacts best represent your thinking and learning of those concepts and processes throughout the semester. While examining artifacts and relating them to your learning make a clear and concise decision on how you will chart out and discuss your growth. You may decide to make comparisons between two particular artifacts, chart changes in your understandings of concepts, skill at processes, or personal understandings or roles, examine the learning process; review your reflective thinking, or critique the decisions you have made.

The selection process is one that requires intense planning and reflection. Look at your artifacts against the competencies you intend to evidence. However, you need to understand the competency or standard. Recall the story of the Fuzzy in Chapter 3. Had the Fuzzy known what to look for in the "goodest of men" he would have kept his legs. The same might be said about competencies. Make sure you have a clear understanding of the competency before you go out looking for the artifact. You might also keep in mind that your peers could be of much value in providing support in this effort. When selecting entries you should bear in mind that each piece is part of a much larger whole and that together, carefully selected artifacts, along with well thought-out rationale statements, make a powerful statement about your individual professional development. Questions similar to those listed in Figure 8.3 will guide you in the decision-making process.

It becomes a challenge to reach a decision on what to include in the portfolio if you don't have much of a choice. You cannot make a selection decision if you only have a limited number of artifacts to work with. You may also find it to be a challenge when you have them. In other words, it is a catch-22 either way. However, it is much easier if you have faithfully accumulated your artifacts. Remember the approach discussed in Chapter 7? If you have a paper trail evidencing your growth and development, it may be helpful to look at each artifact and ask yourself, "What would including this item add that has not already been said or shown?" Remember that a portfolio creates representative records of your professional development and is not to be comprehensive.

Figure 8.3: Questions to Guide your Decision-making Process

- ❖ What do I want my portfolio to show about me as an aspiring teacher?
- ❖ What are my attributes as a prospective teacher?
- ❖ What do I want my portfolio to demonstrate about me as a learner?
- ❖ How and what have I learned?
- ❖ What directions for my future growth and development does my self-evaluation suggest? How can I show them in my portfolio?
- ❖ What overall impression do I want my portfolio to give a reviewer about me as a learner and as a teacher?
- ❖ Does this artifact support the kind of learning that the competency statement calls for?

As you seek to document growth and learning, it is important to remember that the absolutely best work should be included. If you received superior grades on three papers, which papers must you include in your portfolio? The most appropriate paper to include in the portfolio is the one that adequately responds to a competency outcome. You may also consider including one that represents you, your background or you personality. Further, diversity and quality of materials should be a first consideration.

Reflection Summary Essay

The importance of a reflective quality in a portfolio cannot be understated. Paraphrasing the realtor's mantra—location, location, location—developing an exemplary portfolio requires reflection, reflection, reflection. There is no illusion that a portfolio lacking of true, bona fide, reflection will thwart efforts to evidence professional growth and development. The last document in your portfolio is a reflection summary essay. The reflection summary essay is a concise document that ties together the portfolio. It summarizes the portfolio as it points to specific knowledge, skills, and dispositions gained. A well developed portfolio speaks for itself. A portfolio needs to capsulate its content in a brief essay. We would like to think of a reflective summary essay as some form of a rebuttal even though that terminology is inadequate. It is here that you get your last chance to state your case. However, we hesitate to call it a rebuttal because the reflection summary ought to be honest enough to note your strengths, weaknesses and opportunities. Here you will want to point out where you are as a developing teacher. You will want to talk about your strengths—of course, you can toot your horn here and even place a feather or two on your hat. By the same token, though, you need to examine yourself and admit your weakness and shortcomings and describe how you plan to overcome them. Undoubtedly, it is not uncommon to readily admit weaknesses even though the evaluation is focused on strengths. A portfolio provides an opportunity for transparency. A portfolio offers a new and better perspective of looking at ourselves. The fact that you can observe a weakness in yourself is strength of its own!

A few words of wisdom: abandon the idea that someone other than yourself may be an expert of your learning. Of course, they are experts about learning but not experts about your learning. Remember, many a portfolio evaluator plays his own version of "tinker, tailor . . ." in order to decide what to be when they grow up—in this case, what a good portfolio will look like. Lastly, get over the common myths of assessment, the myth of audience, and the myth of decision-maker. Accept the need to create an argument in your portfolio. It is at this point that you need to carefully look at your reflection abstract sheets with a keen eye on the rationale. While the performance outcomes or competencies that your portfolio is centered around may have been explicated, do not hesitate to promote broader meanings about them. A portfolio is meant to provide a forum to play double agent and is thus open to duality. However, make sure that your interpretation is tactful, sound and documentable.

A well articulated reflection summary essay portrays organization and coherence. Such qualities can only be achieved if you are willing and determined. This, then, requires writing, rewriting, and rewriting. If possible, set the draft aside for a day or at least a few hours. Any amount of time can be helpful. The idea behind it is the need to return to it with a fresh brain. Other approaches that you may find to be of benefit include:

❖ Reading your reflection summary essay aloud to yourself.
   This is a good way to "hear" problems that you cannot see.

❖ Having a friend read your reflective essay (to him or herself, or out loud to you). This approach has great potential in bringing about dividends in that another pair of eyes will be able to tell you if your flow of thoughts make sense. This will allow you concentrate on the logic and organization without getting distracted by visual errors.

Summary of Key Points

This chapter has provided a discussion touching on a number of documents that might be contained in your pre-service. While acknowledging that there is no single or right way to "do" a portfolio the discussion has suggested that your philosophy of education can become the lynchpin in your pre-service teacher portfolio. The philosophy of education document can anchor the portfolio and provide effective scaffolding for the evidence that follows.

The inclusion of a resume and an autobiographical sketch communicates adequate information to your audience to gain interest as they see you as a real person with skills and desire to grow as a professional. In addition, your portfolio needs a cover letter. This introduces you as pre-service teacher and is also the place where faculty examine your disposition. Equally important to your philosophy of education are *reflection abstract pages* which are written narrative descriptions of your artifacts. Reflection abstracts are very important components of your portfolio because they give your artifacts a voice and leave a lasting impression of the content. Within reflection abstract sheet are statements of your rationale. Artifacts need to be introduced by rationale statements. For each artifact included in the portfolio you must have a brief rationale statement justifying the decision to select it. An effective rationale statement includes a brief description of the context in which the artifact was created. This description informs the reader of pertinent circumstances surrounding the development of the artifact itself.

This chapter has presented two important planning considerations. First, you must recognize that the format of the artifacts must suit the requirements of your teacher education program. Second, you must continuously ask yourself the question: Can the artifact chosen fit into my portfolio? If it does not, can the artifact be reproduced without altering its effectiveness? Will someone else be able to easily examine the artifact? As you seek to document your growth and learning, remember that your absolute best work must be included.

References

APA. (2001). *Publication manual of the American Psychological Association*. Washington, DC: American Psychological Association.

Brookfield, Stephen. (1990). *The skillful teacher: Technique, trust and responsiveness in the classroom*. San Francisco, CA: Jossey-Bass.

Campbell, D. M, Melenyzer, B. J., Nettles, D. H., & Wyman, R. M. (2000). *Portfolio and performance assessment in teacher education*. Boston, MA: Allyn and Bacon.

Covey, S. (1989). *The 7 Habits of Highly Effective People: Powerful Lessons in Personal Change*. New York: Simon & Schuster.

Goodyear & Allchin. (1998). *Statements of Teaching Philosophy*. http://www.utep.edu/cetal/pub/stofteac.html. (Retrieved June 19, 2003).

Guillaume, A. M., & Yopp, H. K. (1995). Professional portfolios for student teachers. *Teacher Education Quarterly*, 22 (1), 93-101.

Palmer, P.J. (1998). The courage to teach: Exploring the inner landscape of a teacher's life. San Francisco: Jossey-Bass.

Chapter 9

Portfolio Template

Orientation

In addition to introducing you to the portfolio as a lifelong, ongoing project, the teacher preparation program in your institution has a more immediate purpose for requiring one: it provides a formal exercise in self-evaluation and allows you to demonstrate certain college-designated competencies. It also places responsibility on you to set forth academic and personal goals and to develop a plan for achieving them. Your thoughtful articulation of achievements and future goals will aid your academic advisor in assisting you reach those goals.

Many teacher education programs have neither found a ready-made formula for the perfect portfolio nor devised one. However, many have surveyed practices observed elsewhere, considered their specific goals and settled on a recommended skeletal format and guidelines. Within these guidelines the pre-service teacher is free to present herself in whatever way she thinks is likely to be effective. If this is the case at your institution, a point to remember is that you must envision your audience.

Focus Questions

- What goes into the portfolio?
- What are its various components?
- How is a portfolio organized?
- How are reflection abstracts written? How about a reflection summary essay?

Our discussion of the portfolio process up to this point has focused on the general organizational framework for gathering and processing evidence products. Knowledge of this framework is only a part of the portfolio development process. What, however, is of equal importance is the manner in which these products are presented. Initially your audience includes college advisors and peers. Once it is complete, it moves to a team of evaluators whose determination will have an impact on your progress toward program completion. It will be easier for them to assess your work if it follows an outline they expect. As your audience changes over time, you will want to make appropriate adjustments

Underlying the motivation for developing a portfolio is the need to share your work with others. Now, you can decide how and in what order to present the artifacts gathered from your coursework. Again, consider the perspective of your audience and what type of evidence they will find convincing. Have you selected, organized, and presented the data in a way that brings the most compelling evidence into focus for your readers? Does each piece of evidence serve a purpose, supporting a claim you have made about your teaching? Frequently, the effectiveness of demonstrating your growth and development is stifled by an aversion to providing your product in a well-organized way. Some teacher education programs provide a template for the portfolio. This might not always be true at your institution. To minimize that aversion, we will provide a helpful guide in putting together your portfolio.

The most basic and reasonable bottom-line to a successful portfolio is its quality. Quality can only be measured against the various components and extend to which the various components of your portfolio speak to a set of primary goal of documenting your growth and development as an aspiring teacher. The most important components to consider are those that best present you as a true learner. Of course, format and neatness are vitally important and great, but do they get you where you want to go? That's the question. In this chapter we will look at a simple portfolio template.

Pre-Service Teacher Portfolio

Melanie Davis
Fall 2003

LEMOYNE-OWEN COLLEGE

DIVISION OF EDUCATION

Figure 9.1: Sample Cover Page

PRE-SERVICE TEACHER PORTFOLIO

MELANIE DAVIS

Elementary School Education

Fall 2003

LeMoyne-Owen College

DIVISION OF EDUCATION

Figure 9.2: Sample Title Page

Table of Content

Figure 9.3: Sample Table of Content

SECTION I

ATTESTATION DOCUMENTS

Figure 9.4: Sample Section I: Attestation Documents Divider

MY AUTOBIOGRAPHY

My name is Melanie Davis, a 23 year old African American woman pursuing an endorsement in K-8 Elementary Education in Social Studies/ English Language Arts. I am the youngest of four siblings, Elizabeth, Alonzo, and Chantell. First thing everyone should know about me is that I love cars! My dad is a mechanic at a used car lot in Southaven. I know an unbelievable amount of stuff about cars and all kinds of cars. My dad, my brother Alonzo and I built a Shelby Cobra from a kit car last summer. We did all that work in our own garage. We even painted it there. I am a woman with a lot of talents even though I have not had opportunities to travel or live in other parts of the country.

I attended county schools in Mississippi and graduated from Horn Lake High School where I maintained good grades and was an honor roll student. During my senior year, I was given the prestigious award of valedictorian. I was also an honor student in middle school and ranked number eight at graduation. I received several awards. One of the most important awards that I ever received was from the Rotary Club. The award was given to me for good citizenship. A person chooses what he/she wants to do in life. You may decide to go after the wind or decide to go after a goal.

As a child whose parents had never graduated from high school, my thoughts were on education and my career. My 8th grade teacher, Mrs. Tate, always kept my head up high. She was my History and my "motivational" teacher, and friend. Mrs. Tate told me that I could be whatever I wanted to be. I want to be a teacher so I can give back to the community. I love working with people and if children are our future 'people' I would love to be a part in their lives.

After completing an Associate of Science degree at a junior college, I enrolled at LeMoyne-Owen College. Also, I chose this institution not only because it is closer to home but also because Teacher Education is a flagship program at LeMoyne-Owen College which gives me an assurance that I will gain superior training and knowledge for the teaching profession. Moreover, the school is really small therefore I can be heard and seen.

At LeMoyne-Owen College, I am a member of the Student Government Association, Concert Choir, Alpha Kappa Alpha Sorority Inc., and the Student Tennessee Education Association. Although I consider myself a senior, I have two more full semesters to go before I graduate as a certified teacher. I am determined to become the most successful and outstanding teacher that I can be while emulating the "teacher facilitator of transformative processes" model of the Teacher Education at LeMoyne-Owen College. In addition, I would want to be a role model for my students and support them in becoming what they want to be.

Melanie Davis
August 15, 2003

Figure 9.5: Sample Autobiography

Melanie Davis
7365 N. Shawnee Avenue, Apt. #3E
Memphis, TN 38117

August 16, 2003

Chair, Teacher Education Committee
Division of Education
LeMoyne-Owen College
807 Walker Ave
Memphis, TN 38126

Dear Chair:

Re: Admission to Teacher Education Program

This is my formal application for admission to the Teacher Education Program at LeMoyne-Owen College. I am currently a sophomore with a declared major in Social Studies and a cognate area in English Language Arts. My plan is to receive an endorsement in Elementary Education (K-8). I came to LeMoyne-Owen College in the fall semester from City Community College. My transfer credit hours satisfied 25 of the 42 hours in the General Education (Core II). I successfully completed the remaining 17 hrs except for HLFW 129 which I, regretfully, dropped last fall due to illness. Upon completion of that course by the end of this semester I will have met all the benchmark I requirements except Praxis I Writing and the pre-candidate portfolio evaluation.

The following, therefore, are the requirements that I have met:

- Successful completion of General Core II Program requirements with B in MATH 120; A in MATH 130; and C in ENGL 205. My grade point average right now is 2.53.
- Three favorable recommendations from faculty
- Passing scores of the Praxis I -- Mathematics 174 and Reading 174
- Successful Oral Interview (Personal Interview I)
- Completed Application Form
- Maintaining membership in a professional organization (STEA)

I plan to complete the Writing section of the Praxis I examination in September. I am currently attending the Praxis workshop and making steady progress in my preparation for that examination. In case you need more information or additional documentation for my file, my professional core advisor is Dr. Kenneth Morgan and Dr. Justin Robinson is my major area advisor. I have kept them updated with my progress.

I am, therefore, requesting for provisional admission to the Teacher Education Program. In case you need to get in touch with me for additional information, my telephone number is (901) 343 3477 and my e-mail address is davism765@po loc.edu

Sincerely yours,

Melanie Davis
SSN 498 23 4418

Copy: Dr. Kenneth Morgan, Advisor Professional Core
        Dr. Justin Robinson, Advisor Major Area

Figure 9.6: Sample Formal Letter of Application

Melanie Davis

7365 Shawnee Ave. Apt. #3E
Memphis, Tennessee, 38117
Phone (901) 280 9394 Email davism765@po.loc edu

OBJECTIVE

Gain admission to the Teacher Education Program at LeMoyne-Owen College and acquire skills in preparation for the teaching in K-8 classrooms.

EDUCATION

2000 - Present LeMoyne-Owen College, Memphis, TN
B.S. K-8 Social Studies
1997 - 2000 City Community College, Memphis, TN
A. S. General Science
1993 - 1997 Horn Lake High School, Horn Lake, MS
High School Diploma Honors Diploma with Gold Seal Endorsement

VOLUNTEER SERVICE

Jan. 1999 - May 1999 High School Intern at Homewood Nursing Home, Horn Lake, MS

Aug. 1997 - Dec. 1997 Student Assistant at Horn Lake High School in Horn Lake, MS

1997-1998 Vice President at Eagles Company at Horn Lake High School in Horn Lake, MS

WORK EXPERIENCE

2001 – Present Liberty Land Amusement Park, Memphis TN
Employment Assistant
2000-2001 Curriculum Resources Center, LeMoyne-Owen College, Memphis, TN
Work Study Student

SKILLS

Working knowledge of: Windows 95 and 3.1 operating systems, Microsoft Office 95/97/2000, Resumix, Word Perfect 6 0, AmiPro, Lotus 1-2-3, TurboCad, MathCad, AutoCad/AutoSketch, Turbo Tax, Quicken, Microsoft Publisher 97, Select Phone, Microsoft Automap, Microsoft Works, Claris Works, Aldus Pagemaker. Office hardware/equipment operated: Pentium & Power Mac Computers, AHS Switchboard, HP Laser Jet IV, Lexmark Laser Printer, HP PaintJet, HP ScanJet, Smith Corona Typewriter, Copiers, Fax Machines, and Modems.

PROFESSIONAL MEMBERSHIPS

Student Tennessee Education Association (2001 – Present)

REFERENCES

Dr James P. Takona
Assoc. Prof. of Educ Technology & Media
200A Gibson-Orgill Science and Mathematics Hall
(901) 774 9090
james_takona@nile.loc edu

Dr. Roberta Wilburn
Assoc. Prof. of Education
24A Brownlee Hall
(901) 774 9090

roberta_wilburn@nile.loc.edu

Figure 9.7: Sample Resumé

MY PHILOSOPHY OF EDUCATION

Melanie Davis

The philosophy I have adopted is one that is based on my beliefs and observations as a student and through field experiences activities. There are five components that I consider important and reflective of my beliefs concerning education. The first component is the learner and learning activities. The second component is classroom organization. The third component is motivation of the learners. The fourth component is classroom discipline. Lastly, the fifth component is classroom-climate. My philosophy of education is influenced by my experiences and observations during my service as a special education teacher and during my field experiences. These experiences have molded my vision of what I consider the ideal classroom setting and learning environment.

I believe that there are basic skills that all children must have at any given grade level and within any particular learning activity to be successful. The basic skills are the catapult for application and critical thinking. It is my belief that all children enjoy showing what they have learned and therefore should be active participants in the learning activities. For this reason, I believe that children should participate in cooperative learning activities that foster sharing of information, understanding, and strategies for learning. Learning activities should be developed that allow each student to contribute to the group according to the student's ability level, thereby building confidence and determination.

Learning activities should be very structured and the movement through the lessons and learning activities should very predictable for the students. All learning activities should be presented at a skill or concept level that is easily understood and accomplished. Learning activities should also foster critical and divergent thinking. In order for cooperative learning activities to occur, classroom organization must be considered. Ideally, I prefer to set my classroom up so that there are four to five small group settings. Each group consists of three to five students who work well together. The groups should be heterogeneous in ability level, race, and sex depending on the over-all make-up of the class. The lessons are constructed in a manner that first allows for guided practice and later includes cooperative learning. The students are encouraged to work together during each lesson, providing constructive criticism and peer tutoring.

Assessment of student learning includes teacher observations, isolated skill tests, and group product assessments using a rubric scale developed by the teacher and the students. The results the assessments are used to develop new lessons or to re-teach a skill or concept. To ensure that students are willing to participate in the cooperative learning activities, students must be properly motivated. I believe that one of the greatest motivators for learning in any classroom should be the desire to know. Because of this belief, I try to develop activities that fascinate the students and inspire them to want to dig deeper. During the lesson there are many times when the students' efforts are affirmed verbally and times when the winning team in a spelling bee or a math rally might be awarded a Snickers bar and the other team awarded a Snickers snack as a consolation prize. Because my students will know that I believe in them and their ability, they will be eager to show me that they can complete the tasks assigned to them. The motivation for learning and the classroom disciple needed for productive learning go hand in hand. I believe that disciple in the classroom begins with rules that benefit all involved. The entire class agrees upon the rules and the consequences for breaking these rules. The consequences for breaking the rules must be faced and can range from a loss of centers time to a visit to the principal's office. All classroom rules support the right of each student to learn in a safe environment without feeling threatened emotionally or physically by any other person in the classroom.

The classroom rules also support my right to teach uninterrupted in that same environment. In order for this form of classroom disciple to work there must be a positive classroom climate. The climate in the classroom should be one of mutual respect. I believe that I must earn the students respect and that the two main requirements for earning respect are firmness and fairness. My tone of voice in the classroom will be one that lets the students know that what I ask of them is what I expect. My students will also know that they may ask for assistance anytime during one-on-one instruction and cooperative learning activities.

During one-on-one instruction and guided practice students are given opportunities to make more informed decisions and are encouraged to use the problem solving method that works best for them. The students are encouraged to share their knowledge and be themselves as long as they respect the others around them.

The learners, learning activities, classroom organization, discipline, and classroom climate all work together to create an environment in which everyone enjoys learning and is eager to learn. Idealistically, I would love a classroom in which the students are happy, full of inquiry, full of enthusiasm to share their knowledge, and full of the confidence needed to do so. It is my responsibility as a teacher to be a model, a facilitator, a cheerleader, and a disciplinarian. One of the greatest rewards for me in the classroom is to hear students say that they understand a concept and ask if they may help someone else to understand.

Figure 9.8: Sample Philosophy of Education

COLLEGE ACADEMIC TRANSCRIPT							
Student Name:	Melanie Davis	**Home Phone:**	(901) 456 8724		**SSN:** 498-23-4418		
	7365 N Shawnee Ave Apt	**Email:**	davism765@po loc edu				
FEMALE	Memphis, TN 38117	**Emergency**	(901) 456 8724				

Undergrad/BS/Social Studies (K-8)

2003/Spring

Course	Title	TYPE	SECT	GRDE	CRDT	QPNTS	Repeat
ENGL 307	AMERICAN LITERATURE (1620-1860)	Lecture	A	B	3	9	
ENGL 303	ADVANCE COMPOSITION	Lecture	A	B	3	9	
ART 302	STUDIES IN COMP IMAGE MAKING	Lecture	A	A	3	12	
ENGL 340	CHILDREN'S LITERATURE	Lecture	A	B	3	9	
EDUC424	INTERNSHIP IN TRAINING SETTING	Lecture	A	B	3	9	
		Attempted Credits	Earned Credits	Total Credits	GPA Credits	Transfer Credits	Quality Points	GPA
Term:	15	15	15	15	15	49	3.26
Overall:	108	103	103	105	75	266	2.53

2001/Fall

Course	Title	TYPE	SECT	GRDE	CRDT	QPNTS	Repeat
HIST 201	U S. HISTORY TO 1865	Lecture	A	C	3	6	
POL 201	AMERICAN GOVERNMENT	Lecture	A	B	3	9	
SOCI 307	ANTHROPOLOGY	Lecture	A	C	3	6	
SOCI 306	INTERGROUP RELATIONS	Lecture	A	B	3	9	
SPAN 102	METHODS OF ELEM. LANGUAGE ARTS	Lecture	A	B	2	6	
EDUC410	PRESCHOOL CURRICULUM	Lecture	A	B	3	9	
HLFW129	LIFETIME FITNESS	Lecture	A	WD	2	0	
		Attempted Credits	Earned Credits	Total Credits	GPA Credits	Transfer Credits	Quality Points	GPA
Term:	19	17	17	19	0	45	2 36
Overall:	93	88	88	90	60	217	2.41

2001/Sum1

Course	Title	TYPE	SECT	GRDE	CRDT	QPNTS	Repeat
ARTS301	ART IN DIVERSE ENVIRONMENTS	Lecture	A	I	3	0	
DIVS346	STUDY OF MULTI-ETHNIC EDUCATION	Lecture	A	C	2	4	
		Attempted Credits	Earned Credits	Total Credits	GPA Credits	Transfer Credits	Quality Points	GPA
Term:	5	2	2	2	2	4	2
Overall:	74	71	71	71	60	172	2.42

2001/Spring

Course	Title	TYPE	SECT	GRDE	CRDT	QPNTS	Repeat
EDUC204	FOUNDATIONS OF EDUCATION	Lecture	B	C	2	4	
GEOG102	INTRODUCTION TO GEOGRAPHY	Lecture	A	D	3	3	
		Attempted Credits	Earned Credits	Total Credits	GPA Credits	Transfer Credits	Quality Points	GPA
Term:	5	5	5	5	2	7	1 4
Overall:	69	69	69	69	58	168	2.43

2000/Fall

Course	Title	TYPE	SECT	GRDE	CRDT	QPNTS	Repeat
EDUC320	MEASURES & EVALUATION	Lecture	A	D	2	2	
ENGL205	HUMAN LITERARY HERITAGE	Lecture	A	C	3	6	
		Attempted Credits	Earned Credits	Total Credits	GPA Credits	Transfer Credits	Quality Points	GPA
Term:	5	5	5	5	0	8	1 6
Overall:	64	64	64	64	56	161	2 51

2000/Sum1

Course	Title	TYPE	SECT	GRDE	CRDT	QPNTS	Repeat
COLE201	TEST-TAKING SKILLS AND STRATEGIES	Lecture	A	A	2	8	

Course	Title		TYPE	SECT	GRD	CRDT	QPNTS	Repeat
HUMN202	HUMAN HERITAGE		Lecture	A	B	3	9	
MATH130	COLLEGE ALGEBRA		Lecture	A	A	3	12	

	Attempted Credits	Earned Credits	Total Credits	GPA Credits	Transfer Credits	Quality Points	GPA
Term:	8	8	8	8	8	29	3 62
Overall:	59	59	59	59	56	153	2.59

2000/Spring

Course	Title	TYPE	SECT	GRD	CRDT	QPNTS	Repeat
BIOL104	GENERAL BOTANY	Lecture	A	B	4	12	
COSI119	PROGRAMMING IN BASIC	Lecture	A	D	3	3	
HUMN201	HERITAGE I	Lecture	A	C	3	6	
SOSI111	INTRODUCTION TO POWER & SOCIETY	Lecture	A	C	3	6	

	Attempted Credits	Earned Credits	Total Credits	GPA Credits	Transfer Credits	Quality Points	GPA
Term:	13	13	13	13	10	27	2 07
Overall:	51	51	51	51	48	124	2.43

1999/Fall
City Community College

Course	Title	TYPE	SECT	GRD	CRDT	QPNTS	Repeat
BIOL131B	GENERAL BIOLOGY I	Lecture	A	C	3	6	
EDUC1311	ORIENTATION	Lecture	A	A	1	4	
EPY 2533	HUMAN GROWTH & DEVELOPMENT	Lecture	A	C	3	6	
HPR 1213	HEALTH	Lecture	A	C	3	6	
MAT 1723	REAL NUMBER SYSTEM	Lecture	A	B	3	9	
MUS 1113	MUSIC APPRECIATION	Lecture	A	B	3	9	

	Attempted Credits	Earned Credits	Total Credits	GPA Credits	Transfer Credits	Quality Points	GPA
Term:	16	16	16	16	16	40	2 5
Overall	38	38	38	38	38	97	2 55

1999/Sum1
City Community College

Course	Title	TYPE	SECT	GRD	CRDT	QPNTS	Repeat
COM 1010	COMPUTER LITERACY	Lecture	A	A	3	12	
HIST1520	US HISTORY SINCE 1877	Lecture	A	C	3	6	
SOCI1010	INTRO SOCIOLOGY	Lecture	A	B	3	9	

	Attempted Credits	Earned Credits	Total Credits	GPA Credits	Transfer Credits	Quality Points	GPA
Term:	9	9	9	9	9	27	3
Overall:	22	22	22	22	22	57	2.59

1998/Spring
City Community College

Course	Title	TYPE	SECT	GRD	CRDTS	QPNTS	Repeat
BIOL1131	GENERAL BIOLOGY LAB	Lecture	A	B	1	3	
ENGL1113	ENGLISH COMP I	Lecture	A	C	3	6	
ENGL1123	ENGLISH COMP II	Lecture	A	C	3	6	
SPT 113	ORAL COMMUNICATION	Lecture	A	C	3	6	
PSYC1513	GENERAL PSYCHOLOGY I	Lecture	A	B	3	9	

	Attempted Credits	Earned Credits	Total Credits	GPA Credits	Transfer Credits	Quality Points	GPA
Term:	13	13	13	13	13	30	2 3
Overall	13	13	13	13	13	30	2.3

Figure 9.9: Sample Academic Transcript

THE PRAXIS SERIES
Professional Assessment for Beginning Teachers™

Telephone: (601) 771-7395

DESIGNATED INSTITUTION SCORE REPORT

BACKGROUND INFORMATION

Examinee's Name:	DAVIS, MELANIE					
Candidate ID	022987	Social	410-23-4442	Sex: F	Date of	03/23/1976

EDUCATIONAL INFORMATION

College Where Relevant Training Was Received:		LEMOYNE OWEN COLLEGE	
Undergraduate	SOCIAL STUDIES		
Graduate Major:			
Educational Level:	B.S.		
GPA:	2.5 – 2.99		

SCORE RECIPIENT INFORMATION

Code#	Recipient Name
R1403	LEMOYNE OWEN COLLEGE

Melanie Davis
7365 N Shawnee Avenue,
Apt #3E
Memphis, TN 38117

CURRENT TEST		Examinee's Score	Possible Score Range
Test Code	Test Name		
0524	PRINCIPLES OF LEARNING & TEACHING	171	100 – 200

HIGHEST SCORE AS OF		07/27/2002		
Test Date	Test Code	Test Name	Examinee's Highest Score	Possible Score Range
06/26/2002	0524	PRINCIPLES LEARNING &TEACHING 7-12	171	100-200
06/23/2001	0710	PPST READING	174	150-190
06/23/2001	0720	PPST WRITING	169	150-190
06/23/2001	0720	PPST MATHEMATICS	174	150-190

Figure 9.10: Sample Praxis Series Scores

SECTION II

REFLECTION SUMMARY

Figure 9.11: Sample Section II: Reflection Summary Divider

COMPETENCY # 1

Think creatively, critically, logically and analytically using both quantitative and qualitative methods for solving problems

INTERPRETATION

I perceive creative thinking as the ability to generate possible solutions to a problem and involve skills such as flexibility, originality, elaboration, brainstorming, modification, associative thinking, attribute listing, imagery and metaphorical thinking. Critical thinking is a skill associated with skepticism about a subject or field It is also a technique which allows you to ask the right questions and evaluate the outcomes; logical thinking includes skills such as comparison, classification, sequencing, cause/effect, patterning, webbing, analogies, deductive and inductive reasoning, forecasting, planning, hypothesizing, and critiquing; and lastly, analytical thinking is the ability to stand back from the information given while examining the *what, why where, when* and *how* in detail from multiple angles in light of available evidence for completeness and accuracy. Each of these skills requires that the thinker has the proficiencies associated with a competent practitioner in a professional field. Thinking creatively, critically, logically and analytically are essential skills that are pivotal in problem solving through use of numbers and words.

EVIDENCE
Artifact #1.1:

Name of Artifact: Global Connection: Analysis of Tensions between National Interests and Global Priorities

Date: March 4, 2000

Source: SOSI 111, Introduction to Power, Society, and the Social Sciences

Context: To successfully complete the requirements of SOSI 111, the instructor required that each student engage in a research study using resources from the Internet to compile a critical analysis of societal factors that lead to antagonism and strife

Artifact #1.2

Name of Artifact: *Sarcophaga Bullata* Selectivity Ability of Sugars and a Sugar Substitute Saccharin

Date: Fall 2001

Source: NATS 110, Biological Sciences

Context: As part of the requirement for NATS 110, the instructor assigned us to groups with each having four members. My group's name was "Red Indians." The Red Indians were given the task to test the ability of the blowfly *Sarcophaga bullata* to taste different sugars and a sugar substitute saccharin. Because sucrose is so sweet to people, I expected the flies to taste lower concentrations of sucrose than they would of maltose and glucose Because saccharin is also sweet tasting to people, I expected the flies to respond positively to it as well

RATIONALE

I have chosen to use two artifacts that indicate the growth that I have attained in demonstrating my ability to think creatively, critically, logically and analytically using both quantitative and qualitative methods for solving problems. The first artifact (Artifact 1.1) is a paper that I submitted as a course requirement and demonstrates my ability to articulate and evaluate the rights and responsibilities of an individual in relation to his or her family, social groups, community, and the nation. Evident in my paper is my ability to repackage information from various sources and present them in a logical manner to defend my position on the need to view national interests and global priorities as not a mere demonstration of political correctness but as a way to actually strengthen this nation's long-term strategies and influence. This opportunity allowed me to really think about what I also believe, and that I would do when confronted by issues related to segregation.

The second artifact (Artifact 1 2) is a project requiring that the group that I belonged to to test and provide a definitive report on the ability of blowflies to test different sugar and sugar substitutes. The results supported our first hypothesis that sucrose would be the most detectable sugar by the flies. Flies show a selectivity of response to sugars based on molecular size and structure. Glucose, the smallest of the three sugars, is a monosaccharide. The threshold value of glucose was the highest in this experiment because a higher concentration of this small sugar was needed to elicit a response. Maltose and sucrose are both disaccharide. However, they do not have the same molecular weight or composition. This artifact demonstrates my ability to think logically and analytically in both qualitative and quantitative methods. I got an A on this!

Figure 9.12: Sample Reflection Abstract

[Artifact # 1.1]

Global Connection: Analysis of Tensions
between National Interests and Global Priorities

Figure 9.13: Sample Artifact #1.1

[Artifact # 1.2]

Sarcophaga Bullata Selectivity Ability of Sugars and a Sugar Substitute Saccharin

Figure 9.14: Sample Artifact# 1.2

SECTION III

REFLECTION SUMMARY

Figure 9.15: Sample Section III: Reflection Summary Divider

Reflection Summary Essay

Throughout this portfolio, artifacts have been used to demonstrate my mastery of competencies in academic, cultural, social, and professional areas. This portfolio presents my response to the College's ten competencies. I experienced failure and success in many of the products I created. I still remember all of those feelings that I had to do it again or was satisfied with this product. This portfolio provides a representative display of everything I learned in this program and all of my ability to work in this field.

Putting together this pre-service teacher portfolio was a very worthwhile experience. It allowed me to summarize my philosophy, learning experiences, and provided me to assess my development as a future teacher and how I will accomplish the task of becoming the best teacher that my ability will allow. Creating this portfolio also taught me a plethora about technology, how to use technology, and ways in which I can integrate technology into my classroom.

I feel that the types and amount of evidence that I have included in this portfolio adequately represents my development to become a teacher at the entry level. The artifacts presented along with professional documents such as college transcripts, Praxis Series scores, and the resume are evidence of my academic and professional achievements to become a teacher. As I worked on this portfolio, I came to realize that I need to pay special attention to a couple of competencies. For example, my communication skills were not adequately documented. Writing is one of my weakest areas.

As I reflected on my technology competencies, I felt less confident of my mastery of the skills needed to be an effective teacher. Working with an instructor who helped guide and educate me on the technology was extremely valuable. I feel that this learning process has made me more confident in my abilities to teach using technology. There are so many possibilities awaiting teachers in the field of technology. As our students in elementary schools become more aware of the increase in technology so should I as a teacher. I feel it is my job to keep myself informed and educated on the newest developments in technology as well as my students. The new age is moving away from the ordinary pencil and paper and moving into the extraordinary world of e-mail and web pages. Learning how to use different programs that allow you to scan documents, create web pages and pictures is exciting. To be a part of something so new and fresh was an experience I have grown from and will pass on to others.

The portfolio demonstrates that I have met all of the College's competencies. Each aspect of the portfolio reaches a different competency and my artifacts speak to my development and growth in areas related to teaching strategies, philosophies of teaching, and lesson plans, every competency except the second one that is related to communications. I believe this portfolio proves that I am a knowledgeable and educated teacher that uses my communication, instruction, organization, and classroom management skills. The portfolio demonstrates that I can provide a school district and the students with a dynamic teacher who is well informed about pedagogy, content, and current educational issues.

Figure 9.16: Sample Reflection Summary Essay

Chapter 10

Evaluation of the Pre-Service Teacher Portfolio

Orientation

As an astute pre-service teacher, having a clear understanding of the evaluation process is necessary. In most cases, the portfolio assessment process is articulated in the various handbooks published by your teacher education. Evaluation and the scoring of a portfolio is a time consuming process that requires attention to details. The construction of a portfolio is such that each portfolio is unique and tailored to the individual. Ideally, each portfolio is evaluated without making a comparison with any other portfolio. The second concern of portfolio assessment, the subjectivity in the evaluation of the portfolio, is somewhat problematic. Teacher evaluation, in any form, is subjective. Instructors use rubrics to assess products contained in your portfolio and you can use the same rubrics to provide benchmarks that encourage your own self-evaluation.

Three scoring systems are presented in this chapter: holistic, checklist, and analytic scoring systems. Holistic is that form of evaluation where the examiner observes the quality of various components and attributes of a performance and then assigns a numerical value to the overall quality. It is based on the assumption that a given portfolio conveys a total impression and the score the portfolio earns is based upon that overall impression. After reviewing the portfolio, the panel bases its scores on the general quality of the portfolio (organization, development, and expression) without paying attention to minor errors.

A second approach takes into consideration the use of a checklist to make certain that required components have been included. An analytic scoring approach breaks down the final product into component parts to enable independent scoring. In most instances, analytic scoring approach has the advantage of providing detailed information on the quality of individual items in the portfolio.

Focus Questions

☞ Who assesses the portfolio, what is assessed, and how is it assessed?

☞ List and explain a number of scoring approaches used in portfolio assessment?

☞ What is a rubric and how is it used in assessment?

Proof of Purchase—Where is It?

Now that the portfolio development project is complete the question is—at least for now—do you have it or do you not? What is next? Having reached this juncture, first ask yourself if you have a sense of satisfaction, or a complete experience. Return to your look at the product once more and carefully discern what it is that has given or not given coherence to the work as a whole. It is not enough to put your trust on program faculty and consider them as a total body of experts who know what they expect or recognize the quality and level of your work when they see it. An astute pre-service teacher must have a clear understanding of the evaluation process. You need to become keenly aware of the meaning and consequences associated with unsatisfactory, satisfactory, proficient, outstanding or any other descriptors your institution uses in a rubric. There certainly is a lot that can be said regarding your understanding of the portfolio assessment process. This understanding is key to success in this endeavor. In most cases, the portfolio assessment process is articulated in the various handbooks published at your institution. If you don't have one, look for one. Ask your advisor or another member of the faculty. It is your absolute right to demand to know the procedures needed to be followed in order to submit the portfolio for evaluation.

Evaluation Team

A large cross-section of teacher preparation programs requiring the development of portfolios often stress the need for accurate and consistent data from valid and fair instruments that are free of bias. For that reason the portfolio becomes a multi-audience document. An evaluation of pre-service teacher portfolios is often conducted by teams of dedicated and responsible professionals who are knowledgeable of the principles and practices of the teaching profession. Individuals who form the evaluation team may include individuals outside the professional teacher education department. These could be faculty across campus in the arts and sciences as well as PreK-12 personnel. In some cases, an upper level pre-service teacher may be asked to serve at a specific level in the review panel. In most cases, the evaluation team is formally appointed by the program's governing body and charged with the task to examine portfolios. In some institutions this could be the teacher education committee. Because the results of an evaluation panel appreciates the importance of the task and the need to obtain valid and reliable results, the seriousness of the panel's responsibilities are emphasized and may be described and published in a handbook.

Partnership in Evaluation

An effective portfolio process requires collaboration between pre-service teachers, faculty, and others. Shulman (1998) has eluded that collaboration between pre-service teachers and faculty to design and evaluate portfolios creates a sense of ownership on the part of the pre-service teacher and a stronger desire to continue the process. This really is the beauty of the portfolio process—assessee and assessor work together on "brick and mortar." Wolf (1998) suggests the need to form a "portfolio culture" in schools. Culture requires shared interests and values. It is a give-and-take relationship that support, trust and sincerity. A portfolio culture allows pre-service teachers and faculty to benefit from each others perspective. A portfolio culture demands, "New skills, new visions of being a professional, and the commitment of each school community to its students and teachers" (p. 50). It also means coming to an understanding that portfolios are personal and dynamic, and that there are ways to assess them that allow for these qualities (De Bruin-Parecki, Schmits, Boraz, Shaw, Severson, & Mizaur-Pickett, 1999).

How Will it be Evaluated?

The construction of a portfolio is such that each portfolio is unique and tailored to the individual. The use of a portfolio has been advanced as a tool for evidencing academic learning and professional development and growth. Additionally, a portfolio has become a useful tool for arriving at licensing and other personnel decisions within a school district. The latter reason is served well where comparability between teachers (often from different subject areas) is desired. Face with the lack of standardization to effectively make those personnel decision a portfolio becomes handy.

Just as there is no one model for a good teacher, there is also no one method for evaluation. Again, this is strength of the portfolio, since it means that your teacher education program will need to develop specific criteria for evaluation and make them relevant to specific programs. A decision on criteria is, for the most part, based on what your teacher education program values and seeks to model. These values are often explicated in a conceptual framework document.

A major concern often emerging in any assessment process of a portfolio regards the question on subjectivity. If necessary measures are not taken, subjectivity can become somewhat problematic. Of course, any form of evaluation is prone to have a certain degree of subjective. If such then is true the question then becomes: how will I be assured that my teacher education program will evaluate my portfolios with an unquestionable degree of reliable and valid basis given that portfolios are subjective in nature? You need to take courage in that teacher education programs, generally, have a commitment to excellence and continued improvement. As portfolios become an important tool of assessment, teacher preparation programs engage themselves in the development and refinement of acceptable ways of judging. These may include the use of evaluation panels as well as rubrics. Furthermore, faculty and pre-service teachers are continuously forming partnerships in evaluation. Such a partnership provides a safeguard against subjectivity in evaluation and encourages advances student achievement while promoting life-long learning.

In a responsive and standards-based teacher education program, faculty use portfolio assessments to guide instructional decisions. This is has also picked momentum in PreK-12 classroom. Portfolio assessment is just another evaluation tool that college faculty and PreK-12 teachers have available to them. For the same purpose, teachers assess student learning for a variety of reasons including the following:

- ❖ To identify what the learner knows.
- ❖ To clarify what is expected.
- ❖ To measure degrees of learning.
- ❖ To identify individual learning needs.
- ❖ To observe individual students' thinking skills and dispositions for learning.

Evaluation Tool

A "typical" portfolio contains artifacts that may include those that you have developed including term papers, lesson plans, tests as well as those developed by others. These may include evaluation reports, praxis examination scores, faculty recommendations and so. Since the portfolio shows examples of work over time, and without an appropriate tool, these can be difficult to evaluate. A common solution to this problem requires the development of a rubric focused on predetermined qualities, based on the mandated items. Scoring of a portfolio is a time consuming process requiring attention to details. The evaluator or evaluators must examine reflection abstract sheets noting how they dully provide an adequate description of the artifact in response to the competency in question. Further, the evaluators scrutinize the artifact to ascertain that it is responsive in adequately documenting a specified mastery of a competency. Ratings may then be combined to generate categorical and/or overall ratings. The process of a portfolio evaluation may look at various aspects of the portfolio and may take one or any combination of the four approaches given in Figure 10.1. You need to find out what evaluation approach your institution employs.

Figure 10.1: Four Approaches to Portfolio Evaluation

Type of Evaluation	Focus of Evaluation
Portfolio Checklist Evaluation	This approaches the evaluation with the use of a simple "Yes" and "No" evaluation tool
Portfolio Entry Evaluation	Examines the individual entries to look a how well they address the standards
Portfolio Reflection Evaluation	Looks at the artifacts and places more emphasis on the reflection quality of your work
Portfolio Structure Evaluation	Looks at the structural nature of your portfolio

Performance Rubrics

Earlier chapters of this text described the level of emphasis placed on accountability by the current reform movement. This accountability is based on defined standards. Standards provide targets to strive to achieve. The need for accountability has affected the assessment process because assessment has become a means of providing information on how close pre-service teachers and their teacher education program come to achieving the targets, as well as how far they need to go to achieve the required success. Along with standards, criteria statements may be defined and serve the purpose of identifying appropriate benchmarks.

Unlike most traditional evaluation processes that often appear to operate on a "gotcha" premise, portfolio assessment, when used appropriately, offers opportunities for using defined sets of criteria. These criteria describe the expected levels of performance. The evaluation criteria for individual artifacts may be specified using various rubrics. What is a rubric? Jonassen, Peck and Wilson (1999) have defined a rubric as a "tool used for assessing complex performance" (p. 221) for rating its quality. This term has, in the most recent years, become popular in the classroom. A rubric means a guide for critiquing the effectiveness of a planning activity, a tool for assessment used by teachers and students, and a process of establishing the essential goals and assessment criteria. Rubrics are important because they are intended to be a means of "communicating expectations to learners in advance of the learning" (Cunningham & Billingsley, 2003, p. 152). They state in an organized way the kinds of observable evidence—whether in the form of a product or a performance, or the process that used to reach the product or performance—that will count toward showing that the student has successfully completed the learning experience. Rubrics are often used as a scoring guide that differentiates, on an articulated scale, among a group of sample behaviors or evidences of thought that are responding to the same prompt. They provide unambiguous ways to classify and judge specific components of your portfolio into categories that vary on a continuum. This continuum may range from unacceptable to outstanding. Detailed criteria are delineated and used to discriminate among levels of performance. As an assessment tool, rubrics allow for complex critiques of multimedia projects, presentations, written reports, and other classroom work. Jonassen and his associates (1999) have described characteristics of rubrics that can serve as authentic assessments, to include the following:

❖ All important elements of the behavior are represented as strands to be assessed
❖ Elements are unidimensional (i.e. discrete, not overlapping behaviors)
❖ Rating scales for each aspect of behavior are distinct, comprehensive, and descriptive
❖ The instrument communicates clearly to students and parents
❖ The instrument yields rich information that can help improve a student's level of performance, rather than just serving as a basis for grading

When the criteria for assessment are clearly defined, instructors and pre-service teachers share a common understanding of the project goals and criteria, and the various levels of completing the defined criteria. Since the criteria for assessment is clearly defined, teachers and students share a common understanding of the project goals and criteria, and the various levels of completing the defined criteria. The importance of rubrics lies in their ability to sort out varying degrees of achievement in any given component of a portfolio (quality of the autobiographical sketch, philosophy of education, resume, reflection abstracts, choice of artifacts, etc.). Rubrics are effectual in the assessment of attributes that are directly observable—what a student has done or can do rather than what he claims he can do. For this reason, rubric grading is criteria based. This simply means that the rubric contains criteria for observable performances that are meaningful, clear, concise, unambiguous, and credible.

Herman, et al. (1992) have defined five characteristics of a good scoring rubric. These include:

- ❖ Help teachers define excellence and plan how to help students achieve it.
- ❖ Communicate to students what constitutes excellence and how to evaluate their own work.
- ❖ Communicate goals and results to parents and others.
- ❖ Help teachers or other raters be accurate, unbiased and consistent in scoring.
- ❖ Document the procedures used in making important judgments about students.

Well developed rubrics have, within themselves, embedded values to support judgment in the assessment process. Using rubrics, instructors assess products contained in the portfolio. As a portfolio developer, you can use the same rubrics to provide benchmarks that encourage your own self-evaluation. Using rubrics, the evaluation team gains an objective tool to support the evaluation and may write a report that summarizes the results of their review. At LeMoyne-Owen College, for example, the report describes the extend at which selected artifacts reflect the pre-service teacher's achievement levels.

System of Grading

Become aware of the grading that your institution has established is important. Three scoring systems are given in Box 10.1. Specifically, you need to know the levels of performance that are specified and the criteria needed to be met to achieve the level. Although the premise of portfolio assessment is process rather than product, many teacher education programs require a numeric score or letter grade for reporting purposes. The grading system in most colleges calls for a numeric score that allows scores for all pieces of work to be combined into a percentage which will be allocated either a letter grade (A-F) or a category such as "fail" "pass" "distinction" or "highest distinction." Consider for a moment how many tests or other evaluations have come your way and you had no idea what the expectations for excellent work was and had to rely on your own intuition or some psychic skill to guess what a particular examiner's "standards" might be.

Box 10.1

   🗁   Holistic Scoring
   🗁   Checklist Scoring
   🗁   Analytical Scoring

Holistic Scoring

Holistic scoring is common in figure skating, diving, gymnastic, band recitals, and dances. In such events, numbers are assigned on a 10-point scale, with decimals used to indicate finer gradations of performance. In an evaluation of a portfolio, approach is used when the examiner observes the quality of various components and attributes of a performance and then assigns a numerical value to the overall quality. Holistic scoring is based on the assumption that a given portfolio component conveys a total impression and the score the portfolio earns are based upon that overall impression. After reviewing the portfolio, the panel bases its scores on the general quality of the portfolio (organization, development, and expression) without paying attention to minor errors. Therefore, a holistic approach assumes that each component that makes up the portfolio is related to all of the other components. And, that one component cannot easily be separated from the others. The holistic scoring approach views an artifact as a total work, the whole of which is greater than the sum of its parts and assigns an overall index of performance.

Checklist Scoring

A checklist is an instrument whose dimensions and properties are essentially scored on two levels, "yes" or "no". Analytical checklists provide a master list of information that must be present. The check indicates that either the dimension is present or absent. A checklist could be used in instances where there is no need to judge how well each of a dimension or behavior is displayed, only that they are there. Certain sections of a portfolio can be assessed using this process. For example, a title page, table of contents, membership in a professional organization, transcript records, etc. may not need to call on a value judgment. Checklists provide a method for recording whether required portfolio components have been included. The use of this type of scoring does not generally attempt to address the overall impression of the portfolio.

Analytic Scoring

An analytic scoring approach breaks down the objective or final product into component parts and each part is scored independently. In this case, the total score is the sum of the rating for all of the parts that are being evaluated. When using analytic scoring, it becomes necessary to treat each component or part as separate to avoid bias toward the whole product. Analytical scoring systems generally provide detailed information on the quality of individual items within the portfolio. The task of the evaluation panel is to focus on the various aspects of the performance, judge its quality along a qualitative dimension. Rating scale methods are easy to use and understand. The concept of the rating scale makes obvious sense; both the evaluation panel and you as a pre-service teacher have an intuitive appreciation for the simple and efficient logic of the bipolar scale. The rating scale method offers a high degree of structure for appraisals. Each portfolio entry or attribute is rated on a bipolar scale that may have several points ranging from "poor" to "excellent" (or some similar arrangement).

Who Benefits from the Evaluation?

Portfolio evaluation can only be understood from the context of the person or persons who will use the results. You deserve better. You need to know what the outcomes and expectations for you are and how your performance will be assessed. To gain the full benefit of an evaluation, you need to mindfully reflect on what you have come to know and how you have come to know it. First, consider which processes and concepts you have developed most over a given period of time—for example, while completing a given block of courses. Then determine which artifacts best represent your thinking about and learning of those concepts and processes throughout that period. As you examine artifacts, decide on how you will chart and discuss your growth. You may also decide to make comparison between two particular artifacts; chart changes in your understanding of concepts, skills, and personal understanding or roles; review your reflective thinking; or critique the decisions you have made.

Summary of Key Points

An ardent pre-service teacher possesses a clear understanding of the evaluation process. In most cases, the portfolio assessment process is articulated in the various handbooks that your teacher education program publishes. You will need to consult them or visit with your academic advisor. The construction of a portfolio is such that each portfolio is unique and tailored to the individual.

Unlike some traditional evaluation approaches where the test often appears to operate on a "gotcha" premise, portfolio development assessment systems offer a rubric with specified sets of criteria that describe levels of performance. Issues related to subjectivity cause the evaluation of portfolios to be somewhat problematic. Ideally, each portfolio is evaluated without making a comparison with any other portfolio.

The evaluation criteria for individual artifacts often use a specified set of rubrics. When the criteria for assessment are clearly defined, teachers and students share a common understanding of the project goals and criteria, and the various levels of completing the defined criteria. Using rubrics, instructors assess products contained in your portfolio, and you can use the same rubrics to provide benchmarks that encourage your own self-evaluation. Although the premise of portfolio assessment is process rather than product, many teacher education programs require a numeric score or letter grade for reporting purposes. These scores may be obtained using either (a) a holistic scoring approach were the score is based on the assumption that a given portfolio conveys a total impression and the score the portfolio earns are based upon that overall impression; (b) a checklist scoring approach where specific items are checked included or not included in the portfolio; or (c) an analytic scoring that evaluates a portfolio by breaking down the objective or final product into component parts and each part is scored independently of the other.

References

Cunningham, C. A. & Billingsley, M. (2003). *Curriculum webs: A practical guide to weaving the web into teaching and learning.* Boston, MA: Allyn and Bacon.

Debruin-Parecki, A., Schmits, D., Boraz, M., Shaw, E., Severson, A., & Mizaur-Pickett, A. (1999). *Developing professional portfolios.* Paper presented at the annual meeting of the Association of Teacher Educators, Chicago, Illinois.

Herman, J. L., Aschbacher, P. R., & Winters, L. (1992). *A practical guide to alternative assessment.* Alexandria, VA: Association for Supervision and Curriculum Development.

Jonassen, D. H., Peck, K. L., & Wilson, B. G. (1999). *Learning with technology: A constructivist perspective.* Columbus, Ohio: Merrill.

Shulman, L. (1998). Teacher portfolios: A theoretical activity. In N. Lyons, (Ed.). *With portfolio in hand: Validating the new teacher professionalism.* New York: Teacher College Press.

Wolf, D. (1998). Creating a portfolio culture. In N. Lyons, (Ed.). *With portfolio in hand: Validating the new teacher professionalism.* New York: Teacher College Press.

Chapter 11

An Effective Pre-Service Teacher Portfolio

Orientation

As we had noted in Chapter 9, many teacher preparation programs have neither found a ready-made formula for the perfect portfolio nor devised one. However, many have surveyed practices observed elsewhere, considered their specific goals and settled on a recommended skeletal format. Within these guidelines the pre-service teacher is free to present herself in whatever ways she thinks likely to be effective. If this is the case with your institution, one point to remember is that you must envision a prospective reader. Initially your audience includes college advisors. It will be easier for them to assess your work if it follows an outline they expect. As your audience changes over time, you will want to make appropriate adjustments.

Focus Questions

- ☐ What are the attributes of an effective portfolio?
- ☐ How do you become responsible of your own learning, thinking, and destiny?
- ☐ Why is authentic assessment becoming a preferred way of assessing students?
- ☐ What kind of assessment are Praxis series examinations?

In addition to introducing you to the portfolio as a lifelong, ongoing project, most teacher preparation programs have more immediate purpose for requiring one. First, a portfolio provides a formal exercise in self-evaluation and allows you to demonstrate certain college-designated competencies. Second, a portfolio places responsibility on you to set forth academic and personal goals and to develop a plan for achieving them. Your thoughtful articulation of achievements and future goals will aid your academic advisor in assisting you to reach those goals.

Shaping and Organizing Strategies

There are many unresearched questions about how portfolios can be utilized as effective tools of learning. Several such questions are listed in Box 11.1.

Box 11.1

> What are the skills and techniques need to be effective in developing a good portfolio?
>
> Are there structures that are generic in the organization of a portfolio?
>
> How concerned are pre-service teachers in making sure that they select their best work for the portfolio?
>
> Are there specific ways that of organizing an effective portfolio?

From existing research, it is already clear that learning by doing brings about meaningful learning (Jonassen, 2000) and that meaningful learning as argued by Jonassen, Peck, and Wilson (1999) is:

Active (manipulative/observant)—learners interacting with an environment and manipulating the objects in that environment, observing the effects of their interventions and constructing their own interpretation of the phenomena and the results of the manipulation

Constructive (articulative/reflective)—learners integrating new experiences and interpretations with their prior knowledge about the world, constructing their own simple mental models to explain what they observe

Intentional (reflective/regulatory)—learners articulating their learning goals, what they are doing, the decision they make, the strategies they use, and the answers that they found

Authentic (complex/contextual)—learning tasks that are situated in some meaningful real-world task or simulated in some case-based or problem-based leaning environment

Cooperative (collaborative/conversational)—learners working in groups, socially negotiating a common expectation and understanding of the task and the material they will use to accomplish it.

With a focus on what you have already collected, decide how and in what order to present it. Again, consider the perspective of your audience and what type of evidence they will find convincing. Have you selected, organized, and presented the data in a way that brings the most compelling evidence into focus for your readers? Does each piece of evidence serve a purpose—support a claim you have made about your teaching?

Let us revisit a few words of wisdom introduced in an earlier chapter. First, you need to abandon the idea that someone other than yourself may be the expert of your learning. Second, they are experts about learning but not experts about your learning. Remember, that many a portfolio evaluator plays his own version of "tinker, tailor . . . " as they decide on what to be when they grow up—in this case, what a good portfolio will look like. Lastly, you must acknowledge two common myths of assessment—the myth of audience, and the myth of a decision-maker. You are rightfully a part of your portfolio's audience and you are the decision-maker of your portfolio. As you do that, accept the need to create an argument in your portfolio. This is where you need to carefully examine your reflective abstract pages, especially the rationale section. While the competencies the portfolio addresses may have been explicated by the teacher preparation program or are external, do not hesitate to promote broader meaning about them. Go ahead and tell what your interpretation of the standard is and what it means to you. Moreover, portfolios are meant to provide a forum to play double agent and interpretations are open to duality. In all cases, however, make sure that your interpretation is tactful, sound, and documentable.

How Will You Know When You Got it?

In Chapter 8 we entered into a discussion centered on the question "What should I include in my pre-service teacher portfolio?" Murphy's Law says that anything that can go wrong will go wrong. Admittedly, Murphy's Law is extremely pessimistic. It does, nevertheless, offer an important warning to any portfolio developer. A portfolio is never complete and that there is never a time that you can say the portfolio needs to be shelved away. Only the assembly of a portfolio can be complete its development and enhancement is always ongoing. In addition to deciding what you need to include in the portfolio, you must address the issue of determining when you have an adequate level of mastery of the standard. Finally, after drafting your portfolio, implement a SWOT analysis. SWOT is an acronym for "strengths, weaknesses, opportunities, and threats." In SWOT analysis, you will need to think back for a moment about your purpose and analysis of your audience. As you engage yourself in that analysis, consider whether your portfolio product will achieve their expectations and what you, as an aspiring teacher, set out to do. Does your portfolio give the reader a sense of who you are as a prospective teacher? What is the most striking claim that is evident in pre-service teacher portfolio? Will the evidence presented for this claim be convincing enough to the audience? Are all of the claims and evidence offered for teaching effectiveness relevant? All these questions are focused on the issue of having the "proof-of-purchase" in your hand or not.

When it all fits together, a portfolio must present several assertions: (a) that the object of the portfolio was clear; (b) that the reflection abstracts sheets, which include the rationale, are solid and show evidence of reflection; and (c) the collection of artifact engaging and worthwhile rather than a mere scavenger hunt. The layout of the portfolio is pretty neat and now you have a tidy package that you think is ready to go for evaluation.

A portfolio must end with a brief reflection summary essay encapsulating "Lessons Learned." As with the introductory statement, your philosophy of education and goals, this should be a reflective statement regarding your experiences as a developing teacher. This summary essay should be succinct in its presentation of your mastery level of the set of performance standards you are required to account for. Your reflection summary essay ought to be characterized by honesty. This is the place to talk about those problems and barriers you encountered and how you dealt with them. It is also a place to describe how the goals, strategies and ideas behind your development have evolved and changed over time, and more so since becoming a part of the teacher preparation program. Approach your portfolio as a whole, and tell what it means to you. Try to understand the significance of the evidence you have compiled. What does your portfolio show about your overall understanding and ability? While developing your portfolio, what did you learn about yourself? Was it anything you didn't know before? Of course not! Always remember that the pre-service teacher portfolio should be constructed in such a way as to be relevant to both you as a prospective teacher and to the purposes for which it is directed toward. Use it to describe your growth and development strengths, to record your accomplishments, and generally emphasize your best work. The strength of a portfolio lies in its ability to integrate different scales of success, instead of one single measure of your accomplishments. This could be a good idea to include in your reflection summary. To make a strong and clear argument, use the first person pronoun and sincerely, though emphatically, state your case and attainment. And—this is really the beauty of a reflection summary essay—it is an opportunity to give yourself a pat on the shoulder.

What Color are the Stripes?

No teacher education program expects you to have completed all the major requirements or even to have met all the required competencies. A key stripe of a good portfolio is the self-assessment quality. Recall that a portfolio is both a window and a mirror. As a window, a portfolio allows others to look from the outside into your development as well as allows you to step to the outside and look at yourself. As a mirror, you gain the advantage of seeing yourself in the same way as others look at you. In all cases, your portfolio should include three basic attributes outlined in Box 11.2.

Box 11.2

🗁 Sincere and honest
🗁 Engaging
🗁 Appealing design

Portfolio is Sincere and Honest

Your portfolio should present an accurate representation of you—your personality, your view of education, your style, your accomplishments, and a glimpse of your future goals as a professional educator. The purposes of a pre-service teacher portfolio are to effectively represent your knowledge, skills, and experiences to convince a panel and others that you are ready to enter the teaching profession and that you are a potential candidate. The rationale for selecting certain pieces rather than others has to do with what kind of image you want to present of yourself. Remember that a portfolio is a product that tells a story about you. This appears to be a very simplistic definition. And it is. In essence, your portfolio should consist of what you think represents you as a developing teacher. This representation can be shown by an assortment of best work. Nevertheless, that needs not to be the guiding rule. You might include, for example, drafts of a particular project to demonstrate how your revision process grew during the course of the project. We might add here that the portfolio process tells a story of your journey. It sketches a journey from where you came from, where you presently are, and where you want to be. You might include your worst examination work reflecting that terrible grade and show what you have done to remove that problem.

Portfolio is Engaging

A portfolio is most effective when it provides opportunities to engage in evaluating one's own learning, growth and development. Comparing such opportunities can be in the form of earlier work in terms of development and growth, progress in specific learning areas, selection of specific evidence and comparison of data, and growth in the depth of arguments presented. From this stand point, you can now see that engagement in learning is a not simply a commitment to completing an assigned work. Rather, it is an attempt to interact with your learning environment and assess whether you have a mastery of the knowledge, skills and dispositions that your academic program is intended to provide. The reader of your portfolio, through the records placed in the portfolio, can readily identify aspects of your preparation that have influenced your growth and development process.

Portfolio is Appealing in Design

Every portfolio must have an appealing design. While you might have little control over the design, it must seek to provide an appeal to you and your audience. An effective portfolio should be well documented and organized. Three basic characteristics describe a good portfolio: structure, representative, and selective. What does all that mean? Let's give a closer look at each on of these basic characteristics:

Structured

Careful thought must be put into the portfolio development process to avoid, chaos and clutter that can overshadow its effectiveness. For this reason, a portfolio must be organized, complete, and creative in its presentation. Some questions for you to think about might be: Is my portfolio neat? Are the contents displayed in an organized fashion? Is the content representative for the purpose that it is intended? Here again, you need to ask yourself the question: is my growth and development as a prospective teacher evident? Can others see my growth and development as a prospective teacher? If you cannot see this demonstrated in your portfolio, it is very likely that others will not see it either.

Representative

In the childhood pastime favorites is Bill Martin's (1983), Brown Bear, Brown Bear, What Do You See? The classic line is, "Brown bear, brown bear, what do you see?" and this is followed by the bear's seeing a series of colorful animals: yellow duck, red bird, blue elephant. . . . As each animal is revealed, the bear utters a repetitive line: "I see a ___ ____ looking at me," with the blank filled in with an animal and its color. May be this analogy is far too fetched. In either case, it drives the point home—representation requires creativity. Such representation must be documented. The documentation should represent the scope of your academic and professional growth and development. This documentation should be representative across courses and time. This may include courses you took in your General Education program, major and minor core course experiences as well as the professional core components. It may even include artifacts from a developmental course that you took while a freshman. Some questions for you think about might be: Does my portfolio portray the types of evidence that accurately reflect my growth? Does my portfolio display a cross-section of my learning experiences? What is my judgment or evaluation of the image portrayed by my portfolio? Is it positive or negative? The bottom line here is that you are creating images of your portfolio. In doing so, you become more aware of where your portfolio stands.

Diversity and range of the kinds of experiences that go into the portfolio certainly make your product outstanding. Evidence of these experiences may include artifacts from highly structured learning experiences say an Earth Science course to a less structured course such as Freshman Year Experience or service learning where there was a good measure of independence. In addition, the level of reflection will mark a well thought out portfolio. Portfolio evaluation panels are always impressed with reflections that look back and look forward like. Look at the example below:

> When I was taking the course in Biological Science 201, I needed a lot of support, which I got from the Lab Assistant. She was patient with me even when I had all those mind blocks. When I become a licensed teacher in Middle School Education, I will spend time even outside the classroom to help out slow students.

This opinion feels realistic. Even though you may soon discover that classroom teachers have fewer hours during the day to accommodate too much out of time for the support for their students. Nevertheless, it always interests the portfolio evaluation team to see your success in carving out that role for yourself.

Selective

The natural tendency for anyone developing a portfolio is to have a desire to document everything. However, if a portfolio is being used for either summative or formative purposes, careful attention should be given to conciseness and selectivity in order to appropriately document one's work. However, we suggest that you limit the contents of your portfolio required keeping its purpose in mind. Including too many artifacts may obscure the information that is most helpful in evidencing the mastery of a given set of competencies (Roe, Stoodt-Hill & Burns, 2004). The rationale for selecting certain pieces rather than others has to do with what kind of image you want to present of yourself. Remember that a portfolio is an instrument that tells a story about you. That is a rather simplistic definition. In essence, your portfolio should consist of what you consider your best work. You may, however, include your "before and after" products. For example, drafts of a particular project to demonstrate how your revision process grew during the course of the project.

A checklist is useful in the development of a portfolio. Moreover, when a criterion is translated into a yes or no answer within a checklist, you will gain a better edge in developing a cohesive and complete portfolio. Check with your teacher education program to see if there is a standard checklist that can support and guide your portfolio development project. Chism (1999) has provided a list of questions offered in Figure 11.1. These questions can be especially helpful to pre-services teachers whose field experiences participation affords them opportunity to teach. These questions are worth considering as you reflect on the effectiveness of the content of your portfolio as you document your teaching effectiveness for summative purposes. Carefully look at it and consider printing it out and use it to guide you to evaluate your completed portfolio.

When you Really Have to Work on It

We have already noted the words of Eleanor Roosevelt who once said "the answer to fear is not run and to hide; it is not to surrender feebly without contest. The answer is to stand and face it boldly, look at it, analyze it, and, in the end, act." One of the most thought-provoking discoveries that one can make is realizing what they don't know. The danger inherent in checklists is that they are prone to act as blinders producing a tunnel effect. As a judicious pre-service teacher, you must remain attentive to significant qualities that may not be covered by the checklist. In all cases, you must continuously remind yourself that the dominant purpose for a pre-service teacher portfolio is to provide an opportunity to engage in a self-assessment of progress in fulfilling specified educational and institutional goals. Of course, bear in mind that your advisor or others can play a major role in guiding you through your plans for meeting other long-range educational and career goals (i.e. applying for graduate school, deciding if teaching is for you, identifying other career opportunities, etc.). In either case, a portfolio is just meant for that.

A good portfolio is both expensive to develop but also requires considerable time to prepare. Artifacts must be collected over time and may take months. Reflection abstracts must be written, edited and reflected

Figure 11.1:
Guiding Questions on the Effectiveness of Portfolio Content

Guiding Questions	Yes	No
Did I show the breath and depth of my current knowledge of the content, as demonstrated by the inclusion of course materials in the portfolio?		
Does my portfolio demonstrate my use of effective design principles to facilitate learning in the courses I have taught, as demonstrated by the teaching philosophy statement and course materials?		
Does my portfolio demonstrate that I delivered effective instruction, as indicated by summaries of student evaluation ratings, reports by peers, and review of the products of student learning, such as tests, papers, and project reports?		
Overall, what does your portfolio say about the quality of your growth and what recommendation would you make on this professional decision?		
Is my portfolio effective for formative purposes?		
Does my portfolio contain the type and amount of information needed in order to address the competency elements?		
Do the materials enable me to assess whether there are clear connections between my goals and values (course goal statements, philosophy statements) and actual practices (assessment measures, syllabus format)?		
Does my portfolio contain reflective statements that show engagement with the performance issues?		
Did I provide a sufficient context so that the reviewer will be able to give me good information?		
Is my portfolio organized in such a way to show improvement?		
Have I drawn on other sources of opinion and evidence in compiling my portfolio?		
Did the exercise of putting together the portfolio provide me with new realization about my development as a teacher?		

upon. This stands in contrast to a hastily assembled collection of term papers and other course products. As you work on your portfolio, you will need to make a plan on each of the various portfolio components. This plan may be organized around the following set of questions:

❖ What are they intended to represent?
❖ What points do I want to make?
❖ What kind of documents do I need to include in order making that point?

To answer this set of questions, you must completely understand the purpose of the portfolio, the process of developing it, the meaning of the standards, and the perspective of your teacher education program.

Having identified the documentation that must be contained in your portfolio, you will begin the less challenging task which is the layout of your documents. In all regards, the key to producing a good portfolio is neatness. Stories can be told about pre-service teacher portfolios that we have evaluated. Some looked like an elephant has been stomping on them. Some were stained with jelly or spaghetti sauce, and others contained dog-eared artifacts that appear as if they were out of a recycling dumpster. These may be extremes. However, if you are serious about your development and growth and anticipate meeting the portfolio requirements of your teacher education program, you need to be resolute on the appearance of your portfolio and its contents. Number all your pages and avoid using clear pockets for your artifacts. Although they may look pretty, they are often annoying to the evaluation panel that would want to read or make comments and feedback on your artifacts. You can get by if you insert the section dividers in clear pockets but certainly not your artifacts and especially if they are term papers with multiple pages. In all cases, the appearance of your portfolio should not overshadow its content.

Celebrate Completion

We have learned in this text that the portfolio development process is an evolving activity. However, once the portfolio assembly is complete, it is time to relax and enjoy a little leisure. Developing a portfolio is a stressful event. Experience has proved that a portfolio offers an opportunity to examine your own learning and professional growth and development as well as lead to improvement in your own preparation as a prospecting teacher. Now that you have completed your portfolio, take time to consider the kinds of strengths and weaknesses you have identified. Find ways of working to enhance those strengths and removing identified the weaknesses. Seek guidance from your instructors and network with peers.

Summary of Key Points

In Chapter 8, we became engaged with the question "What should I include in my pre-service teacher portfolio?" Does your portfolio give the reader a sense of who you are as a prospective teacher? What is the most striking claim that is evident in pre-service teacher portfolio? Will the evidence presented for this claim be convincing for this audience? This chapter makes a strong statement to the effect that many teacher preparation programs have neither found a ready-made formula for the perfect portfolio nor devised one. However, there are no experts who are better knowledgeable about your learning than yourself.

A well developed portfolio should present an accurate representation of you —your learning, growth, and development, your personality, your view of education, your style, your accomplishments, and a glimpse of your future goals as a prospective teacher. The purposes of a pre-service teacher portfolio are to effectively represent your experiences and knowledge; to convince a committee that you are ready to enter the profession program; and that you are a potential candidate. Remember that a portfolio is a product that tells a story about you. We might add here that the portfolio process tells a story of your journey.

The format of a portfolio varies considerably from one institution to another. In all cases, however, an efficient portfolio is well documented and organized. We have considered the suggestion that a good portfolio should be (a) structured, (b) representative, and (c) selective. A structured portfolio should be organized, complete, and creative in its presentation. Its representative quality must portray the types of evidence that reflect growth and development of its author. Finally, being selective means that careful attention has been given to conciseness and selectivity for the purpose of appropriately documenting one's work.

An effective portfolio must have a conclusion—often in the form of a brief reflection summary essay: "lessons learned." This essay must approach your portfolio as a whole, and tell what it means to you. What does your portfolio show about your overall understanding and ability? It is important that the pre-service teacher portfolio should be constructed in such a way as to be relevant to both you as a prospective teacher and to the purposes toward which it is directed. The reader of your portfolio, through the records placed in it, is able to can readily identify aspects of your preparation that have influenced your growth and development process.

References

Chism, N. (1999). *Peer review of teaching: A sourcebook.* Bolton, MA: Anker.

Jonassen, D. H., Peck, K. L., & Wilson, B. G. (1999). *Learning with technology: A constructivist perspective.* Columbus, Ohio: Merrill.

Martin, Bill. (1983). *Brown Bear, Brown Bear, what do you see?* New York: Henry Holt & Company, Incorporated.

Roe, B., Stoodt-Hill, B., & Burns, P. (2004). Sunday *school literacy instruction: The content areas* (8th Ed). Boston, MA: Houghton Mifflin Company.

Appendix A

LeMoyne-Owen College
CONCEPTUAL FRAMEWORK
The Teacher as Facilitator of Transformative Processes

Mission of the Institution

Throughout its 139-year history, LeMoyne-Owen College has been a beacon of hope for all students but primarily African Americans seeking higher education. For most of its history beginning in 1862 to the late 1960's, LeMoyne-Owen was the only institution of higher education that African American students could attend in the city of Memphis, Tennessee. However, administrators and faculty members of LeMoyne-Owen College recognized the need to educate professionals for the multicultural nation that the United States was and is. Therefore, in the tradition of historically African American institutions of higher learning, LeMoyne-Owen College has always been and continues to be open to all.

The mission of LeMoyne-Owen College, a historically black liberal arts college, is to prepare students in a nurturing and student-centered community for lives of success, service and leadership. In fulfilling this mission, the administration, faculty and staff of LeMoyne-Owen College strive to:

- Provide an exciting and challenging academic and intellectual atmosphere and culture in which to teach and learn.
- Promote the spiritual and moral development of each student.

- Encourage the spirit of generosity and reinvestment in LeMoyne-Owen College with graduates giving time, talent and financial resources.
- Prepare students to be able to thrive in a diverse community.
- Open new vistas of what is possible in the lives of all students by providing educational opportunities to those for whom these may not be readily available, especially the disadvantaged.
- Foster self-sufficiency, self-confidence, and positive attitudes among our students.
- Render high-quality service to all our constituents—students, faculty, staff, alumni, schools, the community, and all other supporters
- Produce highly quality and sought-after graduates.
- Become a resource to address social and economic issues of the community.
- Contribute to the preservation of African American Culture.

Faculty members, committed to teaching, community service, and research, play a key role in carrying out the mission of the college. Their commitment provides an academic environment that facilitates student transformation.

Under girded by the college mission, the institution's programs and services are designed to enable LeMoyne-Owen College graduates to:

1. Think creatively, critically, logically, and analytically using both quantitative and qualitative methods for solving problems.
2. Communicate effectively (listen, speak, read and write) on formal and informal levels.
3. Distinguish, clarify, and refine personal values for the attainment of richer self-perception and relate those values to the value systems of others.
4. Appreciate, understand, and know the foundations of the Afrocentric perspective.
5. Appreciate, understand, and know the foundations of diverse cultures in the context of a global community.
6. Appreciate, understand, know, and pursue the principles, methods and subject matter that underlie the major discipline(s).

7. Accept social responsibility and provide service to human-kind.
8. Maintain levels of literacy that allow them to understand the impact of science and technology on individuals, society and the environment.
9. Attain motivational, personal management, interpersonal skills, professional development and research experience, as well as resourcefulness that will form the basis for a career and/or further educational experiences.
10. Attain critical skills, frame of reference, and understanding needed to appreciate and discriminate between artistic achievement.

Mission and Philosophy of the Unit

The mission of LeMoyne-Owen College's Division of Education supports and extends the mission of the institution. The Division of Education's mission is to prepare candidates as facilitators of transformative processes who are able to educate students from diverse socio-economic and cultural backgrounds. The purpose of the teacher education programs in the unit is to prepare teacher candidates to engage students in transformative learning processes that prepare them to perform efficiently and effectively within a contemporary global framework. The purpose is under girded by two complementary goals: The first is to provide excellent teaching and learning environments that result in critical literacy and learning for teacher candidates who will in turn mirror these outcomes for the PreK-12 students in their care. The second is to provide, in collaboration with partnership schools, related field experiences and clinical practice where teacher candidates develop and demonstrate the knowledge, skills and dispositions that make them facilitators of transformative processes. The conceptual framework articulates the unit's expectations for candidates from program entry to program completion. In short, candidates are expected to leave the program as skillful, critical, creative thinkers who are able to use transformative processes to facilitate the learning of PreK-12 students. The unit's programs are designed to prepare candidates who are capable of and willing to teach all students with special emphasis on meeting the needs of African American students from urban and rural areas, the population that has for historical and demographic reasons, been our predominant population. This emphasis emerges from LeMoyne-Owen College's legacy, historical and current mission. The fact that LeMoyne-Owen College is a predominantly African American College instills an understanding of race issues and the need for racial equality. Culture and more specifically the culture of African Americans, has traditionally been an integral element of LeMoyne-Owen College. This rich heritage and the need for African Americans to know and be guided by knowledge of their own history and people under gird this program emphasis.

From its inception LeMoyne-Owen College has recognized that African Americans have been disenfranchised and excluded from opportunities. In order to achieve racial and economic parity a strong education is critical for LeMoyne-Owen College's historical and current constituency. Although LeMoyne-Owen College continues to embrace the reality of a strong education for African Americans, it acknowledges and applauds the growing diversity apparent in the United States. Recognizing the need for diversity in the academic community the college continues in the tradition of historical African American institutions of higher education to be open to all. Further, it actualizes an open-door policy of student and faculty recruitment.

As the division's mission is to prepare teachers as facilitators of transformative processes, the terms teaching, facilitator, and transformative processes have special meanings. Teaching is defined as facilitating the development of knowledge, skills and dispositions of learners by bringing out the latent qualities that learners already possess.

A facilitator of learning is one who is able to:

- Recognize innate potential;
- Appeal to the intellect;
- Promote critical and creative thought;
- Inspire the humanity and spirituality of learners;
- Inspire creativity;
- Foster character development in students; and
- Achieve excellence (Hilliard, 1997).

Transformative Processes refers to the employment of self-motivated acts of change:
- From mere knowledge acquisition to knowledge construction;
- From passive thinking to critical, creative, active thinking;

- From actions informed only by external evaluations to actions informed also by self-evaluations;
- From isolated learning to continuous, lifelong learning; and
- From covert adaptations of dispositions to overt adaptations of dispositions.

Teaching, facilitating, and employing transformative processes must be modeled by faculty for candidates, thereby enabling them to perform as teachers who facilitate learning using transformative processes. To become teachers who facilitate transformative processes, candidates must believe in their ability to succeed academically and invest themselves fully in the teaching-learning dynamic. Faculty must encourage this belief by reorienting the curriculum and their pedagogical practices from teaching at to learning with teacher candidates.

Beliefs

Members of the Unit believe that teacher candidates have the human capacity to fulfill their chosen career goals. As Nobles (1986:92) put it: "To be human is to possess 'will and intent' and to have the capacity to develop and change." Secondly, we believe that teacher candidates and the students they will teach have the capacity to grow and continuously transform themselves into competent learners. However many learners, especially those of low-prestige, disenfranchised groups, have been socialized to adopt patterns of helplessness, perceptions and behaviors that impede growth capacity. Thirdly, we believe it is imperative that faculty members, PreK-12 teachers and are able to facilitate teacher candidates use of their own intelligence to control their behaviors as learners; to center in, think, and focus on their own development as constructors of knowledge; critical thinkers, self-evaluators, and continuous learners. The teacher candidate develops these abilities while they master the knowledge, skills, dispositions, and competencies of specific subject matter. In short, we believe that teacher candidates have the capacity to grow and continuously transform themselves into excellent learners who will in turn become excellent teachers of PreK-12 students.

The unit's faculty is committed to facilitating the development of candidates in becoming facilitators of transformative processes. Current research and literature point out that African American students in most instances have not been encouraged and energized by schools; therefore their capabilities have not been discovered or documented extensively enough in recent educational history (Ladson-Billings, 1994; Anderson, 1997; Washington and Andrews, 1998; Hilliard, 1997 and Delpit, 1997). Ladson-Billings (1994 p. ix) points out that "No challenge has been more daunting in the United States than that of improving the academic achievement of African American Students". A history of denial of and exclusion from educational opportunities for students of African descent continues to make the "quest for quality education an elusive dream for the African American community" (Ladson-Billings, 1994 p. ix). Noting this phenomenon and drawing upon the earlier theme of teacher as facilitator, the modified conceptual framework of the Division of Education hinges primarily on studies by Hilliard (1997); Ladson-Billings, (1994); and Foster (1997). They affirm the belief in the power of the learner and the teacher. Furthermore, the conceptual framework grows out of professional, state and national guidelines for best practices.

Program Design

A major learning principle that under girds the Unit's beliefs and practices is that concepts can be taught at any level, increasing in complexity as the learner develops and becomes more sophisticated (Bruner, 1992; Taba, 1962; Harden, 1999; Bernstein, 1985; Kantor, 1983; Tramper, 1996). The spiral has become a symbol that is widely used in education to represent this process (Banks, 1996). The Teacher Education Unit has adopted the spiral to represent teacher candidates' development into facilitators of transformative processes.

The spiral (figure 1) illustrates the candidate's advancement through the four major phases of their preparation for teaching. Phase I, developmental education, is the entering point for candidates who need additional preparation for success in college courses. Phase II, general education, provides students with a broad base of content knowledge. Phase III, the professional core, and major combines course work and clinical experiences and deepen content and pedagogical knowledge. Phase IV, Clinical Practice, requires application of knowledge to practice and includes student teaching and internships. Each level becomes increasingly more complex and sophisticated as candidates develop the knowledge, skills, and dispositions that are represented at the top of the spiral as performance outcomes that demonstrate candidates' competencies as teachers as facilitators of transformative processes. The spiral configuration is intended to illustrate that learning is active and that learners construct new ideas or concepts by combining new knowledge with past knowledge, and that this does not occur in a moment but happens gradually and over time, that the process is developmental and sequential. Development is the process by which an individual grows and changes from one phase of life to another. Finally, the top of the spiral represents the cumulative competencies of candidates that are developed by the end of the program. The facilitator of transformative processes has knowledge, skills, and dispositions in the areas of 1) African culture, 2) communication, 3) ethics, 4) instruction, 5) content knowledge, 6) diversity, 7) cultivating and sustaining excellence, and 8) technology.

Figure 1: Spiral Model

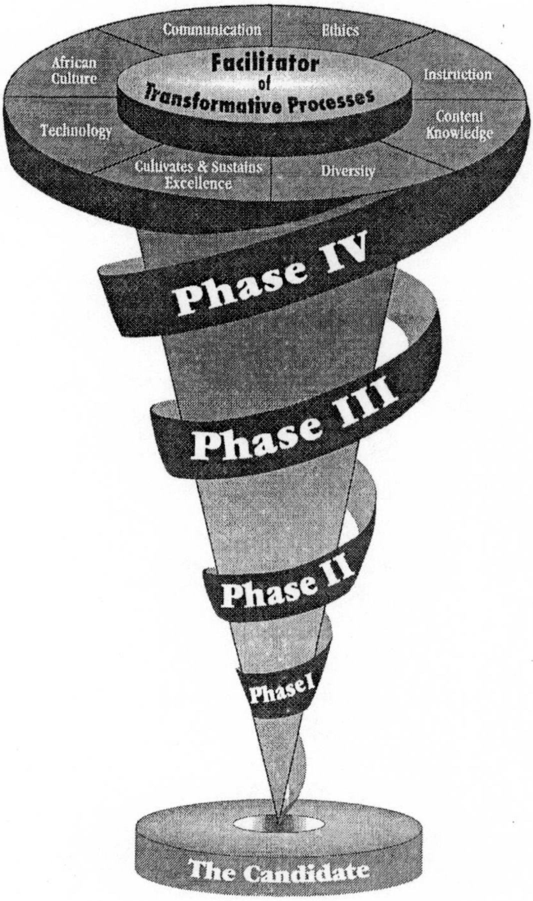

The journey commences when candidates enter the college and begin their progression through a curriculum that is spiral in nature. Beginning with Phase I and II, the pre-candidate (students declaring their intention of becoming a candidate) is presented with a broad base of content knowledge in the liberal arts. Pre-candidates obtain knowledge sufficient enough to support development of the knowledge, skills and dispositions critical to experiencing achievement and academic growth. Taking the required skills and content courses in general education and core course in professional education, the pre-candidate acquires content knowledge and problem solving skills such as identifying, planning, acting, postulating and assessing. Integrating knowledge from a variety of sources, the pre-candidate learns to synthesize ideas, information and data and comes to understand the interdependence among fields of study. In or before the last semester of core courses, pre-candidates make application for entry into their chosen teacher education program. Upon admission to the teacher education program, the status of 'candidate' is conferred.

The candidate then proceeds to Phase III of the spiral, comprised of courses in the major and concentration or cognate area as well as the professional core and related field experiences. This phase of the spiral provides the candidate with the opportunity to learn and demonstrate the content, pedagogical, and professional knowledge, skills, and dispositions necessary to help all students learn. Candidates engage in major and concentration courses that introduce them to more complex information in the content area of the discipline that they plan to teach. The principles and concepts of the discipline are thoroughly examined with candidates using and demonstrating their knowledge through inquiry, critical analysis and synthesis of the subject matter. In Phase II, the candidate is also provided with in-depth knowledge and instructional strategies focusing on pedagogical content knowledge. Pedagogical topics such as principles of learning and teaching, classroom management, strategies of evaluation and assessment, methods of integrating technology into instruction, curriculum, and social and cultural issues are examined. Field experiences offer teacher candidates opportunities to further develop and integrate their knowledge into the teaching and learning environment to facilitate the learning of subject matter by all students.

Further, in Phase III candidates are introduced to the general concepts, theories and research about effective teaching. They explore historical, sociological, philosophical and psychological understandings of schooling and education. They also examine the social, political, and economical context in which their students live. Knowledge about learn-ing, diversity, technology, professional ethics, legal and policy issues, pedagogical and the role and responsibilities of the teaching profession are also studied. These topics are introduced in survey courses while opportunities for applications are provided via Level I and Level II field experiences. Level-I field experiences offer candidates opportunities to observe education and school related activities in educational settings. Level II field experiences provide, through microteaching, initial prac-tice using knowledge about learning, diversity, and technology. Candi-dates illustrate more complex structures for analyzing, synthesizing and evaluating information as they construct new concepts and ideas by com-bining knowledge gained in Phase I and II with the new knowledge that is presented and constructed in Phase III.

Phase IV provides candidates opportunities under the supervision of clinical faculty and seminar instructors to use their content area, peda-gogical and professional content knowledge, skills and dispositions to plan, implement, and reflect on their instruction to facilitate learning of all students. In clinical practice candidates show increased competence in the eight performance outcome areas that designate them as a facilita-tor of transformative processes at a more complex and sophisticated level. They analyze, synthesize and evaluate schools, family and community context in which they work. Candidates work to improve learning by collaboratively partnering with other candidates, clinical faculty, coop-erating teachers, administrators and other school personnel. They gain hands-on practice with employing the transformative processes of knowl-edge construction, active thinking, self-evaluations (reflections), con-tinuous learning, and adaptations of dispositions. Teacher candidates demonstrate their more complex understanding in the ways they assess students, use assessment in instruction, and develop meaningful learning experiences for all students. Throughout both field experiences and clinical practice, clinical faculty assess and provide feedback to the candidates so that the information, when coupled with reflection, leads to an effective facilitator of transformative processes.

In sum, the spiral conveys that the candidate advances and constructs new knowledge in each new phase with information from the preceding phase. At each of the phases, faculty members: (a) encourage candidates to continually discover and construct new knowledge building upon what they have already learned; (b) present an organized body of new knowl-edge that is linked and related to information taught in the preceding phase; (c) model the practices that they teach; and (d) create environments appropriate to the candidates' state of understanding, thereby providing the candidate with a scaffold transformational experience. Eggen and Kauchak have described scaffolding as "assistance that allows candidates to complete tasks that cannot be completed independently when first introduced" (2001, p.58). Scaffolding supports candidates while they are being introduced to and becoming familiar with a competence. As the candidates' understandings and skills increase, less guidance and support is provided, thereby enabling them to eventually complete the competence independently. Because understanding the body of knowledge that is specific to teacher education requires persistence and hard work, faculty members teach, model, and encourage effective learning and problem-solving strategies as candidates advance through each phase toward becoming the facilitator of transformative processes.

Performance Outcomes

The teacher education unit recognizes that effective facilitators of transformative processes must demonstrate competencies that characterize the facilitator of transformative processes. Using the areas deemed as important to becoming effective teachers, the following performance based outcomes are designated as targets for development and assessment. Specifically the facilitator of transformative processes:

- Demonstrates mastery of content on African culture and can disseminate that knowledge to P-12 students to improve learning and self-esteem.
- Communicates effectively.
- Models ethical and professional behavior in all contexts
- Uses a variety of developmentally-appropriate pedagogical strategies in instructional settings.
- Demonstrates a broad base of content knowledge
- Is an effective teacher of PreK-12 students from diverse populations?
- Holds high expectations for self and all PreK-12 students.
- Is technologically proficient.

Professional Commitments and Dispositions

The Unit's conceptual framework draws on a knowledge base of theory and research, as well as practice that is aligned with the Tennessee State Department of Education Office of Teacher licensing. Guidelines and the Interstate New Teacher Assessment and Support Consortium (INTASC). The conceptual framework provides theoretical bases for the Unit's professional commitments and the dispositions that faculty must exhibit and candidates must attain to be effective facilitators of transformative processes. Faculty members in the Unit have observed that values they would like teacher candidates to posses are often set forth in isolation of the performances that are expected of them. The result is that many times candidates are unable to see the connections that are inherent in beliefs, values and actions.

Dispositions are defined in the Professional Standards for the Accreditation of Schools, Colleges and Departments of Education as "The values, commitments, and professional ethics that influence behaviors toward students, families, colleagues, and communities and affect student learning, motivation, and development as well as the educator's own professional growth. Dispositions are guided by beliefs and attitudes. . . . Dispositions are not usually assessed directly; instead they are assessed along with other performances in candidates' work with students' families, and communities." Unit faculty members affirm this definition and believe that all actions have dispositions, beliefs and values that serve as their foundation. For these reasons Unit faculty members carefully considered each of the performance outcomes of the conceptual framework to identify the deep-seated values that are within each of them. After many hours of reflection, consideration, and discussion, Unit faculty members identifies dispositions they deemed critical to becoming facilitators of transformative processes who are able to help all students learn. The facilitator of transformative processes:

- Respects cultural identity.
- Seeks first to understand.
- Models ethical and professional behaviors in all contexts.
- Demonstrates an appreciation of the need for the connectedness in teaching.
- Nurtures intellectual curiosity in self and others.
- Is respectful and open-minded.

- Demonstrates a commitment to life-long learning.
- Fosters a probing spirit in self and others.

As faculty members exhibit and model behaviors critical to helping all students learn, candidates are more likely to be successful in embodying these behaviors. Therefore, faculty members in the Teacher Education Unit model behaviors, and dispositions that are consistent with the Division's philosophy, purpose and conceptual framework. Unit faculty members continually evaluate their own teaching behaviors using principles of learning and teaching, current research, and best practices as knowledge bases. Thus, teaching methods and strategies implemented by unit faculty include the following actions:

1   Setting and articulating clear standards
2. Continuing professional growth and development in preparation for teaching
3. Creating an open teaching and learning environment that is accepting of all students' ideas
4. Providing a broad structure that defines expectations for candidate performance yet allows them to set their own pace
5. Assessing regularly to re-teach concepts and skills that have not been mastered
6. Modifying instructional methods, practices, strategies and curricula to include technology and innovative reforms as needed and as identified through continuous assessment and evaluation
7. Supporting learning for all candidates by integrating diversity concepts across the curriculum
8. Using and integrating educational and informational technology across the curriculum to help all candidates learn

Commitment to Diversity

The Unit's conceptual framework guides the preparation of candidates as they advance through the program and towards becoming facilitators of transformative processes, ultimately enabling them to help all students achieve. Unresponsive and dysfunctional education systems and practices plague not only African ancestry citizens but other communities as well. Specifically, Native American/Indian, Hispanic/Latino communities and other peoples, who represent diverse cultural worldviews, are marginalized and under-served by educational practices in the United States. Dave Else (2000) in Issues Facing People of Color in Education reports Octavio Paz as saying "life is plurality, death is uniformity. Every view that becomes extinct, every culture that disappears, diminishes a possibility of life." Banks, (2001) asserts "Issues, problems, and opportunities related to diversity are still paramount for the nation at the beginning of the twenty-first century." Students in the United States are becoming more diverse while the nations' teachers are becoming more European American and female. Coupled with the fact that "few of our nation's schools have become multicultural in their vision or practice" (Bennett, 1999), it is very likely that students will attend schools where their culture and worldviews are not valued. "A teaching force unbalanced in its representation of the nation's population is inappropriate at best and has profound implications for the country. The United States cannot have a functioning democracy without respect for and involvement of all of its citizens. . . . To do so, would be to deny the contributions of many American citizens and an even greater number of the world's citizens" (Else, 2000 p. 1). Banks (2001 p. xxi) points out that a major goal of Teacher Education Programs should be to help all teachers acquire the knowledge, values, and behaviors needed to work effectively with students from diverse groups." Acknowledging these conditions and needs, Unit faculty explicated as major commitments, knowledge, skills and dispositions, related to diversity and integrated them throughout the curriculum, field experiences and clinical practice. They are delineated in the rubric that is a part of this document.

Commitment to Technology

Jonassen, Peck and Wilson (1999) maintain that the primary goal of education at all levels should be to engage students in meaningful learning, which occurs when students are actively making meaning. Students need to learn how to "recognize and solve problems, comprehend new phenomena, construct mental models of those phenomena, and set goals to regulate their own learning (learn how to learn)" (Jonassen, Peck and Wilson 1999). Technology can be employed to actively engage students in their own learning and in thinking about their own thinking (metacognitive processes). They include:

- Technology as tools to support knowledge construction
- Technology as information vehicles for exploring knowledge to support learning-by-constructing
- Technology as context to support learning-by-doing
- Technology as social medium to support learning by conversing
- Technology as intellectual partner to support learning-by-reflecting

The Unit is committed to assuring that candidates experience technology in ways that facilitate the development of the above skills. To that end, outcomes for the teacher candidate have been aligned with professional literature, state guidelines and International Society for Technology in Education (ISTE) standards and set forth in the conceptual framework. Specifically teacher candidates who complete teacher education programs at LeMoyne-Owen College will use technology in developmentally and culturally appropriate ways to educate all students. Therefore they will be competent in the following areas:

- Technology and instruction
- Technology and professional growth and productivity
- Computer operation skills
- Design and management of learning environments/resources
- Technology use and diversity

The Unit offers opportunities for teacher candidates to examine various paradigms, canons, and knowledge systems that under gird the dominant as well as little known curricula. Technology is a major tool used by the unit to enhance teacher candidate's ability to make meaning, reflect, communicate, collaborate and evaluate teaching and learning.

Knowledge Bases

Ladson-Billings (1994 p. ix) points out that "No challenge has been more daunting in the United States than that of improving the academic achievement of African American Students." A history of denial of and exclusion from educational opportunities for students of African descent continues to make the "quest for quality education an elusive dream for the African American community" (Ladson-Billings, 1994 p. ix). A chronicle of the history of Africans in the United States illustrates the importance that the African American community places on education. From clandestine schools during slavery, to public school legislation initiated and passed by Black legislators during the Reconstruction Congress, to the initiation and implementation of private academies and colleges, to the civil rights movement, to school reform, African Americans have demonstrated that they believe that education is the primary means to a better quality of life in these United States. Anderson (1997 pp. 189-90) reports that "following emancipation, no measures were taken to identify and correct the psychological, social, economic and educational damage that 260 years of slavery and abuse had inflicted on African people. The dominant society pretended that slavery had never happened. While a peonage system was being prepared for blacks, the new public policies introduced them into separate and inferior public schools. But, even under these poorest of educational conditions, blacks were able to reduce their illiteracy from 98% in the mid-1860s to 40% by 1900, and to just 20% by 1920." Spring (1997) supports the findings and reports an illiteracy rate for African Americans of only 10% in 1950.

Today, while still holding fast to this belief in the power of education, people of African ancestry in the United States find they are representing a historical anomaly. African Americans are on a downhill course, with each succeeding generation completing fewer years of school than the last (Anderson, 1994; Ladson Billings, 1994; Ornstein, 1999; and Washington and Andrews, 1998). Washington and Andrews in Children of 2010, a 1998 publication, reveal that African American and Hispanic American students score lower than their white peers on standard academic achievement measures. They point out that school counselors continue to advise these students into non-college bound academic and vocational tracks that not only do not prepare them for college but also do not prepare them to enter into the job market with adequate skills to compete for life sustaining employment. Ladson-Billings (1994) states it thusly:

> African American students lag far behind their white counterparts on standard academic achievement measures. At the same time, the very society that experienced a civil rights revolution finds itself locked in the grips of racism and discrimination and a seemingly eternal ideology of white supremacy (italics added). Almost forty years after a Supreme Court decision declaring separate but equal schools to be illegal, most African American students still attend schools that are in reality segregated and unequal.

Today segregation occurs within the same building—ability tracking and resource room—and from building to building—magnet schools, optional schools and other specialized programs as in Advanced Placement (AP) and Gifted Education. Joel Spring (1997) contends that "[t]he history of African American education is highlighted by both the denial of education in order to continue economic exploitation and the use of segregated education to assure an inexpensive source of labor."

Unfortunately, in United States educational systems, a manipulative and destructive myth about African students and their potential for being excellently educated has prevailed over time. The myth is "without access to white culture, white teachers, white schools, and white leadership, black people cannot adequately educate their children, nor hope to create a decent future for them" (Delpit in Foster, 1997, p. ix). The Civil Rights movement inadvertently assisted in constructing the idea that African Americans agreed with the larger society's view of African ancestry peoples' abilities and intensified the myth. Research as well as popular media has attested that the real reason for the struggle was to gain the same benefits and resources for black children that were ordinarily supplied for white children. "But truth has little ammunition against a destructive myth" (Delpit 1997), when that myth reinforces the ideal of the nation—that of white supremacy. An outcome of this myth is that African American students and their families are socialized, through educational systems and institutions as well as research and literature, to believe that their abilities and achievements emanate from sources outside themselves. Consequently, rather than believing that their academic success is a result of their own genius, capacity and efforts to study, learn, develop and change, the students and their families believe that their academic successes lie in the will and intent of the teacher, the school system or 'luck'. As a consequence, they attempt to live in accord with the definitions of reality established by the socialization they receive in the schools. They then adjust their thinking and learning to conform to those definitions of reality. As a result, African ancestry students in United States Schools often do not become competent and able learners and thinkers. (Ennis, 1998) describes the critical thinker as one who is able to "use evidence skillfully and impartially, to organize thoughts and articulate them concisely and coherently, to suspend judgment when sufficient evidence is not present, to support a decision, and to apply problem-solving techniques in domains other than those in which they are learned. Unfortunately many students graduate high school without these abilities. Moreover, African American students graduate having little knowledge of themselves as African peoples temporally, chronologically, geographically, historically or culturally.

Hilliard (1997) reports forecasts for African Americans made by W.E.B. DuBois four years after the Brown decision in *Whither Now and Why* (1960). Dubois forecasted that in years to come in the United States: 1) there would be fewer African teachers, 2) African children would be taught in a physically and emotionally uncomfortable environment, 3) there would be an increase in the African student dropout rates and a decrease in Black college attendance, 4) African universities would disappear, and 5) African history would be taught rarely, if at all. Recent educational history has confirmed DuBois' predictions.

Education systems do not only under serve and under develop African Ancestry citizens of the United States; students from other communities and diverse populations are also disenfranchised and underserved. "Issues, problems and opportunities related to diversity are still paramount for the nation at the beginning of the twenty-first century" (Banks, 2001 p. xxi). Students in the United States are becoming more and diverse while the nation's teachers are becoming more and more European American and female. Banks points out that a major goal of Teacher Education Programs should be to "help teachers acquire the knowledge, values, and behaviors needed to work effectively with students from diverse groups." Additionally, "teachers need to acquire the knowledge and skills required to help European American students develop cross-cultural knowledge and competencies" (Banks, 2001 p. xxi). A major assumption here is that the primary goal of teachers is to foster intellectual, social, emotional, physical and spiritual development of all students so that they might reach their highest potential. A correlating idea is that each student must then be provided with an equal opportunity to learn. As cognitive (learning) styles are to a great extent culturally based, an education that is multicultural is an imperative if all students are to be provided the opportunity to learn. Bennett (1999) asserts, "Few of our nation's schools, have become multicultural in their vision or practice" (p. xi). She states, "They are hampered by societal policies and practices, often beyond their control, that impede reform of formal and hidden curricula." Bennett also later states, "teachers who are uninformed about cultural diversity, whose knowledge of history and current events is monocultural in scope, and who are unaware of their own prejudices are likely to hinder the academic success and personal development of many students, however unintentional this may be."

LeMoyne-Owen College administrators, staff and faculty members are committed to addressing the current crisis areas in the education of African American students and to actively work toward transforming its surrounding community—a community that reflects the predictions made by DuBois in 1960. LeMoyne-Owen College has initiated and assumed the leadership role in the development of a Community Teaching and Learning (Alliance). The foundation for the Community Teaching and Learning Alliance has been established through a series of meetings with leaders of community agencies that are directly involved in the development, socialization and education of children and youth in the LeMoyne-Owen College area. This community group, along with LeMoyne-Owen College faculty and other leading educators, defined The Community Teaching and Learning Alliance and its mission as follows: "The Community Teaching and Learning Alliance is a collaborative cohesive collective, committed to promoting a caring environment for children families, and elders. The focal point of the Alliance is the development of critical literacy and the actualizing of critical consciousness by all members of the community. The Alliance will work to nurture, support, and transform the total learning processes of community members and thereby transform the total person. It values the involvement of all constituents in the community." LeMoyne-Owen College continues to facilitate a planning process that will formalize the Alliance, establish principles of collaboration, develop its membership, actualize its mission and define its operations.

Members of the LeMoyne-Owen College family believe that the Alliance is an important partner in the transformation of schools, teacher training and thereby the community. As such, the Division of Education is committed to educating teachers who are dedicated to, and skilled in, facilitating transformative processes for themselves, their students and consequently their communities. Hilliard (1997) supports this idea by asserting:

> African teachers hold the future of African people in their hands. If the African teachers and other teachers [italics added] who have access to our children are prepared, conscious, and willing, the development of African children knows no bounds. Preparation, however, is the key and before beginning the educational relationship with students, Afri-

can teachers must first become transformed, (italics added) whole, productive, and conscious beings. Only then can they transform students (p.99).

Hilliard goes on to say:

Any approach to educating African teachers, and any teachers who will work to transform African students, must take into account two realities: 1) the African cultural tradition and 2) the political and economic environment within which people of African descent are situated—especially for the last four centuries. The intersection of culture and the political economy has produced the context for socialization and education, which is African Americans' current problem.

When educating teachers who will work to transform students, major considerations that must be taken into account are knowledge construction and transformative approaches to education. Knowledge and the control of knowledge is a powerful tool of the dominant culture and serve to maintain the power structure within the United States. Knowledge and paradigms consistent with the interests, goals, and assumptions of the dominant culture are institutionalized within the schools and universities as well as within the popular culture. A concealed yet purposeful function of such knowledge is to legitimize the dominant political, economic, and cultural arrangements within society. Teacher candidates must be educated to investigate what knowledge they are exposed to as well as the ways in which they acquire, and are taught to examine, and evaluate knowledge. The examination as well as the practice of knowledge construction must become an indispensable part of teacher education programs so that teacher candidates begin to understand the limits of knowledge and the extent to which knowledge is a social construction that reflects the social, political, and cultural context in which it is formulated. Participating in this process will enable teacher candidates to understand how the dominant culture in the nation formulates, shapes, and disseminates knowledge that supports their interests and legitimizes their power (Banks 1994 p. 148).

Disenfranchised groups frequently object to the dominant cultural group's paradigms, knowledge systems, and perspectives to little avail because institutionalization of these structures within the nation leave almost no room for purposeful and meaningful change that will result in a better education for all students. This coupled with the presentation of a curriculum that holds European American ideals as the norm and standard diminishes democratic values and beliefs. Banks (2001) proffers a *Transformative Approach* to curriculum and teaching. He maintains that a *Transformative Approach* changes the basic assumptions of the curriculum and enables students to view ideas, issues, themes, and problems from several cultural perspectives and points of view. The key curriculum issues involved in the *Transformative Approach* does not mean adding a long list of ethnic groups, heroes, and contributions rather, it represents the infusion of various perspectives, frames of reference, and content from various groups that will extend students' understanding of the nature, development and complexity of societies.

Historically and currently teacher candidates, most often, acquire knowledge in a non-analytical milieu and in environments that do not engage them in knowledge construction and transformative processes. Consequently candidates exit teacher education programs with many misconceptions about themselves as well as members of other cultural groups, not knowing how to assess, evaluate and transform themselves, the curriculum or their students.

Students learn—develop and change—from experiencing multiple occurrences that include other people, objects, events, activities, actions, behaviors, procedures and operations. Learners' translations of their experiences are formulated as a result of what they already know, their thinking about, and reflecting on their experiences and their thinking processes. Jerome Bruner (1990) called this process "meaning making," which is the foundational framework on which constructivist education is built. Jonassen, et. al. (1999) states in Learning With Technology that their methods of using technology for learning are grounded in Constructivist ideas about teaching and learning. Those ideas embody the Unit's philosophy that teaching is facilitating the development of knowledge, skills, dispositions and the intellect of students—bringing out the latent qualities that students already possess. Constructivism supports the belief that all learners have, existing within them, the capability and competence to fulfill their chosen career goals. Constructivism supports the beliefs that "To be human is to possess 'will' and 'intent'—divine intelligence—and to have the capacity to develop and change" (Nobles, 1986 p. 92). Jonassen, et. al (1999 pp. 3-11) catalog the major assumptions that under gird Constructivism; and in doing so illustrate this belief.

1. Knowledge is constructed, not transmitted.
2. Knowledge construction results from activity, so knowledge is embedded in activity.
3. Knowledge is anchored in and indexed by the context in which the learning activity occurs.
4. Meaning is in the mind of the knower.
5. There are multiple perspectives in the world.
6. Meaning making is prompted by a problem, question, confusion, disagreement, or dissonance (a need or desire to know) and so involves personal ownership of that problem.
7. Knowledge building requires articulation, expression, or representation of what is learned (meaning that is constructed.)
8. Meaning may also be shared with others, so meaning making can also result from conversation.
9. Meaning making and thinking is distributed throughout our tools, culture, and community.
10. Not all meaning is created equally.

Further, Jonassen, et al. (1999) maintain that the primary goal of education at all levels should be to engage students in meaningful learning, which occurs when they are actively making meaning. Students need to learn how to learn. "If technologies are used to support learning they will not be used as delivery vehicles (such as in computer-assisted instruction, tutorials, drill-and-practice)" (pg. 13). Technology can be employed to actively engage students in their own learning and in thinking about their own thinking (metacognitive processes). Jonassen, et. al (1999) has suggested some useful roles for technology in learning. They include:

Technology as tools to support knowledge construction:
> for representing learners' ideas, understandings, and beliefs
> for producing organized, multimedia knowledge bases by learners

Technology as information vehicles for exploring knowledge to support learning-by-constructing:
> for accessing needed information
> for comparing perspectives, beliefs, and world views

Technology as context to support learning-by-doing:

> for representing and simulating meaningful real-world problems, situations and contexts.
>
> for representing beliefs, perspectives, arguments, and stories of others

Technology as social medium to support learning by conversing:

> for collaborating with others
>
> for discussing, arguing, and building consensus among members of a community
>
> for supporting discourse among knowledge-building communities

Technology as intellectual partner (Jonassen 1996) to support learning-by-reflecting:

> for helping learners to articulate and represent what they know
>
> for reflecting on what they have learned and how they came to know it
>
> for supporting learners' internal negotiations and meaning making
>
> for constructing personal representations of meaning
>
> for supporting mindful thinking. (pp. 13-14).

Grabe and Grabe (2001) affirm Jonassen's suggestions and assert that "when students play a more active role in their own learning the teacher's role shifts from dispenser of knowledge to facilitator of learning". This supports the idea that the students accomplish learning and the teacher's role is to consider how to assist the students. (p. 12). An assessment of the use of technology in the schools consistently contends that technology in academia isolates students from each other and from the teacher. When technology is used within the structure of Constructivist ideas students and teachers are engaged in a learning community that supports and strengthens each participants learning.

As we prepare teachers who are facilitators of transformative processes we provide opportunities for teacher candidates to examine various paradigms, canons, and knowledge systems that under gird the "dominant curriculum" (Banks, 2001). Teacher candidates also have the opportunity to examine knowledge systems, paradigms, and canons that writers of the "dominant curriculum" avoid. Technology is a major tool used by the unit to enhance teacher candidate's ability to make meaning, reflect, communicate, collaborate, and evaluate teaching and learning.

Candidate Assessment

The Division of Education's assessment system outlines the means by which the candidate's proficiencies are regularly assessed. Measures for evaluating candidate proficiencies are delineated in the rubric below. Further, the Division of Education's performance outcomes are aligned with the College's graduating senior competencies, which are also stated on the rubric.

LeMoyne-Owen College Division of Education
Performance Outcomes

LeMoyne-Owen College Graduating Senior Competence(s):
1 – Think creatively, critically, logically and analytically using both quantitative and qualitative methods for solving problems.
4 -- Appreciate, understand and know the foundations of the Afro-centric perspective.
10 -- Attain critical skills, frame of reference and understanding to appreciate and discriminate between artistic achievement

Division of Education Performance Outcome(s): 1 -- Demonstrates mastery of content on African Culture and can disseminate that knowledge to PreK-12 students to improve learning and self-esteem. (Hilliard 1997)

Competency Rubric					
Indicators	Unsatisfactory	Satisfactory	Proficient	Outstanding	Evidence
A African cultural deep structure and peoples	Has limited knowledge of African cultural structures and describes African peoples from the worldview of the Colonizers and the perpetrators of the slave trade. Articulates information about African American culture as though it originated in the U. S. and has little to do with Africa	Knowledge of African Cultural structures is at the surface level Candidate gathers information from limited sources in the dominant curriculum and is able to summarize the information.	Describes and uses knowledge of African cultural deep structures and peoples. The candidate draws information from several sources including those not from the dominant curriculum The candidate identifies cultural structures, concepts, ideas, and practices that have been maintained by African ancestry people living in the United States.	Analyzes and evaluates African cultural deep structures drawing on several references and distinguishes between varying points of view. The candidate identifies cultural structures, concepts, philosophies, ideas, ideologies and practices that have been maintained in the African Diaspora and can explain them making connections between Continental Africans and those in the Diaspora. Candidate relates the knowledge to the teaching and learning process to transform educational curricula and practices.	Course embedded, Benchmark & Portfolio assessments Reflections Journals
B African peoples History and Geography	Candidate relies heavily on mainstream textbooks to superficially describe and chart African history and cultural themes from enslavement and colonization onward citing themes in popular media and deficit model literature	Candidate is consistently able to describe and chart African history and cultural themes from ancient times identifying changes in thought and practices over time within the evolution of African history and culture.	Candidate distinguishes between African history and cultural themes from ancient times identifying changes in thought and practices that occurred as a result of evolution, time and space (Geography).	Candidate diagrams and categorizes African history and cultural themes from ancient times and can explain and interpret changing patterns in relation to evolution, time, space and political context.	Course embedded assessments Portfolio assessments Reflections Journals Field Experiences and Clinical Practice assessments
C Political economy and contexts	Describes the history of education in the United States as though it was a parallel experience for all people living in the U S (shared history syndrome)	Accurately describes the history of education for African Americans in the United States. The candidate can match the economic conditions of the country with the kinds of education that were publicly provided for African Americans	Accurately describes the history of education for African Americans in the United States The candidate can relate how the political economy produced differential contexts for the socialization and education of African descent people in the United States	Candidate accurately describes African American education history in the U S The candidate analyzes the political economy and links it to the type of education available to African Americans The candidate relates the connection between "Mis-education" and the political economy.	Course embedded assessments. Portfolio assessments. Reflections Journals Field Experiences and Clinical Practice assessments

LeMoyne-Owen College Division of Education
Performance Outcomes

LeMoyne-Owen College Graduating Senior Competence(s):
1 – Think creatively, critically, logically and analytically using both quantitative and qualitative methods for solving problems
4 -- Appreciate, understand and know the foundations of the Afro-centric perspective
10 -- Attain critical skills, frame of reference and understanding to appreciate and discriminate between artistic achievement.

Division of Education Performance Outcome(s): 1 -- Demonstrates mastery of content on African Culture and can disseminate that knowledge to PreK-12 students to improve learning and self-esteem. (Hilliard 1997)

Competency Rubric					
Indicators	Unsatisfactory	Satisfactory	Proficient	Outstanding	Evidence
D. White supremacy: power & education	Limited awareness of the impact of white supremacy on Education in the United States. The candidate isolates school activity from that of the broader society and uses a mono-cultural perspective to examine school effectiveness for **all** students	Places school activities within the context of the greater U S society and examine the ways that school policies, procedures, materials, and resources are distributed among students to maintain the *status quo*	Examines, analyzes school policies, procedures, materials, and resource distribution and describes how white supremacy influences the distribution of goods and services in education systems The candidate can identify how this impacts educational outcomes	Deconstructs school policies and procedures, the dominant curriculum, the use and allocation of materials and resources to assist students in analyzing and reconstructing knowledge about their ancestry, families and personal abilities and to become fully engaged in their own learning.	

LeMoyne-Owen College Division of Education
Performance Outcomes

LeMoyne-Owen College Graduating Senior Competence(s):
1 – Think creatively, critically, logically and analytically using both quantitative and qualitative methods for solving problems.
2 -- Communicate effectively (listen, speak, read and write) on formal and informal levels.
10 -- Attain critical skills, frame of reference and understanding to appreciate and discriminate between artistic achievement
Division of Education Performance Outcome(s): 2 -- Communicates effectively

Competency Rubric					
Indicators	Unsatisfactory	Satisfactory	Proficient	Outstanding	Evidence
A Communication.	Rarely uses appropriate standard English when speaking and writing	Speaks and writes clearly, correctly and distinctly to communicate the objectives to the learners and to guide instruction	Uses standard English and knowledge of effective verbal and non-verbal communication to foster active inquiry, collaboration and supportive interaction in the classroom. (INTASC)	Consistently uses standard English and knowledge of effective verbal and non-verbal communication to foster active inquiry, collaboration and supportive interaction in the classroom and professional forums	Course embedded assessments Portfolio assessments Reflections Journals Field Experiences and Clinical Practice assessments
B Non-Verbal Cues	Limited understanding and use of non-verbal cues in communication.	Understands how non-verbal cues affect communication and demonstrates the use of non-verbal cues in positive ways	Understands and frequently uses non-verbal cues to enhance communication and transform the teacher-learning process	Consistently uses non-verbal cues to enhance communication with students, parents and professionals to transform the teaching learning process	Course embedded assessments. Portfolio assessments Reflections Journals Field Experiences and Clinical Practice assessments
C Audiences and settings	Limited ability to effectively communicate in speaking and writing to various audiences	Identifies intended audience and setting to select and use appropriate modes for effective communication	Differentiates between audiences and settings based on abilities and cultural differences to communicate effectively (SDE)	Identifies and distinguishes among setting, audiences' cultures and abilities to converse effectively via multiple modes in classrooms and various forums.	Course embedded assessments Portfolio assessments. Reflections Journals Field Experiences and Clinical Practice assessments
D Communication of student's progress	Limited ability to communicate progress and results to students, parents, and colleagues	Maintains useful records of student work and progress and communicates results to the students, parents and appropriate colleagues.	Maintains useful records of student work and progress and communicates results to the student, parents, and colleagues to foster positive interaction	Consistently maintains useful records of student work and progress and communicates results to the students, their parents and appropriate colleagues Fosters positive interaction with parents and colleagues to engage them in support of student learning.	Course embedded assessments Portfolio assessments Reflections Journals Field Experiences and Clinical Practice assessments
E Technology.	Limited ability to select appropriate technology tools to communicate concepts.	Selects appropriate technological tools for communicating concepts and solving problems.	Selects and designs appropriate technological tools for communicating concepts and solving problems	Selects, evaluates and creates appropriate technological tools for communicating concepts and solving problems.	Course embedded assessments Portfolio assessments Reflections & Journals Field Experiences and Clinical Practice assessments

LeMoyne-Owen College Division of Education
Performance Outcomes

LeMoyne-Owen College Graduating Senior Competence(s):
1 – Think creatively, critically, logically and analytically using both quantitative and qualitative methods for solving problems
3 – Distinguish, clarify and refine personal values for the attainment of richer self-perception and relate those values to the value systems of others
10 -- Attain critical skills, frame of reference and understanding to appreciate and discriminate between artistic achievement

Division of Education Performance Outcome(s): 3* – Models ethical and professional behavior in all contexts

Competency Rubric					
Indicators	**Unsatisfactory**	**Satisfactory**	**Proficient**	**Outstanding**	**Evidence**
A Reflective practitioner (INTASC)	Seldom reflects about practice and evaluates the effect of his/her choices and actions on others Seldom seeks opportunities for professional growth	Is a reflective practitioner who continually evaluates the effects of his/her choices and actions on others (students, families, and other professionals in the learning community)	Is a reflective practitioner who evaluates the effects of his/her choices and actions and analyzes the results to transform professional and classroom activities	Is a reflective practitioner who evaluates the effects of his/her choices and actions, analyzes the results, and creates a better process for transforming classroom practice	Course embedded assessments Portfolio assessments Reflections Journals Field Experiences and Clinical Practice assessments
B Intercultural competence skills (Bennett)	Limited effort is made to strengthen his/her intercultural competence skills	Continually studies and works to strengthen his/her intercultural competence skills.	Analyzes areas of need for improvement and growth and continually studies and works to strengthen his her intercultural competence skills to transform classrooms	Investigates his/her intercultural competence skills and identifies areas that need improvement The Candidate compiles and evaluates new materials for incorporation in his/her knowledge, skills, and dispositions to transform him/herself and his/her students.	Course embedded assessments Portfolio assessments Reflections Journals Field Experiences and Clinical Practice assessments.
C School, parent and community relationships *Both a performance outcome and disposition	Limited effort to foster relationships with school colleagues, parents and agencies in the larger community to support student's learning and well being	Fosters relationships with school colleagues, parents, and agencies in the larger community to support student's learning and well-being.	Fosters relationships with schools colleagues, parents and agencies and analyzes how these groups can develop new initiatives for student learning and to facilitate transformative processes	Fosters relationships with school personnel, colleagues, parents and agencies to support learning Analyzes how these groups can develop and create new activities, and evaluate resulting transformation of student's learning.	Course embedded assessments. Portfolio assessments. Reflections Journals Field Experiences and Clinical Practice assessments

LeMoyne-Owen College Division of Education
Performance Outcomes

LeMoyne-Owen College Graduating Senior Competence(s):
1 – Think creatively, critically, logically and analytically using both quantitative and qualitative methods for solving problems
6 -- Appreciate, understand, know and pursue the principles, methods and subject matter, which underlay the major discipline.
10 -- Attain critical skills, frame of reference and understanding to appreciate and discriminate between artistic achievement

Division of Education Performance Outcome(s): 4 -- Uses a variety of developmentally appropriate pedagogical strategies in instructional settings.

		Competency Rubric			
Indicators	Unsatisfactory	Satisfactory	Proficient	Outstanding	Evidence
A. Student Learning, Development, and Assessment	Marginally understands stages of development and principles of learning as a means to assess student needs for planning instruction	Explains how children learn and develop Uses this knowledge, subject matter, curriculum and learning theory to plan instruction	Designs and implements developmentally appropriate instructional plans using data from assessment of student needs, and knowledge of subject matter, learning and curriculum theory	Evaluates, designs and implements developmentally appropriate instructional plans, methods, materials, and technology using data from assessment of student needs, and knowledge of subject matter, learning and curriculum theory	Course embedded assessments Portfolio assessments Reflections Journals Field Experiences and Clinical Practice assessments
B. Principles of effective Instruction	Selects and creates an integrated learning experience that is minimally appropriate, and not based upon principles of effective instruction	Demonstrates ability to select and create integrated learning experiences that are developmentally appropriate, relevant to students' developmental needs, and are based on principles of effective instruction.	Selects, and creates integrated learning experiences that are developmentally appropriate, relevant to students, and are based upon principles of effective instruction including technology	Evaluates, selects, creates, and implement integrated learning experiences that are developmentally appropriate, relevant to students, using instructional methods, materials, and technology that are based upon principles of effective instruction	Course-embedded assessment Portfolio Assessment Clinical Practice interview Field Experiences and Clinical Practice assessments
C. Learning Experience Connected to Real Life	Limited ability to implement instruction that connects learning to real life	Identifies, selects and implements long-range instructional goals that are connected to the student's experiential background.	Produces long-range instructional goals that are connected to the student's experiential background and implement daily lesson plans, which effectively integrates subject matter goals and real life experiences of the student.	Discriminates among, produces and implements interdisciplinary long-range instructional goals that are connected to the student's experiential background.	Course-embedded assessment Portfolio Assessment Field Experiences and Clinical Practice assessments
D Assessment Strategies	Minimal use of formal or informal assessment strategies to communicate learning results with respect to student abilities, skills, and core concepts	Understands and uses formal and informal assessment strategies to ensure the continuous intellectual, social, and physical development of the learner	Differentiates among and uses formal and informal assessment strategies to assess learning and provide integrated instruction that supports the transformation of the intellectual, social, and physical abilities of the learner	Compares formal and informal assessment strategies to implement appropriate methods for assessing student learning and to produce integrated instruction that supports the transformation of the intellectual, social, and physical abilities of the learner.	Course-embedded assessment Portfolio assessment Lesson Plans Field Experiences and Clinical Practice assessments.
E. Family and Community Relationships	Limited awareness of relationship of the subject matter, student, the family, and the community to curriculum goals.	Understands the relationship of the subject matter, student, the family, and the community to curriculum goals (INTASC)	Consistently modifies instruction based on knowledge of subject matters student, family and the community relationship to curriculum goals	Reflects on and evaluates instruction based on knowledge of subject matter, and the student, family and community relationships to curriculum goals.	Portfolio assessments. Reflections Journals Field Experiences and Clinical Practice assessments

LeMoyne-Owen College Division of Education
Performance Outcomes

LeMoyne-Owen College Graduating Senior Competence(s):
1 – Think creatively, critically, logically and analytically using both quantitative and qualitative methods for solving problems
6 -- Appreciate, understand, know and pursue the principles, methods and subject matter, which underlay the major discipline
10 -- Attain critical skills, frame of reference and understanding to appreciate and discriminate between artistic achievement

Division of Education Performance Outcome(s): 5 – Demonstrates a broad base of content knowledge

Competency Rubric					
Indicators	Unsatisfactory	Satisfactory	Proficient	Outstanding	Evidence
A Structure of Discipline(s)	Displays limited awareness of the central concepts, tools of inquiry, and structures of the discipline(s) he/she teaches	Understands the central concepts, tools of inquiry, and structures of the discipline(s) he or she teaches (INTASC)	Creates learning experiences that make the central concepts, tools of inquiry, and structures of the disciplines meaningful for students	Uses tools of interdisciplinary approaches to teaching and learning that engages students in interpreting ideas from a variety of perspectives	Course embedded assessments. Portfolio assessments Reflections Journals Unit Plans Lesson Plans Teaching Video
B Interdisciplinary Knowledge	Has limited knowledge of the interdisciplinary relationships of various disciplines	Uses interdisciplinary learning experiences that allow students to integrate subject matter, skills, and methods of inquiry	Creates interdisciplinary learning experiences that allow students to integrate subject matter, skills, and methods of inquiry	Evaluates, modifies and incorporates interdisciplinary learning experiences that allow students to integrate subject matter, skills, and methods of inquiry.	Course embedded assessments Portfolio assessments Reflections Journals Unit Plans Lesson Plans Teaching Video
C Instructional Strategies	Uses limited methods of instruction relying heavily on direct instruction to teach students content knowledge.	Uses and describes a variety of instructional strategies (INTASC) to teach students a broad base of content knowledge	Prepares and uses a variety of instructional strategies (INTASC) to teach students a broad base of content knowledge Candidate facilitates student's development of critical thinking, and problem solving, skills to interpret and use content	Appraises and modifies a variety of instructional strategies (INTASC) to teach students a broad base of content knowledge. Candidate facilitates student's development of critical thinking, and problem solving, skills to interpret and use content	Course embedded assessments. Portfolio assessments Reflections Journals Unit plans Lesson plans Teaching videos Field experiences and Clinical Practice assessments

LeMoyne-Owen College Division of Education
Performance Outcomes

LeMoyne-Owen College Graduating Senior Competence(s):
1 – Think creatively, critically, logically and analytically using both quantitative and qualitative methods for solving problems
5 -- Appreciate, understand and know the foundations of diverse cultures in the context of a global community; and
7 -- Accept social responsibility and provide service to humankind
10 -- Attain critical skills, frame of reference and understanding to appreciate and discriminate between artistic achievement.

Division of Education Performance Outcome(s): 6 -- Is an effective teacher of PreK-12 students from diverse populations

Competency Rubric					
Indicators	**Unsatisfactory**	**Satisfactory**	**Proficient**	**Outstanding**	**Evidence**
A Culture and Learning	Has limited understanding of how students differ in their approaches to learning and how cultures drive the differences	Understands how students differ in their approaches to learning and how culture drives the differences (INTASC)	Understands how students differ in their approaches to learning and how culture drives the differences and creates instructional opportunities that are adapted to diverse learners.	Consistently creates and adapts instructional techniques to students of diverse cultural and language backgrounds and creates an inclusive learning community in which individual and cultural differences are respected	Course embedded assessments. Portfolio assessments Reflections Journals Field experiences and Clinical Practice assessments
B Multiple historical perspectives (Bennett)	Has limited awareness of multiple historical perspectives of students attending schools in the United States	Knows and can explain multiple historical perspectives – particularly those of students attending schools in the United States	Identifies, points out and explains multiple historical perspectives and can integrate the knowledge into instruction	Consistently compares and contrasts historical perspectives; and gathers, organizes and integrates appropriate information instruction.	Course embedded assessments. Portfolio assessments Reflections Journals Field experiences and Clinical Practice assessments
C Intra (Richardson, 2000) and Inter (Banks, 2001 and Bennett, 1999) cultural competence	Has limited content area knowledge that reflects his/her own culture and that of others	Uses content area knowledge that reflects his/her own culture and that of others and can integrate this knowledge into instruction	Can categorize and compile content area knowledge that reflects his/her own culture and that of others and can integrate this knowledge into instruction to transform teaching.	Interprets and appraises content area knowledge that reflects his/her own culture and that of others and can integrate this knowledge into instruction to transform teaching	Portfolio assessments Reflections Journals Field experiences and Clinical Practice assessments.
D Content Integration (Banks, 1999)	Has limited awareness of content information about various cultural groups, which make up the United States	Has knowledge of and can effectively use the knowledge about selected groups' histories, perspectives and worldviews	Has an informed historical perspective, including an understanding of how one's own society developed in relation to other societies; and can communicate that knowledge to others	Integrates a variety of cultural perspectives and world views as well as group histories in order to illustrate key concepts, principles, generalizations and theories of discipline that are being taught.	Portfolio assessments Journals Field experiences and Clinical Practice assessments
E Equity Pedagogy (Banks, 2001)	Has limited ability to modify teaching in ways that will facilitate academic achievement of students from diverse racial, cultural, and social class groups	Selects methods and materials to modify teaching in ways that facilitate academic achievement of students from diverse racial cultural and social class groups	Designs and incorporates teaching strategies consistent with the racial, cultural and social class of the students	Evaluates and modifies teaching strategies consistent with the racial, cultural and social class of the students to transform the teaching and learning process	Portfolio Reflections Journals Field experiences and Clinical Practice assessments.
F Global Society	Demonstrates a limited awareness of a global perspective	Has an informed historical perspective, including an understanding of how one's own society developed in relation to other societies; and can communicate that knowledge to others.	Demonstrates knowledge of the state of the planet and global dynamics including prevailing world conditions, trends, and development (Bennett, 1999).	Use strategies and activities, which increases student knowledge and involves them in thinking about critical global issues (Bennett, 1999)	Portfolio Reflections Journals Field experiences and Clinical Practice assessments

LeMoyne-Owen College Division of Education
Performance Outcomes

LeMoyne-Owen College Graduating Senior Competence(s):
1 – Think creatively, critically, logically and analytically using both quantitative and qualitative methods for solving problems
5 -- Appreciate, understand and know the foundations of diverse cultures in the context of a global community; and
7 -- Accept social responsibility and provide service to humankind
10 -- Attain critical skills, frame of reference and understanding to appreciate and discriminate between artistic achievement

Division of Education Performance Outcome(s): 6 -- Is an effective teacher of PreK-12 students from diverse populations

Competency Rubric					
Indicators	Unsatisfactory	Satisfactory	Proficient	Outstanding	Evidence
G Knowledge Construction (Banks, 2001)	Has limited awareness of how cultural assumptions, frames of references, perspectives, and biases influence the ways in which knowledge is constructed	Demonstrates the ability to recognize cultural assumptions, frames of references, perspectives, and biases as related to the ways in which knowledge is constructed. (Banks, 2001)	Investigates, how cultural assumptions, frames of references, perspectives, and biases influence the ways in which knowledge is constructed	Investigates, analyzes, and determines how implicit cultural assumptions, frames of references, perspectives, and biases influence the ways in which knowledge is constructed and engages students in activities to examine knowledge construction.	Portfolio Reflections Journals Field experiences and Clinical assessments

LeMoyne-Owen College Division of Education
Performance Outcomes

LeMoyne-Owen College Graduating Senior Competence(s):
1 – Think creatively, critically, logically and analytically using both quantitative and qualitative methods for solving problems
9 -- Attain motivational, personal management and interpersonal skills, professional development and research experience, as well as resourcefulness that will form the basis for a career and/or further educational experiences
10 -- Attain critical skills, frame of reference and understanding to appreciate and discriminate between artistic achievement

Division of Education Performance Outcome(s): 7 -- Holds high expectations for self and all PreK-12 students

Competency Rubric					
Indicators	Unsatisfactory	Satisfactory	Proficient	Outstanding	Evidence
A. Reflective Teaching	Rarely reflects on teaching practices	Reflects on teaching practice by continually evaluating the effects of instruction.	Reflects on teaching practices and modifies methods of presenting lessons Candidate changes the ways that materials are selected to make them more appropriate for instruction	Continually evaluates the effects of instruction and integrates resources available from professional organizations, field trips and commercial materials to increase the effectiveness of teaching.	Portfolio assessments Reflections Journals Field experiences and Clinical Practice assessments
B Personal and Professional Growth	Self-evaluation is not considered as a part of professional growth	Engages in self-evaluation for personal and professional growth and seeks out professional literature, colleagues, professional organizations, and other resources to improve personally and professionally to transform teaching and learning	Continually self-evaluates and seeks out professional literature, colleagues, professional organizations, and other resources to improve personally and professionally to transform teaching and learning	Continually self-evaluates and seeks out professional literature, colleagues, professional organizations, and other resources to improve personally and professionally to transform teaching and learning Modifies teaching according to findings	Portfolio assessments Reflections Journals Field experiences and Clinical Practice assessments

LeMoyne-Owen College Division of Education
Performance Outcomes

LeMoyne-Owen College Graduating Senior Competence(s):
1 – Think creatively, critically, logically and analytically using both quantitative and qualitative methods for solving problems
8 -- Maintain literacy for the understanding of the impact of science and technology on individuals, society and the environment
10 -- Attain critical skills, frame of reference and understanding to appreciate and discriminate between artistic achievement.

Division of Education Performance Outcome(s): 8 -- Is technologically proficient

			Competency Rubric		
Indicators	**Unsatisfactory**	**Satisfactory**	**Proficient**	**Outstanding**	**Evidence**
A Technology and Instruction	Demonstrate minimal skills or use of technology to support instruction	Applies computers and related technology to support instruction.	Integrates instructional technology into the classroom to facilitate interdisciplinary teaching and learning, supplement instructional strategies, design instructional materials, and enhance hands-on experiences and problem solving	Designs, develops, publishes and presents products (e.g. videos) using appropriate technology resources that demonstrate and communicate curriculum concepts to audiences inside and outside of the classroom and use technology in communication, collaboration, conducting research and solving problems and promotes equitable, ethical and legal use of technological resources	Course-embedded assessment Portfolio assessments Field experiences and Clinical Practice assessments
B Technology and Professional Growth and Productivity	Evidence of limited understanding and use of technology tools to enhance learning, increase productivity and promotes creativity	Applies tools of technology to enhance professional growth and productivity; uses technology in communication, collaboration, conducting research and solving problems, promotes equitable, ethical and legal use of technological resources	Demonstrates ability to use computer-based tools to create presentations	Designs, develops, publishes and presents products (e.g videos) using appropriate technology resources that demonstrate and communicate curriculum concepts to audiences inside and outside of the classroom and use technology in communication, collaboration, conducting research and solving problems and promotes equitable, ethical and legal use of technological resources	Course-embedded assessment Portfolio assessment and Clinical Practice assessments
C Computer Operation Skills	Struggles to cope with technology	Skillfully runs software programs, access, generate, and manipulate data. Performs basic operating systems tasks, software functions, and minor troubleshooting on the most current and available systems.	Recognizes and understands that computer programs (software) are sets of sequential instructions that enable the computer to sort, calculate, print, and other functions	Demonstrates a sound understanding of the nature of operation of technology systems. Creates and implements an environment for him/herself and others where technology is used effortlessly to enhance teaching and learning. Constantly experiments with new technology.	Course-embedded assessment Portfolio Assessment Field experiences and Clinical Practice assessments

LeMoyne-Owen College Division of Education
Performance Outcomes

LeMoyne-Owen College Graduating Senior Competence(s):
1 – Think creatively, critically, logically and analytically using both quantitative and qualitative methods for solving problems
8 -- Maintain literacy for the understanding of the impact of science and technology on individuals, society and the environment
10 -- Attain critical skills, frame of reference and understanding to appreciate and discriminate between artistic achievement.

Division of Education Performance Outcome(s): 8 -- Is technologically proficient

Competency Rubric					
Indicators	Unsatisfactory	Satisfactory	Proficient	Outstanding	Evidence
D Design and Management of Learning Environments/ Resources	Demonstrates limited application of technology to support active student involvement, inquiry and collaboration	Demonstrates knowledge through practical application of technology to support active student involvement, inquiry, and collaboration	Consistently performs tasks that require students to locate an analyze information, draw conclusions, and use variety of media to communicate results clearly	Selects and creates learning experiences that are appropriate for curriculum goals, relevant to learners, based upon principles of teaching and learning; incorporates the use of media and technology for teaching to support learner expression in a variety of media	Course-embedded assessment Portfolio Assessment Field experiences and Clinical Practice assessments
E. Technology use and Diversity	Demonstrates limited skills in the use of media and technology to support learning for students with diverse needs.	Demonstrates skills in the use of media and technology to support learning for students with diverse needs	Consistently selects and uses media and technology to effectively support learning for students with diverse needs.	Can select and evaluate media and technology to effectively support learning for students with diverse needs	Course-embedded assessment Portfolio Assessment Field Experiences and Clinical Practice assessments

LeMoyne-Owen College Division of Education **Performance Outcomes**					
Professional Commitments and Dispositions					
Competency Rubric					
Indicators	Unsatisfactory	Satisfactory	Proficient	Outstanding	Evidence
Outcome 1: Respects Cultural Identity	Limited understanding of education's relationship to group and self-identity	Understands the concept of an education process that bonds the individual to his or her ethnic group, the community and the nation. (Hillard, 1998)	Understands and appreciates the concept of an education process that bonds the individual to his or her ethnic group, the community and the nation. Candidate seeks knowledge and skills to facilitate such bonds	Understands and appreciates the concept of an education process that bonds the individual to his or her ethnic group, the community and the nation. Candidate creates learning environment that facilitates such bonds	Course embedded assessments. Portfolio assessments. Reflections Journals Field experiences and Clinical Practice assessments Exit interview Exit survey Personal Interview IV
Outcome 2: Seeks first to understand (Covey, 1994)	Seldomly seeks to understand, when talking to others.	Consistently listens with care to gain understanding.	Listens with care, questions and restates to better understand	Listens with care, questions, examines, and restates to assure understanding	Course embedded assessments. Journals Self-assessments. Field experiences and Clinical Practice Assessments
Outcome 3: Models ethical and professional behavior in all contexts	Seldomly use knowledge of legal and ethical responsibility, and educational policy to guide professional behavior	Uses knowledge of legal and ethical responsibilities, and schools and educational policy to guide professional behavior	Applies knowledge of legal and ethical responsibilities to analyze how professional behavior can improve classroom learning	Synthesizes and uses knowledge of legal and ethical responsibilities to evaluate his/her professional behavior, incorporates additional actions into his/her behavior and evaluates results in relation to student learning	Course embedded assessments Portfolio assessments Reflections Journals Field experiences and Clinical Practice assessments Exit interview Exit survey
Outcome 4: Demonstrates an appreciation of the need for connectedness in teaching	Seldom looks for connections between and among subject matter and teaching the learner	Looks for relationships between and among subject matter and develops integrated instruction that demonstrates connections critical to meaning making and transformational learning	Investigates relationships between and among subject matter and develops integrated instruction that demonstrates connections critical to meaning making and transformational learning.	Organizes and explains relationships between and among subject matter and develops integrated instruction that demonstrates connections critical to meaning making and transformational learning	Portfolio assessments Reflections Journals Field experiences and Clinical Practice assessments Self-assessments Exit interview Exit survey
Outcome 5: Nurtures intellectual curiosity in self and others	Shows little interest in learning more about content knowledge than is required of assignments.	Seeks to increase knowledge to better understand the content area(s) that he or she is teaching	Seeks to increase knowledge about content areas, and ways to integrate it into instruction to transform his or her teaching	Consistently increases his or her knowledge bases in multiple content areas. Evaluates and synthesizes new knowledge to effectively integrate it into instruction to transform his or her teaching	Course embedded assessments. Portfolio assessments Reflections Journals Unit plans Lesson plans Teaching videos Field experiences and Clinical Practice and Self assessments Exit interview Exit survey

LeMoyne-Owen College Division of Education					
Performance Outcomes					
Professional Commitments and Dispositions					
Competency Rubric					
Outcome 6: Is respectful and open-minded	Seldom demonstrates a willingness to explore multiple ways of knowing and perspectives	Identifies multiple ways of knowing and perspectives and is willing and respectfully integrate them into instruction.	Identifies and investigates multiple ways of knowing and perspectives and is willing to respectfully integrate them into instruction	Consistently identifies, investigates and analyzes multiple ways of knowing and perspectives and respectfully integrate them into instruction	Course Portfolio Journals Field experiences and Clinical Practice and self assessments Exit interview Exit survey
Outcome 7: Demonstrates a commitment to life-long learning	Expresses the need for advanced study in terms of merely a higher degree or personal gain or (more money).	Expresses the need for advanced study and specialized training to fulfill a set of criteria having to do with his or her personal/professional development	Expresses the need for continuous and advanced study and specialized training to fulfill personal goals that are related to strengthening thinking skills that will enhance his/her teaching performance	Continuously evaluates need for advanced and specialized study to fulfill goals that are related to strengthening knowledge, skills and dispositions of a facilitator of transformative processes	Portfolio assessments Reflections Journals Exit Survey Exit Interview Field experiences and Clinical Practice assessments Exit interview Exit survey
Outcome 8: Fosters a probing spirit in self and others	Seldom explores uses of technology in instruction	Explores and examines technology and its uses in instruction and how it can support teaching and learning	Searches for varied technologies and multiple media forms to support and transform the teaching and learning process in developmentally and culturally appropriate ways	Combines and uses varied technologies and multiple media forms in developmentally and culturally appropriate ways to support and transform teaching and learning	Course-embedded assessment Portfolio Assessment Field experiences and Clinical Practice assessments Exit interview Exit survey

Continuous, course embedded and field experiences assessments are constructed in accordance with professional state and institutional standards that are outlined in the rubric. As candidates progress through the program their individual performance is assessed at specific benchmark points. They are listed below.

Benchmark I: Admission to Teacher Education

1. Successful completion of General Core II Program requirements with C or better in Mathematics and English
2. GPA of 2.50 or higher
3. Three favorable recommendations from faculty (one of which must be from EDUC 202 instructor)
4. Pre-Candidate Portfolio assessment with a mean rating of 2.5

5. Passing scores of the Praxis I series at State Levels
6. Successful Oral Interview (Personal Interview I)
7. Introductory Letter (Application)
8. Completed Application Form
9. Maintaining membership in a professional organization

Benchmark 2: Checkpoint Assessment

1. Successful completion of all Level I courses with related Field Experiences and a passing grade of C or better
2. Level I Portfolio assessment with a mean rating of 2.5
3. Passing the PLT at State levels
4. Maintaining a 2.5 GPA and a grade of C or higher in the Professional Core Courses
5. Maintaining membership in a professional organization

Benchmark 3: Admission to Clinical Practice

1. Successful completion of all major/supplemental/cognate and professional core courses
2. Maintaining a 2.5 GPA and a grade of C or higher in the Professional Core Courses
3. Level II Portfolio assessment with a mean rating of 2.5
4. Passing Content Knowledge sections of Praxis II series at State levels
5. Successful Oral Interview (Personal Interview II)
6. Introductory letter
7. Three favorable recommendations from faculty (College and Cooperating teachers)
8. Maintaining membership in a professional organization

Benchmark 4: Exit

1. Maintaining a 2.5 GPA and a grade of C or higher in the Professional Core Courses
2. Successful completion of Clinical Practice (student teaching /internship) with a grade of B or better
3. Level II I Portfolio assessment with a mean rating of 3.0
4. Completion of Exit Survey
5. Completion of Group Interview

6. Passing the remaining Praxis II series sections (Pedagogy) at State levels
7. Maintaining membership in a professional organization

References

Banks, James A. (2001). Cultural *diversity and education: Foundation, curriculum, and teaching*. Boston, Massachusetts: Allyn and Bacon.

Banks, James. (2002). *An introduction to multicultural education*. Boston: Allyn and Bacon.

Banks, James. (1996). *Multicultural Education, transformative knowledge, and Action: Historical and contemporary Perspectives*. New York: Teachers College Press.

Banks, J. (1994). *Educating citizens in a multicultural society*. New York: Teacher College Press.

Bennett, Christine. (1999). *Comprehensive multicultural education: Theory and practice*. Boston: Allyn and Bacon.

Bruner, J. (1992). *Acts of Meaning*. Boston, MA: Harvard University Press.

Bernstein, B. (1996). *Pedagogy, symbolic control and identity: Theory, research, critique*. London: Taylor and Francis.

Campbell, Duane E. (2000). *Choosing democracy: A practical guide to multicultural education*. Columbus, Ohio: Prentice Hall.

Covey, S. (1989). *The 7 Habits of Highly Effective People: Powerful Lessons in Personal Change*. New York: Simon & Schuster.

Darling-Hammond, Linda. (1994). *Graduation by portfolio At Central Park East Secondary School*. New York, NY: NCREST.

Delpit, Lisa. (1997). *Other people's children: Cultural conflict in the classroom*. New York: The New Press.

Eggen, P., & Kauchak, D. (2001). *Educational psychology: Windows on classrooms*. (5th Edition). Upper Saddle River, NJ: Merrill.

Else, D. (2000). *Issues facing people of color in education*. Monograph Series Volume II, Number 2. http://www.uni.edu/coe/iel/colsum.html. (Retrieved 09/09/2001).

Foster, Michelle. (1997). *Black teachers on teaching*. New York: The New Press.

Grabe, M & Grabe, C. (2000). *Integrating technology for meaningful learning*. Boston, Ma: Houghton Mifflin

Gollnick, D. & Chinn, P. (2000). *Multicultural education in pluralistic society*. Columbus, Ohio: Charles E. Merrill Publishing Company.

Good, Thomas L. & Brophy, Jere, E. (1986). *Educational psychology: A realistic approach*

Hilliard, A.G. III. (1997). *SBA: The reawakening of the African mind*. Gainesville, Florida: Makare Press.

Jonassen, D. H., Peck, K. L., & Wilson, B. G. (1999). *Learning with technology: A constructivist perspective*. Columbus, Ohio: Merrill.

Ladson-Billings, Gloria. (1994). *The dreamkeepers: Successful teachers of African American children*. San Francisco: Jossey-Bass Publishers.

Noble, Wade W. (1985). Africanity and the Black family: The development of a theoretical model. Oakland, CA: Black Family Institute.

Ornstein, A. (1999). *Educational Administration: Concepts and Practices*. Belmont, CA: Wadsworth Publishing Company.

Spring, Joel. (1994). *Deculturalization and the struggle for equality: A brief history of the education of dominated cultures in the United States*. New York: McGraw-Hill, Inc.

Taba, Hilda. (1962). *Curriculum development: Theory and practice*. New York: Harcourt, Brace & World.

Washington, V. & Andrews, B. (1998). *Children of 2010*. Washington D. C: Children of 2010.

Watkins, W. H., & Lewis, J. H. (2001). *Race and education: The roles of history and society in educating African American students*. Needham Heights, MA: Allyn and Bacon.

Wittmer, J., & Myrick, R. (1989). *The teacher as facilitator*. Minneapolis, MN: Educational Media Corporation.

Wittrock, M. (1986). *Handbook of research on teaching*. New York: Macmillan; London: Collier Macmillan.

Appendix B

Philosophy of Education Critique Checklist

		Yes	No
1.	Is it written in the first person?	____	____
2.	Does the introductory paragraph clearly give an overview of their philosophy?	____	____
3.	Does it clearly state how the philosophy was developed?	____	____
4.	Does it clearly state his/her beliefs are about teaching?	____	____
5.	Does it clearly state his/her beliefs are about learning and the learning environment?	____	____
6.	Does it clearly state his/her beliefs are about students?	____	____
7.	Does it clearly state his/her beliefs are about parents?	____	____
8.	Do the paragraphs following the introduction support what is stated in the first paragraph?	____	____
9.	Is the philosophy of education essay?	____	____
10.	Does it have less than 3 typos or grammatical errors?	____	____

Score 1 point for each "Yes" response for a maximum of 10 points

KEY

less than 7	Needs substantial rewriting	
7 – 8	Good needs some work	Rating Score _____
9 – 10	Excellent	

Comments: List at <u>least</u> three suggestions for improving the autobiography.

1. _____

2. _____

3. _____

4. _____

5. _____

Glossary of Terms

Achievement test—An examination that measures educationally relevant skills or knowledge about such subjects as reading, spelling, or mathematics.

Authentic task—A task performed by students that has a high degree of similarity to tasks performed in the real world.

Average—A statistic that indicates the central tendency or most typical score of a group of scores. Most often average refers to the sum of a set of scores divided by the number of scores in the set.

Criterion-referenced test—A measurement of achievement of specific criteria or skills in terms of absolute levels of mastery. The focus is on performance of an individual as measured against a standard or criteria rather than against performance of others who take the same test, as with norm-referenced tests.

Diagnostic test—An intensive, in-depth evaluation process with a relatively detailed and narrow coverage of a specific area. The purpose of this test is to determine the specific learning needs of individual students and to be able to meet those needs through regular or remedial classroom instruction.

Holistic scoring—Scoring based upon an overall impression (as opposed to traditional test scoring which counts up specific errors and subtracts points on the basis of them). In holistic scoring the rater matches his or her overall impression to the point scale to see how the portfolio product or performance should be scored. Raters usually are directed to pay attention to particular aspects of a performance in assigning the overall score.

Informal test—A non-standardized test that is designed to give an approximate index of an individual's level of ability or learning style; often teacher-constructed.

Inventory—A catalog or list for assessing the absence or presence of certain attitudes, interests, behaviors, or other items regarded as relevant to a given purpose.

Norm—Performance standard that is established by a reference group and that describes average or typical performance. Usually norms are determined by testing a representative group and then calculating the group's test performance.

Performance assessment—An evaluation in which students are asked to engage in a complex task, often involving the creation of a product. Student performance is rated based on the process the student engages in and/or based on the product of his/her task. Many performance assessments emulate actual workplace activities or real-life skill applications that require higher order processing skills. Performance assessments can be individual or group-oriented.

Performance criteria—A predetermined list of observable standards used to rate performance assessments. Effective performance criteria include considerations for validity and reliability.

Performance standards—The levels of achievement students must reach to receive particular grades in a criterion-referenced grading system (e.g., higher than 90 receives an A, between 80 and 89 receives a B, etc.) or to be certified at particular levels of proficiency.

Portfolio—Is not a scavenger hunt that results in the creation of scrapbook. Rather, it is a purposeful and responsive activity that engages reflective capacities of a pre-service teacher to isolate and document growth and development within learning incidences against preset criteria.

Process—The intermediate steps a student takes in reaching the final performance or end-product specified by the prompt. Process includes all strategies, decisions, rough drafts, and rehearsals-whether deliberate or not-used in completing the given task.

Published test—A test that is publicly available because it has been copyrighted and published commercially.

Rating scales—A written list of performance criteria associated with a particular activity or product which an observer or rater uses to assess the pupil's performance on each criterion in terms of its quality.

Reliability—The extent to which a test is dependable, stable, and consistent when administered to the same individuals on different occasions. Technically, this is a statistical term that defines the extent to which errors of measurement are absent from a measurement instrument.

Rubric—A set of guidelines for giving scores. A typical rubric states all the dimensions being assessed, contains a scale, and helps the rater place the given work properly on the scale.

Standardized test—A form of measurement that has been normed against a specific population. Standardization is obtained by administering the test to a given population and then calculating means, standard deviations, standardized scores, and percentiles. Equivalent scores are then produced for comparisons of an individual score to the norm group's performance.

Standard scores—A score that is expressed as a deviation from a population mean.

Validity—The extent to which a test measures what it was intended to measure. Validity indicates the degree of accuracy of either predictions or inferences based upon a test score.

Bibliography

Alverno College. (1996). *Ability-based learning program: teacher education*. Milwaukee, WI: Alverno College Institute.

Anderson, R.C., Wilson, P.T., & Fielding, L.G. (1988). Growth in reading and how children spend their time outside of school. *Reading Research Quarterly*, 23, 285-303.

APA. (2001). *Publication manual of the American psychological association*. (5th Edition). Washington, DC: American Psychological Association.

Arter, J.A. & Spandel, V. (1992). Using portfolios of student work in instruction and assessment. *Educational Measurement: Issues and Practice*, 11(1), 36-44.

Astin, A.W. (1993). *Assessment for excellence*. New York, New York: Collier Macmillan.

Atkinson, C. & Maleska, E.T. (1965). *The story of education*. New York: Bantam Books.

Banks, J. (1994). *Educating citizens in a multicultural society*. New York: Teacher College Press.

Banks, James A. (2001). *Cultural diversity and education: Foundation, curriculum, and teaching*. Boston, Massachusetts: Allyn and Bacon.

Banks, James. (1996). *Multicultural Education, transformative knowledge, and Action: Historical and contemporary Perspectives*. New York: Teachers College Press.

Banks, James. (2002). *An introduction to multicultural education*. Boston: Allyn and Bacon.

Bembridge, T. (1992). A MAP for reading assessment. *Educational Leadership*, 49, 46-48.

Bennett, Christine. (1999). *Comprehensive multicultural education: Theory and practice*. Boston: Allyn and Bacon.

Bernstein, B. (1996). *Pedagogy, symbolic control and identity: Theory, research, critique*. London: Taylor and Francis.

Blake, J., Bachman, J., Frys, M., Holbert, P., Ivan, T., & Sellitto, P. (1995). A portfolio based assessment model for teachers: Encouraging professional growth. *NASSP Bulletin*, 79 (573), 37-46.

Bloom, B. S., Englehart, M.D., Furst, E., Hill, W.H., & Krathwohl, D. R., (Eds). (1956). *Taxonomy of educational objectives: The classification of educational goals. Handbook I: Cognitive domain*. New York: David McKay.

Borko, H., Michalec, P., Timmons, M., & Siddle, J. (April, 1996). *Student teaching portfolios: A tool for promoting reflective practice*. Paper Presented At The annual meeting of the American Educational Research Association, New York City, NY.

Boyer, E. (1990). *Scholarship reconsidered: priorities of the professoriate*. Princeton, NJ: Carnegie Foundation for the Advancement of Teaching.

Bracey, Gerald. (2002). *The war against American public schools: Privatizing schools, commercializing education*. Boston, MA: Allyn and Bacon.

Brookfield, S. D. (1995). *On becoming a critically reflective teacher*. Jossey Bass, San Francisco.

Brookhart, S.M. (1999). The art and science of classroom assessment: The missing part of pedagogy. *ASHE-ERIC Higher Education Report*. 27(1).

Brophy, J., & Good, T. (1986). Teacher behavior and student achievement. In M. Wittrock (Ed.), *Handbook of research on teaching* (pp. 340-370). NY: Macmillan.

Bruner, J. (1992). *Acts of Meaning*. Boston, MA: Harvard University Press.

Buros, O. K. (ed). (1965). *The mental measurements yearbook*. Highland Park, New Jersey: Gryphon Press.

Cambourne, B., & Turbill, J. (1990). Assessment in whole language classrooms: Theory into practice. *Elementary School Journal*, 90, 337-349.

Campbell, D. M, Melenyzer, B. J., Nettles, D. H., & Wyman, R. M. (2000). *Portfolio and performance assessment in teacher education*. Boston, MA: Allyn and Bacon.

Campbell, Duane E. (2000). *Choosing Democracy: A Practical guide to multicultural education*. Columbus, Ohio: Prentice Hall.

Carr, Judy F., & Harris, Douglas E. (2001). *Succeeding with standards.* Alexandria, VA: ASCD.

Catteral, J. (1991). A reform cooled out: competency testing required for high school graduation. *The High School Journal.* 75 (1), 7-16.

Cerbin, W. (1993). Inventing a new genre: The course portfolio at the University Of Wisconsin-La Crosse. In P. Hutchings (Ed.). *Making teaching community property: A menu for peer collaboration and peer review.* Washington, DC: American Association for Higher Education.

Chambers, D.P. & Stacey, K. (1999). *Authentic tasks for authentic learning: Modes of interactivity in multimedia for undergraduate teacher education.* Paper presented in the 10th Annual Conference of Society for Information Technology & Technology Teacher Education International Conference (San Antonio, TX, February- March, 1999).

Chauncey, H. and Dobbin, J.E. (1963). *Testing: Its place in education today.* New York: Harper & Row.

Chism, N. (1999). *Peer review of teaching: A sourcebook.* Bolton, MA: Anker.

Clarke, Anthony. (1995). Professional development in practicum settings: Reflective practice under scrutiny. *Teaching and Teacher Education.* 11(3):243-261.

Cohen, M. (1978). Whatever happened to interdisciplinary education? *Educational Leadership.* 36(2), 122-126.

Cooley, J. P. (1991). State-wide student assessment. *Educational Measurement: Issues and Practice.* 10 (4), 3-6, 15.

Covey, S. (1989). *The 7 Habits of Highly Effective People: Powerful Lessons in Personal Change.* New York: Simon & Schuster.

Cunningham, C. A. & Billingsley, M. (2003). *Curriculum webs: A practical guide to weaving the web into teaching and learning.* Boston, MA: Allyn and Bacon.

Cureton, L. E. (1971). The history of grading practice. *NCME Measurement in Education*, 2 (4) 1-8.

Darling-Hammond, L. (1991). The implications of testing policy for quality and equality. *Phi Delta Kappan.* 73 (3), 220-225.

Darling-Hammond, L., & Wise, A. (1985, January). Beyond standardization: State standards and school improvement. *Elementary School Journal*, 315-336.

Darling-Hammond, Linda (1984). *Beyond the commission reports: The coming crisis in teaching.* Santa Monica, Ca: The Rand Corporation.

Darling-Hammond, Linda. (1994). *Graduation by portfolio At Central Park East Secondary School.* New York, NY: NCREST.

De Bruin-Parecki, A., Boraz, M., Shaw, E., Yeager, E., Visscher, S., & Lehan, M. (March, 1997). *Pre-service teachers and the development of their self-initiated professional portfolios.* Paper presented at the annual meeting of the Michigan Reading Conference, Grand Rapids, MI.

De Bruin-Parecki, A., Schmits, D., Boraz, M., Shaw, E., Severson, A., & Mizaur-Pickett, A. (February, 1999). *Developing professional portfolios.* Presented at the annual meeting of the Association of Teacher Educators, Chicago, Illinois.

Delpit, Lisa. (1997). *Other people's children: Cultural conflict in the classroom.* New York: The New Press.

Dewey, J. (1933). *How we think: A relation of reflective thinking to the educative process.* Chicago: Henry Regnery.

Diez, Mary E., and Hass, Jacqueline. (1997). No more piecemeal reform: Using performance-based approaches to rethink teacher education. *Action in Teacher Education.* 19 (2), 17-26.

Dorr-Bremme, D. & Herman, J. (1986). *Assessing student achievement: A profile of classroom practices.* A Center for the Study of Evaluation Document. Los Angeles, CA.

Doyle, D.P. (1994). The role of private sector management in public education. *Phi Delta Kappan.* 76(2), 128-32.

Dressel, P. (1983). Grades: one more Tilt at the windmill. In A.W. Chickering. *AAHE Bulletin.* 35 (8), 10-13.

Driscoll, M. (2000). *Psychology of learning for instruction,* (2nd ed.). Boston, MA: Allyn and Bacon.

DuBois, P. H. (1966). A test-dominated society: China, 1115 B.C.-1905 A.D. In A. Anastasi, ed., *Testing problems in perspective.* Washington, D.C.: American Council of Education. pp. 29-38.

Edgerton, Russell, Patricia Hutchings, and Kathleen Quinlan. (1992). *The teaching portfolio: Capturing the scholarship in teaching.* Washington, D.C.: American Association for Higher Education.

Eggen, P. & Kauchak, D. (2001). *Educational psychology: Windows on classrooms.* (5th Edition). Upper Saddle River, N.J. : Merrill.

Eisner, E. W. (1994). Educational reform and the ecology of schooling. In A. C. Ornstein & L. S. *Behar* (Eds.), *Contemporary issues in curriculum* (pp. 390-402). Boston, Mass: Allyn & Bacon.

Else, Dave (2000). *Issues facing people of color in education.* Monograph Series Volume II, Number 2. http://www.uni.edu/coe/iel/colsum.html. (Retrieved 09/09/2001).

Evans, J.F. & Pollicella, E. (2000). Changing and growing as teachers and learners: A shared journey. *Teacher Education Quarterly*, 27(3), 55-70

Falk, Beverly (2000). *The heart of the matter: Using standards and assessment to learn.* Portsmouth, NH: Heinemann.

Flood, J., & Lapp, D. (1989). Reporting reading progress: A comparison portfolio for parents. *The Reading Teacher,* 42, 508-514.

Foster, Michelle. (1997). *Black teachers on teaching.* New York: The New Press.

Fox, J. (1999, March 10). Math problems often linked to language. *What works in teaching and learning*, pp. 1-2.

Frazier, D.M., & Paulson, F.L. (1992, May). How portfolios motivate reluctant writers. *Educational Leadership,* 49(8), 62-65.

George, Thomas F. 1996. *The teaching portfolio at Washington State University.* Online Document. URL: http://www.wsu.edu/provost/teaching.html. (Retrieved November, 27, 2002).

Gollnick, D. & Chinn, P. (2000). *Multicultural education in pluralistic society.* Columbus, Ohio: Charles E. Merrill Publishing Company.

Gomez, M.L., Grau, M.E., & Block, M.N. (1991). Reassessing portfolio assessment: Rhetoric and reality. *Language Arts*, 68, 620-628.

Goodlad, J. I. (1984). *A place called school: Prospects for the future.* New York: McGraw-Hill.

Goodyear & Allchin. (1998*). Statements of Teaching Philosophy.* http://www.utep.edu/cetal/pub/stofteac.html. (Retrived June 19, 2003).

Grabe, M & Grabe, C. (2000). *Integrating technology for meaningful learning.* Boston, Ma: Houghton Mifflin

Gronlund, Norman E. (1998). *Assessment of student achievement.* (6th ed.). Boston: Allyn & Bacon.

Guillaume, A. M., & Yopp, H. K. (1995). Professional portfolios for student teachers. *Teacher Education Quarterly,* 22 (1), 93-101.

Hall, I., Campbell, C. H., Miech, E. J. (1997). *Class acts: Teachers reflect on their own classroom practice.* Boston, MA: Harvard Educational Review.

Haney, W. & Madaus, G. (1989). Searching for alternatives to standardized tests: Whys, whats and whithers. *Phi Delta Kappan.* 70 (9), 683-687.

Hansen, J. (1992). Literacy portfolios: Helping students know themselves. *Educational Leadership*, 49, 66-68.

Herman, J. L., Aschbacher, P. R., & Winters, L. (1992). *A practical guide to alternative assessment*. Alexandria, VA: Association for Supervision and Curriculum Development.

Herman, J., & Golan, S. (1991). Effects of standardized tests on teachers and learning—Another look. *CSE Technical Report #334*. Los Angeles: Center for the Study of Evaluation.

Herman, J.L. & Golan, S. (1993). The effects of standardized testing on teaching and schools. *Educational Measurement: Issues and Practice*. 12 (2), 20-26.

Herrington, J., and Oliver, R. (2000). An instructional design framework for authentic learning environments. *Educational Technology Research and Development*. 48(3), 23-48.

Hiebert, E.A. (1992). Portfolios invite reflection—From students and staff. *Educational Leadership*, 49, 58-61.

Hilliard, A.G. III. (1997). SBA: *The reawakening of the African mind*. Gainesville, Florida: Makare Press.

Interstate New Teacher Assessment and Support Consortium (INTASC). (1992). *Model standards for beginning teacher licensing and development: A resource for state dialogue*. Washington, DC: Council of Chief State School Officers.

Jaeger, R.M. (1991). Legislative Perspectives on statewide testing: Goals, hopes and desires. *Phi Delta Kappan*. 73 (3), 239-242.

Johnson, D.W., & Johnson, R.T. (1992). What to say to advocates of the gifted. *Educational Leadership*, 50, 44-47.

Johnston, P. (1984). Assessment in reading. In P.D. Pearson (Ed.), *Handbook of reading research* (147-182). New York: Longman.

Jonassen, D. (1994). *Technology as cognitive tools: Learners as designers,* [Website]. ITForum. Available: http://itech1.coe.uga.edu/itforum/paper1.html [2002, March 2].

Jonassen, D. H., Peck, K. L., & Wilson, B. G. (1999). *Learning with technology: A constructivist perspective*. Columbus, Ohio: Merrill.

Jonassen, David H. (2000). *Computers as mindtools*. Upper Saddle River, New Jersey: Merrill.

Kaplan (Ed.), *To improve the academy*. Stillwater, OK: New Forums Press and the Professional and Organizational Development Network in Higher Education.

Killion, J., & Todnem, G. (1991). A process for personal theory building. *Educational Leadership*, 48(6), 14-16.

Krause, S. (1996). Portfolios in teacher education: Effects of instruction on pre-service teachers' early comprehension of the portfolio process. *Journal of Teacher Education*, 47, (2), 130-138.

Ladson-Billings, Gloria. (1994). *The dreamkeepers: Successful teachers of African American children.* San Francisco: Jossey-Bass Publishers.

Lamme, L.L., & Hysmith, C. (1991). One school's adventure into portfolio assessment. *Language Arts,* 68, 629-640.

Lanese, J.F. (1992). Statewide proficiency testing: Establishing standards or barriers. *ERIC Document* 347 196.

Linn, R., & Gronlund, N.E. (2000). *Measurement and assessment in teaching.* Englewood Cliffs, NJ: Prentice Hall.

Linn, R., Baker, E., & Dunbar, S. (1991). Complex performance-based assessment: Expectations and validation criteria. *Educational Researcher*, 20, 15-21.

Lissitz, Robert & Schafer, William. (2002). *Assessment in educational reform: both means and ends.* Boston, MA: Allyn and Bacon.

Lyons, N. (1998). Portfolio possibilities: Validating a new teacher professionalism. In N. Lyons (Ed.), *With Portfolio in Hand: Validating the New Teacher Professionalism* (Pp. 9-22). New York: Teachers College Press.

Mager, Robert F. (1984). *Goal analysis.* Belmont, CA: David S. Lake Publishers.

Martella, R. C., Nelson, J.R., & Marchand-Martella, N.E. (2003). *Managing Disruptive Behaviors in the Schools.* Boston, MA: Allyn & Bacon.

Martin, Bill. (1983). *Brown Bear, Brown Bear, what do you see?* New York: Henry Holt & Company, Incorporated.

Matthews, J.K. (1990, February). From computer management to portfolio assessment. *The Reading Teacher*, 43, 420-421.

Mclaughlin, M. & Vogt, M. E. (1996). *Portfolios in teacher education.* Newark: DE: IRA.

Mehrens, W.A. (1992). Using performance assessment for accountability purposes. *Educational Measurement: Issues and Practice.* 11 (1), 3-9.

Meyers, C.A. (1992). What's the difference between authentic and performance assessment? *Educational leadership*, 49, 39-41.

Mitchell, R. (1992). *Testing for learning: how new approaches to evaluation can improve American schools*. New York: The Free Press.

Morrow, L.M. (1985). Retelling stories as a diagnostic tool. In S. Glazer, L. Searfoss, & L. Gentile (Eds.), *Reexamining reading diagnosis* (128-149). Newark, DE: International Reading Association.

Murray, Frank. (2001). Accreditation reform and the preparation of teachers for a new century, in Wang, M. and Walberg, H. (ed). *Tomorrow's teachers*. Richmond, Ca: McCutchan Publishing Corporation.

National Board for Professional Teaching Standards (1996). *What teachers should know and be able to do*. Detroit, MI.: NBPTS.

North Central Regional Educational Laboratory. (2002). *From High-Stakes Testing to Assessment for School Improvement*. http://www.ncrel.org/policy/pubs/html/beyond/stakes.htm [Retrieved July 7, 2003].

National Commission on Excellence in Education (1983). *A Nation at risk: The imperative for educational reform*. Washington, DC: Government Printing Office.

National Commission On Teaching And America's Future. (1996). *What matters most: Teaching for America's future*. New York: NCTAF.

National Council for the Accreditation of Teacher Education (March, 1999). *NCATE 2000 Standards revision* [On-Line]: http://www.ncate.org/specfoc/2000stds.pdf.

National Education Goals Panel. (1997). *National education goals: Building a nation of learners* [Online]. Available: http://www.negp.gov/negp/reports/97report.pdf [Retrieved November 30, 2002].

NCATE. (2000). Groundbreaking teacher preparation standards to be used beginning next year revolution in teacher preparation and training just ahead. http://www.ncate.org/2000/pressrelease.htm

Nettles, M.T. & Nettles, A.L. (1995). *Equity and excellence in educational testing and assessment*. Boston: Kluwer Academic Publishers.

Nickerson, Raymond. (1987). *Reflective reasoning*. Hinsdale. NJ: Lawrence Erlbaurn Assoc.

Nitko, Anthony J. (2001). *Educational assessment of students*. (3rd ed.). Upper Saddle River, New Jersey: Merrill Prince Hall.

Noble, Wade W. (1985). *Africanity and the Black family: The development of a theoretical model*. Oakland, CA: Black Family Institute.

O'Neil, J. (1992). Putting performance assessment to the test. *Educational leadership*, 49, 14-19.

Office of Technology Assessment, U. S. Congress (1992, February). *Testing in American schools: Asking the right questions (OTA-SET-519)*. Washington, DC: U.S. Government Printing Office.

Ornstein, A. (1999). *Educational Administration: Concepts and Practices*. Belmont, CA: Wadsworth Publishing Company.

Palmer, P.J. (1998). *The courage to teach: Exploring the inner landscape of a teacher's lif*e. San Francisco: Jossey-Bass.

Pett, J. (1990). What is authentic evaluation? Common questions and answers. *Fair Test Examiner*. 4, 8-9.

Posner, G. (1992). *Field Experiences: A guide to reflective thinking*. New York, N.Y.: Longman Publishing Company.

Pultorak, E.G. (1993). Facilitating reflective thoughts in novice teachers. *Journal of Teacher Education*. 44 (4), 288-295.

Ravitch, D. (1996). *National standards in American education: A citizen's guide*. Washington, D.C.: Brookings Institute Press

Richert, A. E. (1990). Teaching students to reflect: A consideration of program structure. *Journal of Curriculum Studies,* 22, (6), 509-527.

Roe, B., Stoodt-Hill, B., & Burns, P. (2004). *Sunday school literacy instruction: The content areas* (8th Ed). Boston, MA: Houghton Mifflin Company.

Rose, L. C. & Gallup, A. M. (2002). The 34th Annual Phi Delta Kappa/ Gallup Poll of the Public's Attitudes toward the Public Schools. *Phi Delta Kappan*, 84 (1), 41-56.

Ross, D., & Bondy, E. (1996). The continuing reform of a university teacher education program: A case study. In K. Zeichner, S. Melnick, & M.L. Gomez (Eds.). *Currents of reform in pre-service teacher education*. New York: Teacher College Press

Roth, R. A. (1996). Standards for certification, licensure, and accreditation. In J. Sikula, T. J. Buttery, & E. Guyton (Eds.), *Handbook of research on teacher education* (2nd ed., pp. 242-278). New York: Macmillan.

Rudner, L.M., & Boston, C. (1994). Performance assessment. *The ERIC Review,* 3(1), 2-12.

Sarason, Seymour B. (1995). *School change: The personal development of a point of view*. New York: Teacher College Press.

Schon, D. (1987). *The reflective practitioner: How professionals think in action*. New York: Basic Books.

Schon, D.A. (1983). *Educating the reflective practitioner: Toward a new design for teaching and learning in the professions*. San Francisco: Jossey-Bass.

Schuttloffel, M.J. (1999a, July5-6). *Reflective practice for principal professional development*. Retreat Sponsored By National Association Of Secondary School Principals For Middle School Principals Of Corpus Christi, Texas And Jefferson County, Kentucky. Las Vegas Nevada.

Schuttloffel, M. J. (1999b). *Character and the contemplative principal*. Washington, DC: National Catholic Educational Association.

Scriven, M. (1991). *Evaluation thesaurus* (4th ed). Thousand Oaks, Ca: Sage.

Seifert, K. L. (1999). *Reflective thinking and professional development*. Boston: Houghton Mifflin.

Sergiovanni, T. J. (1992). *Moral leadership: Getting to the heart of school improvement*. San Francisco: Jossey-Bass.

Sergiovanni, T.J. (1991). *The principalship: A reflective practice perspective*. Boston: Allyn and Bacon.

Shavelson, R.J. (1992). What we've learned about assessing hands-on science. *Educational Leadership,* 49, 20-25.

Shore, B., Foster, S., Knapper, C., Nadeau, G., Neill, N., & Sim, V. (1986). *The teaching dossier: A guide to its preparation and use*. Ottawa, Ontario: Canadian Association of University Teachers.

Shulman, L. (1993, November/December). Teaching as community property: Putting an end to pedagogical solitude. *Change*, 6-7.

Shulman, L. (1998). Teacher Portfolios: A Theoretical activity. In N. Lyons (Ed.), *With portfolio in hand: Validating the new teacher professionalism* (Pp.23-37). New York: Teachers College Press.

Smith, M.L. & Rottenberg, C. (1991). Unintended consequences of external testing in elementary schools. *Educational Measurement: Issues and Practice.* 10 (4), 7-11.

Snyder, J., Lippincott, A. & Bower, D. (1998). Portfolios in teacher education: Technical or transformational. In N. Lyons (Ed.), *With portfolio in hand: Validating the new teacher professionalism* (Pp.123-142). New York: Teachers College Press.

Spinelli, Cathleen G. (2002). *Classroom assessment for students with special needs in inclusive settings*. Upper Saddle River, NJ: Prentice Hall

Spring, Joel. (1994). *Deculturalization and the struggle for equality: A brief history of the education of dominated cultures in the United States.* New York: McGraw-Hill, Inc.

Stake, R. (1991). The teacher, the standardized test and prospects of a revolution. *Phi Delta Kappan.* 72 (11), 243-247.

Steiner, B. and Phillip, K. (1991). *Journal keeping with young people.* Englewood, Colo.: Teacher Ideas Press.

Stiggins, R. (1994). *Student-cantered classroom assessment.* Ontario: Macmillan College Publishing Co.

Stoll, Clifford. (1996). *Silicon snake oil: Second thoughts on the information highway.* New York: Doubleday Press.

Sunstein, B. (1992). *Portfolio Portraits.* Portsmouth, NA: Heinemann.

Swanson C. B. & Stevenson, D. L. (2002). Standards-based reform in practice: Evidence on state policy and classroom instruction from the NAEP state assessments. *Educational Evaluation and Policy Analysis.* 24(1) 1-27.

Sweeny, B. (1999). Content standards: Gate or bride? *Kappan Delta Phi.* 35(2), 64-67.

Taba, Hilda. (1962). *Curriculum development; Theory and practice.* New York: Harcourt, Brace & World.

Takona, J. (1999). *Distribution of undergraduate Examination questions among the specified levels: A case of an African university.* Clearinghouse Research Report No HE033165. (ERIC Document Reproduction Service No. 444429).

Takona, J. P. (2001). *Perspective on grade assignment at east Africa's state universities.* Clearinghouse Report No: TM033172. (ERIC Document Reproduction Service No. ED455312).

Tierney, R.J., Carter, M.A., & Desai, L.E. (1991). *Portfolio assessment in the reading-writing classroom.* Norwood, MA: Christopher-Gordon Publishers.

Tyler, R. W. (1950). *Basic principles of curriculum and instruction.* Chicago: The University of Chicago.

U.S. Department of Education. (1998). Goals 2000: Reforming education to improve student achievement *http://www.ed.gov/pubs/g2kreforming/g2ch1.html*

U.S. Department of Education. (1993). *Digest of Education Statistics.* Washington, DC: US Department of Education.

U.S. Department of Education. (2002).No Child Left Behind. On-line document: *http://www.nochildleftbehind.gov/next/overview/ index.html*

U.S. Department of Labor. (1991). *Secretary's commission on achieving necessary skills*. Washington, D.C.: Government Printing Office.

Valencia, S.W. & Pearson, P.D. (1987, April). Reading assessment: Time for a change. *The Reading Teacher,* 43, 726-732.

Valencia, S.W. (1990, January). A portfolio approach to classroom reading assessment: The whys, whats, and hows. *The reading teacher*, 43, 338-340.

Wade, R. C., & Yarbrough, D. B. (1996). Portfolios: A tool for reflective thinking in teacher education? *Teaching & Teacher Education*, 12 (1) 63-79.

Ward, A. W., & Murray-Ward, M. (2000). *Assessment in the classroom.* Belmont, CA: Wadsworth Publishing Company.

Washington, V. & Andrews, B. (1998). *Children of 2010.* Washington D. C: Children of 2010.

Watkins, W. H., & Lewis, J. H. (2001). *Race and Education: The roles of history and society in educating African American students.* Needham Heights, MA: Allyn and Bacon.

Wenslaff, T. & Cummings, K. (1996). The portfolio as a metaphor for teacher reflection. *Contemporary Education,* 67 (2), 109-112.

Wiggins, G. (1990, June). *The truth may make you free, but the test may keep you imprisoned: Toward assessment worthy of the liberal arts.* Paper presented at the fifth AAHE conference on assessment in higher education, Washington, DC.

Wiggins, G. (1989). A true test: toward more authentic and equitable assessment. *Phi Delta Kappan.* 70 (10), 703-713.

Wiggins, G. (1992). Creating tests worth taking. *Educational Leadership*, 49, 26-33.

Wiggins, G. (1993). *Assessing student performance: Exploring the purpose and limits of testing.* San Francisco, CA: Jossey-Bass Publishers.

Wilcox, B. (1996). Smart portfolios for teachers in training. *Journal of Adolescent and Adult Literacy*, 40 (3), 172-179.

Winograd, P., Paris, S., & Bridge, C. (1991). Improving the assessment of literacy. *The Reading Teacher,* 45, 108-116.

Wise, A. E., & Leibbrand, J. (1996). Profession-based accreditation: A foundation for high-quality teaching. *Phi Delta Kappan,* 78, 202-206.

Wittmer, J., & Myrick, R. (1989). *The teacher as facilitator.* Minneapolis, MN: Educational Media Corporation.

Wittrock, M. (1986). *Handbook of research on teaching.* New York: Collier Macmillan.

Wolf, D. (1998). Creating a portfolio culture. In N. Lyons (Ed.). *With portfolio in hand: validating the new teacher professionalism,* (Pp.41-50). New York: Teachers College Press.

Wolf, D., Bixley, J., Glenn, J., & Gardner, H. (1991). To use their minds well: Investigating new forms of student assessments. In G. Grand (Ed.). *Review of Research in Education,* 17, 31-74). Washington, DC: AERA.

Wolf, D.P. (1989). Portfolio assessment: Sample student work. *Educational Leadership.* 46, 35-39.

Wolf, K. (1996). Developing an effective teaching portfolio. *Educational Leadership.* 53 (6), 34-37.

Wright, B. D. (1997). Evaluating learning in individual courses. *Handbook of the undergraduate curriculum.* J. Gaff & J. Ratcliff, Eds., San Francisco: Jossey-Bass.

Zarrillo, James. (2000). *Teaching elementary social studies: principles and applications.* Upper Saddle River, NJ: Merrill.

Zeichner & Tabachnick (Eds.). (1991). *Issues and practices in inquiry-oriented teacher education.* London: Falmer Press.

Ziomek, R. (1997, March). *The concurrent validity of ACT's Passport Portfolio Program: Initial validity results.* Paper presented at the annual meeting of the National Educational Research Association, Chicago, IL.

Zubizarreta, J. (1994). Teaching portfolios and the beginning teacher. *Phi Delta Kappan.* 76 (4), 323-326.

Zumwalt, K. (1989). Beginning professional teacher: The need for a curricular vision of teaching. In M. C. Reynolds (Ed.). *Knowledge base for the beginning teacher.* New York: Pergamon Press.

About the Authors

James P. Takona is Associate Professor of Educational Technology and Media as well as chair of the Division of Education, LeMoyne-Owen College where he specializes in instructional technology and assessment. He is the author of *Educational Research: Principles and Practice* and *Pre-Service Teacher Portfolio Development*. Takona has published in numerous scholarly journals worldwide and contributed at various professional conferences around the world. He received his doctorate from Loyola University of Chicago in 1991. Since then, he has worked in various institutions of higher education both in the US and internationally.

Roberta J. Wilburn received her doctorate from George Washington University in Washington, D.C. in 1982. Since then she has held various professional positions in higher education, public schools and community-based programs. She has been a program administrator, child development specialist, consultant, special education teacher, researcher, and grant writer. Dr. Wilburn has been actively advocating for children and families for over twenty years. She has given numerous presentations both nationally and internationally, and she has published articles in scholarly journals. She is currently Associate Professor and Director of Early Childhood Education in the Division of Education at LeMoyne-Owen College in Memphis, TN.